THE QUAKER TAPESTRY

Title Panel. The prism

THE QUAKER TAPESTRY

A celebration of insights

JOHN ORMEROD GREENWOOD

Prologue by Anne Wynn-Wilson

i

Impact Books

First published in Great Britain 1990
by Impact Books, 112 Bolingbroke Grove, London SW11 1DA

© Text and illustrations: The Quaker Tapestry Scheme 1990

ACKNOWLEDGEMENTS
The committee of the Quaker Tapestry Group
wishes to acknowledge its profound gratitude to
Edward H. Milligan, Mary S. Milligan and Howard F. Gregg
for all that they have done in preparing
John Ormerod Greenwood's final draft for publication.
Photographs of the Quaker Tapestry panels were
taken by Mr R.N. Harvey of Long Ashton, Bristol.
The scene from the Bayeux Tapestry p.5 is reproduced
by kind permission of the *Ville de Bayeux*.

ISBN 0 245 60017 5

Phototypeset by Photoprint, Torquay, Devon
Printed and bound in Italy
by arrangement with Graphicom SRL, Vicenza

Contents

CONTENTS

List of panels

LIST OF PANELS

Panels not illustrated in this book are marked *n. i.*

By the needle you shall draw the thread,
and by that which is past, see how that which
is to come will be drawne on.

George Herbert,
Outlandish Proverbs (1640) No. 329

The experience of the Tapestry Group:
For a moment (for these things come only in moments)
all came into focus: former Friends and we ourselves,
faith and the work of our hands,
death as a part of life, all one.

Betty Harris, writing on a workshop
held at Jordans in Buckinghamshire,
26–29 April 1985

Prologue – The making of the tapestry

ANNE WYNN-WILSON

'To those who look and listen a thing well-made causes the past to call to the future.'
Haida chief from British Columbia

Since the dawn of recorded history, craftspeople have used their skills to tell stories. Such a record is The Quaker Tapestry – a series of seventy-five separate crewel embroidered panels, each measuring 25″ wide by 21″ deep, and thus small enough to be easily transported and exhibited. The Tapestry is not an academic history, but a celebration of insights – that is perceived wisdom – that have motivated the Religious Society of Friends (Quakers) since their founding in 1652 by George Fox.

How it all began

The idea of making the Tapestry began in Somerset, England, in January 1981, when one eleven-year-old boy and myself, his teacher, were attempting to solve a problem. From such unexpected beginnings came the ten-year project which has been continuously shared with others until they now number well over two thousand Friends in Britain, Ireland, Australia, New Zealand, Canada, the United States, Holland and Switzerland. The youngest to contribute is a three-year-old Canadian boy and the most senior is an Englishwoman of ninety-six. They are all members of a co-operative activity striving to encourage communication between children and adults in Meeting, to forge a sense of community by connecting members in scattered Meetings, and finally to extend friendship to groups throughout the world. The outcome is an experiment in education and communication made possible by embroidery and story-telling.

Two questions are often asked about the embroidery: 'How did you think of the project?' and, 'Where will it finally be exhibited?' – the alpha and the omega, the beginning and the end; and in-between a wealth of stories! Sometimes an unspoken question is quite recognisable: 'How has a successful project come from a whimsical idea?' The words of a song from *Sound of Music* come to mind: 'Nothing comes from nothing, nothing ever could . . .'. Every experience influences our capacity to be creative; everyone has something to offer. As George Fox remarked, 'All are serviceable'. 1981 is quoted as the beginning of the project: with hindsight, the origins were a lifetime's experience. Two of the influential strands are that during 1974 I returned to College, as a part-time student at the Taunton College of Art & Technology, to undertake a four-year City & Guilds embroidery course. After a lifetime's embroidery experience, interlaced with teaching home economics, organising political work and owning a craft business (making toys), I wished to widen my textile knowledge and co-ordinate my teaching material in preparation for becoming a freelance lecturer. During this time one of my special studies was the Bayeux Tapestry.

The other strand concerned my experience of Quaker Meetings. I have lived in many parts of Britain and during the past twenty-five years have become part of four Meetings with very different personalities. I attended Jordans, a beautiful 17th century meeting house, where the Friends were experienced in Quaker service and the Society of Friends traditions. We moved to Heswall, and I was welcomed as a member of an active, young Meeting, enjoying modern premises. Our next Meeting, Taunton, long established, quiet and retiring, with very few children, had no young people as companions for our son and daughter. The contrast with our experience of previous Meetings was quite difficult to accept. To my great joy I was appointed to attend Quaker Home Service Representative Council in 1974. This gave me an insight into the administration concerning spiritual caring for Meetings; into adult and children's religious education, Quaker publishing, and outreach.

By listening and sharing experiences with other members I began to understand the hopes and frustrations within the Society: for example, the problems experienced by scattered Scottish Meetings. Within my own Meeting I had the impression that there were other problems: enquirers came but rarely stayed; finding information was difficult; there was a lack of openness. Faithful Attenders seemed apologetic and lonely, their main interest often being the Peace Testimony, without realising its spiritual basis. If I asked a Friend to speak to the children, I sometimes heard the reply, 'I wouldn't know what to say to them'! Was it that they did not know enough about their Quaker heritage and the insights that could speak to our dilemma today? Such was my experience. This it was that persuaded me to prepare for my own Children's

Meeting a programme with a continuous historical thread tracing the insights of the Society. I intended that we should make a frieze of illustrations of the relevant stories, so that even if the children's attendance was irregular, the programme would be constant.

Our meeting house contained a room where we met each Sunday for worship and a small room suitable for 'tinies'. There was also a large, high-ceilinged meeting room which had not been used as such for many years. This was divided by a rough wall and was used as a warehouse. It was gloomy, cold and damp. One half housed old furniture and the other was a storeroom for a toy library. This was where Jonathan Stocks and I held class. The peeling walls and damp cold affected the two of us! Either we could shiver and grumble, or become optimistic and imagine all the improvements that could be made. We borrowed the keys from the caretaker and, taking notice of his warning that the floor was rotten, we peered into the other half. We both knew intuitively that the place should be made into a new children's room. Sometimes wishes do come true. Eventually a new room was built inside the old shell, but that is another story. We made a start with the historical stories, beginning with George Fox in 1643, considering the problems of his time and his reaction to them. To my surprise Jonathan suggested that the insight illustrations 'should be done in embroidery . . .'!

In 1988, while I was Friend in Residence at Pendle Hill, Philadelphia, USA, teaching the Quaker Tapestry, I was surprised to be asked the question, 'Where are you on your spiritual journey?'. Friends in Britain rarely share their spiritual experiences, and I have been reticent about mine. For many years I had practised the mental discipline which Quakers refer to as 'Standing in the Light'. The experience is closely linked in my mind with the gift of creativity. Peak experiences are difficult to describe in words, in my case partly because I often think in patterns. In the early days of January 1981, I felt a sense of freedom and heightened perception, and the interdependent patterns which were to become the Tapestry Project were very clear. One of these concerned the diverse needs of people; another, a large narrative crewel embroidery, linked throughout with a pattern of organisation and time. The whole was a new permutation of existing experience, and I recognised its special meaning.

The experience happened like this: on that January morning I was alone, washing up the breakfast dishes, when I saw the patterns and recognised their significance. I did not see visions outside myself; I knew the idea inside. The room seemed full of sunlight, and the bubbles on my hands shimmered and sparkled. There was a sense of wholeness. The idea was complete and viable. I was happy and laughed at the audacity and magnitude of the undertaking. Put simply but incompletely, my understanding of the experience was the creation of a very large narrative embroidery, too large for any one Meeting to accomplish. The work could only be achieved co-operatively, even shared beyond London Yearly Meeting.

The implications and opportunities were so amazing that I remained quiet in case the vision faded before I had understood it. At the time I confided in no-one but Jonathan, and indeed did not explain the project to Friends for almost four months. Jonathan liked the idea of sharing a large embroidery. I found this added to the quality of concentration and care he put into his story research.

When I was a child there was a painted religious text which hung on the wall of my grandmother's bedroom. It just said, 'Feed my sheep'. I never knew my grandmother, but I often wondered about this text. I now realise there are many unsatisfied people who long for spiritual insight, love, acceptance and the opportunity for communication. These universal needs of people were part of my motivation in preparing the Quaker Tapestry Project: the grand embroidery was happily the means of providing a service. After my excitement about the new idea, there followed a quiet development time. People-centred projects develop a recognisable character which influences decision making. If the first pattern in my vision was of the spiritual needs of people, the second was of the means to help them by sharing resources and providing an opportunity to learn and communicate ideas.

Inspired by the Bayeux Tapestry

My model and inspiration for the new embroideries was the 11th century Bayeux Tapestry, commissioned by Bishop Odo to honour his half-brother, William the Conqueror, by illustrating the story of his conquest of England in 1066. Our embroideries honour Quaker insights by telling their amazing stories, beginning in 1643 in the Civil War, and continuing through the following three-and-a-half centuries.

I designed the new embroidery style in such a way that everyone who wished could join in. Before I describe how the embroideries are made, it is useful to understand two terms: Crewel and Tapestry. Crewel embroidery has appeared in many styles since the 11th century: it is traditionally worked on a twill weave linen: perhaps the best known are the Bayeux Tapestry and the Tree of Life designs of Jacobean embroidery. The word 'crewel' comes from the ancient word describing the curl in the staple, which is the single hair of the wool. Crewel wool has a long staple, which is fine and can be strongly twisted, and crewel work takes its name from the use of this wool. The crewel technique is designed to dance freely across the surface of the fabric, quite distinct from canvas work, which uses wool for stitches that are regulated by the weave of the canvas. Canvas work is sometimes known by the misnomer 'tapestry work'. In a true

A scene from the Bayeux Tapestry

tapestry the design is woven directly into the warp threads, using the special technique of tapestry weaving. It is interesting to note that historically all three methods have been used to make hangings that tell a story. The French word for a worker in these techniques is 'Tapissière'. No wonder there is often confusion in naming these textiles!

The nature of crewel work requires the use of an embroidery frame. Small samplers fit into a ring frame, but larger panels require mounting in the square tapestry frame. The largest commercial frame available in Britain is 36″ wide, and this determined the width for our finished panels, i.e. 25″. The depth within certain limits is set by the length of the embroiderer's forearm, which should comfortably reach the centre of the underside of the stretched embroidery. The Quaker Tapestry is only 1″ deeper than the Bayeux Tapestry, which is 20″ deep and 231 feet long; evidently arms have not changed very much in 900 years! Large embroideries are usually made in central workshops, but the co-operative nature of our wide-ranging project required that the embroideries could be worked at home, and easily transported to meetings or the next embroiderer. The distance between groups of workers is also one good reason why the Quaker Tapestry is designed as seventy-five separate panels, and not a continuous narrative.

The important features of the Bayeux Tapestry incorporated in our style are: the three horizontal divisions of the design, which provides in the top and bottom sections an opportunity for headings and children's work, leaving the centre as a focus for the main story; the embroidered outlines for faces and hands. The latter contrast well with the solid infilling of clothing, which is often embroidered in a distinctive way, known as Bayeux Point or Bayeux Technique. This is achieved by closely laying threads which are tied down with a couched thread (couched refers to small stitches placed across a long thread). The development of the three layers of embroidery is our own, especially the third layer which uses creative stitchery, to be described later.

In addition to Bayeux Technique, I selected only four ancient, well-known stitches. The history of these stitches is very romantic, but they are used today without the worker being aware of their origins. Each has a special personality or quality, which can be used simply or creatively to provide a distinctive line or texture. These stitches are:

Split Stitch, which makes a fine, continuous line or a light-reflecting filling. This stitch was used magnificently by the broderers in the 13th century, at a peak time of craft skill, when the work was known as Opus Anglicanum. In these embroideries a minute spiral of split stitches was used to indicate the high cheek-bones of saints and the reflection of light in the folds of their garments.

[6]

Stem Stitch, which produces a slightly raised, rope-like stitch on the surface and a continuous line of straight stitches on the reverse side. We use this facility for transferring outlines – quilters will recognise the Trapunto technique. It is a useful stitch, much used in Jacobean embroidery. The structure of this stitch pre-dates the weaving of fabrics: I recognised it being used to bind fibres in a basket from Northern Peru dated 7000 BC.

Chain Stitch, which looks like a chain, and can be seen in its traditional form in the embroideries of India for the flat infilling of shapes. We are using this versatile structure for creating descriptive textures.

Peking Knot, which when worked correctly, has a consistent shape and the knot always lies in the same direction. The traditional use is in ancient Chinese embroideries, where it is used for shading infilling for flowers and to describe movement of waves. We use it to represent lace, curly hair, hedges, or just for dotting the i's.

Lettering forms a major part of the design and conveys essential information. It is therefore necessary that it can be easily read. I designed a script suitable for embroidery and a stitch which could cope with the tight curves of the lower case lettering. This stitch is made by compacting Split Stitch and Stem Stitch, which prevents thorns developing on the bends! When I showed a panel to staff of the Royal School of Needlework in London, they questioned me about this stitch, and then recognised it as a new invention. This amazed me, so I took it to the Textile Department of the Victoria & Albert Museum, who confirmed it was so. It is a corded stitch which the workers like to call *Quaker Stitch*.

The design of the lower case lettering was influenced by my enjoyment of the script in 14th century manuscripts and the modern lettering over the Venerable Bede's tomb in Durham Cathedral. The curved E and the small h are incorporated from the calligraphy in the Bayeux Tapestry. Later Joe McCrum, retired Head of Design at the Glasgow School of Art, designed a beautiful alphabet of upper case letters for use in the headings.

The style of the Quaker embroidery was developed by my working several samplers. The first was a typical figure from an L.S. Lowry painting. Simply embroidered in Bayeux Technique, the imagination differentiated between the textures of clothes, boots and hair, and found it quite satisfying. The motif for the second sampler was taken from a small Miro design which enjoyed many similarities to a child's drawing.

The four stitches were used in a linear fashion, totally different from the Lowry sampler, and a most amusing and satisfactory embroidery was achieved. By integrating these experiments, the Quaker Style, based on three layers of embroidery, was created. Later the technique was explored and tested in the making of four early panels. The style consists first of an outline design, which is also the means of transferring the cartoon: it can be seen in the features and hands, etc. The second layer is a plain infilling, using any of the basic stitches. The final layer is of creative embroidery which describes the subject. Together with the lettering, these three processes offer suitable opportunities for people with different temperaments and skills who wish to embroider.

Jonathan and the First Panel

Whilst I was developing the embroidery style, I continued working with Jonathan on the design of the first panel 'George Fox's Convincement' (Panel A1). He enjoyed stories from the early chapters of Elfrida Vipont's book *The story of Quakerism*[1], which we linked for reference to George Fox's *Journal*[2]. Architectural details of the church at Fenny Drayton, Leicestershire, which George Fox attended, were deduced from a photograph. Details of 17th century clothes, uniforms and buildings were collected from school books, which we noticed referred to early Quakers as religious fanatics, and we hoped that the embroideries would explain to people their conscientious convictions. The cartoon was designed to show George Fox as the centre of radiating strands, each one representing a problem he had to strive against. The words reflect his insights. The established church of the 1650s was authoritarian and repressive: its building was considered to be the House of God, but George Fox defined a church as 'the living members of a spiritual household, of which Christ is the head'. He believed that Christ Jesus could speak directly to his needs, without the intermediary of a priest. These ideas represented a great change in thinking, which the authorities would resist. All this was within the children's understanding. Whether the drawings are done by adults or shared with the children, before the illustrator can successfully produce a cartoon that conveys a story, they must be clear about its true motivation and insight. Without this understanding the design will be devoid of the spirit which gives it life.

The work evolved over fifteen weeks and the experiment showed it could be repeated in many other groups. A detailed project was offered to the Children & Young People's Committee who after much scepticism provided the money to buy the original materials. However, they offered little further help which was puzzling. Even the lack of official interest did not kill the idea, ultimately it was advantageous. People have remarked quite humorously that the project had a life of its own: certainly it developed a personality and energy.

A1. George Fox's convincement

Commissioning the fabric

My first responsibility was to commission the weaving of the woollen fabric by Church Farm Weavers in the Quantock Hills, at Kingston St Mary, Somerset. I had recommended a hand-woven woollen fabric because it could be made in our own choice of colours and design, wool is durable and a pleasure to embroider, and a soft-textured fabric does not retain needle marks when mistakes are unpicked. Traditional 17th century crewel work is usually worked on a heavy twill linen, which is stiff when new and expensive. Needle marks made 900 years ago in the plain weave linen of the Bayeux Tapestry are still visible, and show where parts have been changed or are missing. We required a 32" even weave fabric, with a random, insignificant stripe, which would guide the vertical and horizontal embroidery lines. Choosing a mid-tone fabric would allow for lighter and darker embroidery to make an interesting tone pattern. Also, the colour must be convincing for areas of skin, sky or buildings. Talbot Potter and John Lennon, the weavers, were very helpful in experimenting with the weave, and we finally chose nine colours matched to the local Somerset sandstone. Enough wool was bought to weave three lengths (65 yards), but when the number of subjects was increased from fifty to seventy-five, a further length had to be woven and it took a whole year to match the nine wools. To complement the embroidery fabric Appleton Bros. crewel wool was bought in 150 harmonious colours. I intended each panel should use about forty colours chosen in a carefully considered scheme, thus creating a flow of integrated colour throughout the whole Tapestry.

The way forward is to begin where you are

In Somerset, we followed a plan of work that has become familiar to many of the embroidery groups. First, I reported to Monthly Meeting that my proposals for the Tapestry had been accepted; then two working groups were formed. Friends from Wellington and Spiceland (on the Devon border) chose a subject in which they were personally involved during World War II, namely, Quaker relief work abroad. They began the necessary research for the panel, 'The Relief of Suffering' (Panel F7): the Taunton group met to work on practical considerations, experiment with embroidery samplers and teach the children. These Somerset Friends appear in the slide/tape presentation which I made to introduce the ideas to a wider audience.

Enlarging the vision

It was now necessary to extend the research and prove that wider proposals were viable. Research should include visits and conversations as well as written material. I was invited to join a Youth Pilgrimage, staying at the old schoolhouse at Yealand Conyers

(Panel C7). We visited the areas of North Lancashire where George Fox first met the Seekers and gained a great following. We climbed Pendle Hill, where on a clear day he described the estuary as looking like a shining sea, and in the still air the smoke rising from the villages and farms might have shown him where there was 'a great people to be gathered'. On this occasion, as we climbed, the only encounters were a few sheep which lifted their heads and stared through the mist! Later we arrived at Swarthmoor Hall, which became in 1652 the centre of comfort and administration for the new movement (Panel C1). We enjoyed tea seated at the long oak table, warmed by a log fire and the mellow light in the panelled living-room. We could see the small study through the open door to one side of the great fireplace, where Judge Fell used to sit listening whilst Margaret Fell and the household held meeting for worship. After exploring the house, we listened to Elfrida Vipont's wonderful stories about Swarthmoor and Margaret Fell's daughters, and the one son who did not approve (Panel C2), until we could imagine them going about their lives in this old manor house. I took many photographs and stored away memories, to bring life to designs and future story-telling. This visit to the 1652 country influenced my work on the panels 'Swarthmoor Hall' (Panel C1) and 'George Fox Preaching on Firbank Fell' (Panel B1): I, myself, had stood in the churchyard at Sedbergh and climbed on to the rock from which he preached in the high fells. I knew the wide open spaces and could imagine the hundreds of spiritually hungry people climbing up from their valleys to hear his convincing words.

These experiences were shared with the Taunton group and the children. They worked co-operatively on the cartoon for Swarthmoor Hall, which was later embroidered in Cambridge. The children continued their quest with other teachers by following the stories of *The Valiant Sixty*[3] – early Friends who travelled from the north of England to carry the message of 'that of God in everyone' to people all over Britain.

Meanwhile, I was recollecting George Fox's words 'Keep your feet upon the top of the mountains and sound deep to that of God in every man'. I had also become interested in his experience of visions, particularly the Lichfield episode, which I included in a panel headed 'Turn from Darkness to Light and know the Spirit of God in your heart' (Panel D1). Friends confided that they did not think the statement about Lichfield was very nice, and should be left out of the embroidery. The story is, however, understandable: George Fox left Derby Gaol after many months' imprisonment, lowered physically by the treatment he had received. When he was finally released, it was winter and he was on foot. He began to walk towards Leicestershire, but felt impelled to turn towards Lichfield where he experienced a vision of the streets flowing with blood. In his *Journal* there is reference to the Roman legions committing frightful slaughter in Lichfield. We know also by comparing dates, that he would have seen the three spires of Lichfield Cathedral, one broken by cannonfire during the recent years of civil war. During my enquiries about this episode, the Dean of Lichfield informed me that the last woman to be burnt for heresy in England was burnt at Lichfield. She came from the same village, Mancetter, where George Fox had served his apprenticeship and he must have known of these happenings. His reaction, either conscious or unconscious, to all these examples of 'Man's inhumanity to man', was to cry 'Woe to the bloody city of Lichfield!'.

Experiments in embroidery technique

I worked alone, experimentally, on a group of early panels, to find out technically how the embroidery style could be developed and how symbolically it could express ideas. In the Lichfield panel, the style shows clearly the three layers of embroidery already mentioned: (1) the use of line in the Roman soldier; (2) the plain infilling of people and spires, contrasted with (3) the creative layer of embroidery as seen in the fire. I experimented by using the components of Bayeux Point separately, i.e. laid threads and couched bundles, to describe the cathedral buildings and the wooden framed houses. I also experimented on the crowd scene in the use of minimal creative embroidery to depict perspective. The same colours are used for the sunset and the fire as both are intrinsically good – it is the use to which the fire is being put which is evil. If 'Man's inhumanity to man' represents the dark, the people to be gathered hold the possibility of the light within. In the words of George Fox, 'I saw an ocean of darkness and death, but an infinite ocean of light and love, which flowed over the ocean of darkness'. The people are gathered from all periods of our three-hundred-year story: a few can be recognised as members of Friends House staff, our committee, or my own Meeting.

Getting to know the new fabric

Meanwhile the weavers had delivered the first length of fabric. Their care and skill was evident: they had achieved the random stripe which provided its unique personality. It was beautiful. The texture was soft and open, suitable to be mounted on calico or linen and stretched on a frame before embroidering. When I tried to transfer the 'George Fox's Convincement' cartoon, I noticed that the surface was more hairy than I had expected, which precluded the traditional methods of transferring designs. For two days I was puzzled by the problem, but then remembered the Trapunto quilting I had done, and realised that the same technique could be adapted for embroidery. This entailed tracing the design on to the back of the calico and then

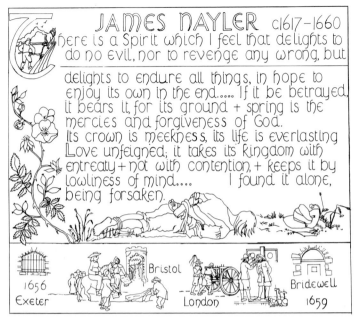

A2. James Nayler

A6. John Woolman

outlining the design in stem stitch, which would bring the design through to the front as a continuous line of small straight stitches. The method was so serviceable it was difficult to understand why it had not always been used as good embroidery practice. The embroidering of this first panel continued: ideas which had been developed on samplers took their place in it, and in the Spring of 1982 Jonathan successfully embroidered the drinking party. That panel was the culmination of the original research that Jonathan and I had begun in January 1981.

Working with the children in Taunton

There were now six children in my class, and a new room was being prepared for our work together on Sundays: it was a lovely summer, and they came to my garden, where we found that acting the story before drawing it helped their illustrations to communicate feelings and energy. The story-telling followed George Fox's early journeys in search of truth. Castles, dungeons and the market cross became unusually interesting to all of us, and the local stocks were looked at with different eyes when a model was needed for the Derby Gaol panel (F1). Early in his *Journal*, George Fox recommends stating a fair price when selling goods instead of the customary haggling. Also, to mean what you say: 'Let your yea be yea and your nay be nay', and 'Keep to the truth and the light within'. We understood this advice to be essential to a peaceable world, and we linked all this teaching with the statement to the soldiers in Derby Castle, 'Live in the virtue of that life and power that takes away the occasion of all wars.' We considered 'Derby Gaol' to be the first Peace Panel. It is interesting to note that this episode happened before the Lichfield experience, Firbank Fell or George Fox's arrival at Swarthmoor Hall, and several years before the establishment of the Society of Friends. I used this particular embroidery as a demonstration panel at the Yearly Meeting exhibition at Warwick, 1982, and later it was completed at Derby.

As the children considered more stories, it became evident in their drawings that even the younger ones were very perceptive. We considered the plight of Richard Sellar (A4) as it appeared in *Quaker Saints* and found the same story in Besse's *Sufferings of the People Called Quakers*. Richard Sellar was a conscientious objector and a fisherman who was illegally press-ganged into the Navy. The children were able to illustrate his disgraceful treatment more directly than an adult could. The story is simple but complex, and apposite to today. I found Richard Sellar's experience of the still small voice, enabling him to speak words of wisdom whilst under the threat of death, very moving. These drawings are by the youngest children to contribute: a four-year-old girl was able to put a few stitches into this panel. These children's drawings also tell the story of 'Elizabeth Fry and the Patchwork Quilts' (Panel E6) and in 'Personal

Devotion' (Panel D3) their understanding of the distraining of goods and the incredible loneliness of imprisonment. Children's work is wonderful: they express what they experience. Notice the drawing of the child on tip-toe, pushing an invalid chair, in 'Workcamps' (Panel F15).

My home at Taunton was a hive of industry: there was production at every stage. 'George Fox's Convincement' (Panel A1), the first panel to be completed, was also the proving ground on which I based the *Stitch manual*, a standard reference to ensure that the completed Tapestry would be cohesive. This began as a ten-page booklet; it has since been augmented and reprinted four times as *The Quaker Tapestry manual*. There was a necessity to teach many people the techniques; also more money was needed to carry the administration forward. The sale of a Sewing Kit would help to solve both problems. Three varieties were produced, using Appleton wools, the ten-page *Stitch manual*, and cartoons from the first three panels. My Tapestry group raised more money by organising a harvest lunch in the garden, to which the children made personal invitations. With hindsight this may have been the first of many Tapestry tea parties: shared meals became a recognised part of many groups' activities, and a focal point of our experiences when travelling abroad in America, Canada and Australia.

An exhibition of opportunities – The Tapestry at Warwick

Early in 1982, because I was lacking help from the Children Committee of Quaker Home Service, it was necessary to find out if individual members of the Society supported the project and if they did, to form a committee. This could be achieved by mounting a comprehensive exhibition during the residential Yearly Meeting at Warwick, the preparation of which was a major personal undertaking. The exhibition included proposals for the selection of subjects, the research, design and embroidery style. The new embroidery technique was described in a prepared manual and the finished panel 'George Fox's Convincement' was displayed. It took eight months to prepare all aspects of the scheme which were printed in an eight-page leaflet of which over a thousand were distributed: below the heading appeared the quotation from George Herbert (1640), 'By the needle thou shalt draw the thread and by that which is past see how that which is to come will be drawn'. I truly hoped that, by considering the insight of past generations, we might recognise the availability of guidance in our own time. In retrospect it was this careful planning which made it possible to produce an integrated embroidery made by over two thousand persons.

The Tapestry room was next door to the Quaker Fellowship of the Arts exhibition, so we attracted their patrons and were rarely without visitors. Well-wishers stayed to help, and gradually it became clear that a nucleus of interested people were returning several times, and bringing others with them. It was from these people that the first committee was formed.

We arranged a Special Interest Group meeting in the exhibition room and about sixty Friends crowded in. They expressed great enthusiasm and encouragement for the Tapestry, and a supporters' group was formed, which they decided to name The Quaker Tapestry Group, and they accepted the proposed Committee. We were thankful to have this encouragement, but were also aware of criticism of the project from some Friends. When I closed the doors at 9pm, I would find that somehow they were opened again, and influential Friends were taking a quiet look round, some shaking their heads at this unconventional art creeping into Quakerism!

The new committee met as a sub-committee of the Children & Young People's committee on 4 September 1982, and formally defined its terms of reference. From this time onwards I was glad that decisions would be shared. The first workshops for teaching embroidery were held at Wellington (Somerset) and at Dorchester. By the time the first newsletter was despatched in January 1983, four workshops had been organized – in York meeting house (April), at Westhope College, Shropshire (May), at Woodbrooke, the Quaker Study Centre, Selly Oak, Birmingham (October); and at Lattendales, a Quaker guesthouse in Cumbria (October). Everyone was welcome to join us. A report in the Quaker weekly, *The Friend*, said of the first workshops at Charney:

> Fifteen people attended: I think we felt that our skills might be meagre, but the project was exciting and we wanted to be part of it. During an exhausting but rewarding weekend we practised the five different stitches, including the one invented especially, and the Group named it the 'Friendly' stitch. Everyone enjoyed one another's company. We were inspired by Anne Wynn-Wilson, organized by Margaret Simpson and made very comfortable by the staff of Charney Manor. (Later, the 'Friendly' stitch was changed by usage to the Quaker Stitch).

The programme for a weekend remained constant, opening with a warm welcome and introduction of Friends before dinner on Friday evening, followed by a talk with slides and a short epilogue. Saturday was devoted to practical work, with an optional free time after lunch, and extra studio time was always available; after tea there was a demonstration of embroidery techniques, and in the evening a second talk and discussion. The epilogue usually included music and was designed to quieten the racing mind! On Sunday morning, Friends were often found in the workroom long before breakfast. Meeting for worship was followed by more practical work and many

A3. James Parnell: Meetings for Sufferings

last minute questions. Friends were free to depart after lunch, but we noticed they were often reluctant to break the circle of friendship.

In the early workshops we discussed the aims and organisation of the project and the research required for designs. Embroidery samplers were made. The programme soon included lettering and the precise work of dressing a large frame, tracing cartoons and transferring a particular design. To achieve all this I soon needed other teachers to help me; Ann Castle was the first to join me, and then Ann Nichols joined us in 1984: together we were known as 'The Three A's'! Meetings became increasingly fascinating when members returned to discuss nearly-finished embroideries, and the completed panels provided talking points and tangible evidence of success.

Three types of workshop developed: the residential type already described; the meeting house workshop which lasted one day and gathered Friends from a wide area; the hostess meeting, an informal gathering of one or two small groups and a teacher. An important feature of our workshops was the opportunity they gave for participants – both members and non-members of the Society of Friends – to meet together across the boundaries of monthly meetings (the area organization of the Society). Friends in Ireland particularly enjoyed these shared gatherings, which opened opportunities to meet Friends from the other side of the border. This happy experience of attending workshops led to the desire for Tapestry holidays, to provide more time not only for embroidery, but to enjoy friendship and explore the local area. The Tapestry holidays began in 1986 at Glenthorne, Grasmere; in 1987 we stayed at Charbonnières, a Quaker chateau in Normandy; and in 1988 at The Mount School in York. The experience of these holidays is another story to be told later.

Selection of subjects for inclusion in the Tapestry

This important decision was postponed until the Spring of 1983, to allow time for thought. Everyone was invited to take part in the edifying exercise of recognizing Quaker insights from the past which could speak to our condition today. Four hundred and three suggested subjects were received: the Committee recognized that all life is one, but to keep the balance in our selection between many types of experience throughout the 350 years, we needed a plan. Individually we submitted our ideas, each expressed differently, but we were in accord that the headings taken from *Christian faith and practice*[4] provided the ideal expression of our intentions.

Some subjects were popular and became single items in the chart; others were shining examples for inclusion. There were groups of insights that could be combined to appear under new headings, and others remained to be considered. This work was undertaken prayerfully, and continued as a caring trust which affected us deeply. The subject chart was published in the second newsletter in May 1983, and it was open for all who wished to adopt subjects. The intended fifty panels increased to sixty and by the end of the year fifty-four had been adopted. As time went on, important insight stories were suggested by historians or groups of Friends with special interests, until the final number of panels grew to seventy-five. No doubt suitable subjects will continue to come to mind and may serve independent groups who wish to mark a celebration in their Meeting.

Organization of groups: Keeping a nice balance between freedom and responsibility

A group adopting a subject became responsible for its welfare: this needed good organization, imagination and diplomacy. The first requirement was to consider the subject and research the facts; then to select the quotations and the story surrounding the insights; finally to compile visual information needed to make the design convincing. The original intention was that the design work would be done centrally, and whilst it was being completed the group should continue learning the embroidery skills. In time, when the design and their skills were ready, one of the embroidery teachers would discuss the work with them, and the materials and frame necessary for making the panel would be available without payment. Each group was asked to support the project financially according to their ability and inclination to raise money. In this way the larger groups could help the smaller ones, and could contribute to the costs not only of the embroidery materials but the mounting boards, photography and printing connected with each panel.

The groups were encouraged to organise themselves to serve their particular needs and pleasure. Each developed its own personality. There were both large and small groups, some centred on one person's home, whilst others ranged over a large area the size of a county. A few groups undertook detailed research, others preferred embroidery; some included children, others not. There are many personal stories connected with the embroidery, which no doubt will continue to be collected and become part of the saga of the Tapestry. Rosa Aylward wrote about the experiences of the Leicester group as follows:

It all started much as probably most other panels have started: someone 'caught' a bit of the vision set before us by Anne Wynn-Wilson. Our love for the Society, and an urge to express it visually, did the rest. But there were blockages on the way. We had chosen the life of Stephen Grellet because of the moving account in *The book of Quaker saints* — what a lovely centrepiece the story 'Preaching to Nobody' would make! We thought it right to find the original mention of the event in Stephen Grellet's own account, somewhere in his diaries. We could not find it anywhere, so referred the matter to the Librarian at Friends House. We were utterly stunned when we were told that the story is legendary, attributable to another Friend, and to crown it all, was probably due to less than careful editing when the story was published for the first time! However, we started to read, and re-read, the original diaries, and found untold treasure in doing so. In those pages there came to life not only a gallant French nobleman, a messenger of the 'Good News of God's Love for his World', but also many other fine people, some of humble, others of high estate. We got truly hooked, there could be no going back. As a record of social conditions in many parts of Europe during the time of the French Revolution and its aftermath, Stephen Grellet's diaries must be counted a most useful and exciting source of information, worthy of any historian's attention. Of course, our concern was the Quakerly aspect of it all. Here, too, we found ample material and we are trying to catch some of it in our panel: his deep concern for the poor and disadvantaged, for children and prisoners; his meetings with many famous and powerful people of his time: the Pope, the Czar, the King of Spain . . . his great love for his native country, France, the bond with his mother, and how the ordinary people flocked to hear him speak. It moves me almost beyond words when I recall what he wrote after one such occasion: 'The Gospel fell upon them like dew onto new grass'.

We are stitching, learning, not always finding it easy to do justice to what we would like to convey. But deep down we are grateful for all that is happening to us: the things we have learnt, the joyful friendships made, the skills acquired. Above all, it is good to feel part of something much bigger than ourselves.

In the lower section of the Leicester panel (Panel B5), there is a delightful illustration of Stephen Grellet talking to a crowd gathered in an orchard by lantern light. I had selected it from a package of children's drawings sent to me that I might compose the lower border. This drawing, describing the crowd enthralled by the preacher, was so complete and imaginative that it could stand in its entirety. I was told later that it was made by a boy who was usually unco-operative, but since his drawing had appeared on the panel and been very much admired, he was quite different. A simple happening, but one we enjoy.

In addition to the original intention of providing communication channels between the children and the adults, the friendship enjoyed within some adult groups is remarkable. On Tapestry days daughters bring elderly parents to enjoy the company and share lunch whilst they concentrate on the embroidery. The quiet conversation whilst embroidering often turns to heartfelt subjects and kindly shared counselling. Ann Nichols writing about her experiences within groups:

finds common denominators – the caring and dedication which has gone into the panel of each of the groups; the occasional anxieties and feelings of insecurity gradually being replaced by greater confidence in themselves and trust in their group. I have often heard, as a group nears completion of their panel, 'I never thought we would have been able to produce anything like this.' or 'In some way, this embroidery, which meant tackling something

A4. Richard Sellar

entirely new and working within it, has made me more confident – even adventurous!' For the group as a whole the words are 'We now know one another in a wider, deeper sense'.

In many cases a group can recall with pleasure that a 'lapsed' member has been drawn back into the meeting because they were invited to participate in the Tapestry and, finding friendship in this common purpose, appeared once again in meeting for worship. Shy attenders, on the edge of a big Meeting possibly, have found friendship in the smaller group. Not only embroiderers, but often non-embroiderers have offered hospitality to a workshop and willingly been general dogsbody, preparing soup and coffee and joining in with the discussions.

Research can take you to unexpected places

The research for the details for the Queen's gown and the old House of Lords in the John Beller's panel (Panel E2) led members of the Hammersmith group to ask the Keeper of the Queen's pictures for permission to see Queen Anne's portrait in St James Palace. As he accompanied them, he enquired why they were interested. During the conversation about the embroideries, ermine and the robes, they were given an introduction to visit our present Queen's robemakers; pursuing the Tapestry opens many unexpected doors!

The Librarian at Friends House was pleased that few weeks went by without someone from a Tapestry group coming in to check facts. When I was researching the story of the good ship *Woodhouse* (Panel A5), I was excited to find that the points of the story were confirmed by the Captain's contemporary account, and the fate of each passenger on board known from reference to their Journals. The small houses representing New Amsterdam were copied from an etching made within six years of the landing of the *Woodhouse*. The skyscrapers were a mischievous addition referring to a later time when New Amsterdam would become New York. Robert Fowler, the builder and captain of the ship, and his passengers felt they were guided on their journey: God's guidance is represented in the Bayeux Tapestry as a hand extended from a cloud; in the design, I echoed the same idea above the ship. Joe McCrum drew the cartoon, which has been much admired: his research was meticulous about the detailed structure of a Scarborough coble, but not quite so good about the rigging of the boat: after it was questioned, it was referred to the National Maritime Museum at Greenwich. We do our best to get things right! Faithfulness to detail is also demonstrated in the 'Delegation to the Czar' (Panel F5) by our alteration to the puffs of smoke coming from the train when we learned that a two-cylinder engine would puff in a particular way. Research takes many forms!

Somehow we developed an awareness of the needs of the Tapestry wherever we went. Daniel Wheeler's ship (Panel F4), which we understood was a converted packet-boat, was compared with the painting of another packet-boat on the walls of a hotel in Bayeux; the skyline of Leningrad in the same panel was from my hostess's travel poster when I visited the group in Dublin: bits of the jigsaw of relevant facts are found in most unexpected places! Details are sometimes checked by conversation with people who have served in the team represented. This was the case with the Maternity Hospital in Chalons, France, in the panel 'Relief of Sufferings' (Panel F7); also with the dreadful lorries that kept breaking down on the China road in the panel 'Friends Ambulance Unit' (Panel F8). Sometimes it is possible to tape-record memories, an activity I hope we shall continue. Some Friends still possess clothing which belonged to ancestors – especially attractive are the bonnets: the drawing of the bride and groom in the 'Marriage' panel (Panel C8) was copied from a well-known painting and a hundred years later the family still treasure the groom's outfit: it was fascinating to notice the details. In the original embroidery cartoon, based on the painting, the bride's mother appears as depicted, wearing a lace cap with her bonnet on her knee. The research group did not find it convincing, so it was altered; now we know that women ministers who might feel called upon to speak, in order that their voices were not muffled and so they would not disturb the Meeting with rustling movements, sometimes removed their bonnets before Meeting began.

It was evident that the historical research provided many groups with an enjoyable interest. Their interpretation and suggestions for designs, including the children's drawings, demonstrated the vitality of their work. Single episode stories, such as the humorous 'Balancing the cash' ('Bankering' Panel E3) and the influential trial of Penn and Meade (Panel F2), were relatively easy to research and straightforward to illustrate. Complex life stories were not always confined to their popular image but represented by an outstanding insight. Elizabeth Fry has two panels which provide interesting contrasts, both in design and making. One panel represents the little-known story of her courage in caring for the women to be deported to Australia, and her perception in providing for their long journey, a personal bag of useful things, for example everything necessary to make a patchwork quilt (Panel E6). This embroidery travelled with Ann Castle when she introduced the Tapestry to Australia. The second panel (Panel E7) was made, with the help of her friends, by an embroiderer confined to her home. The design is complex; in the bottom section it shows Elizabeth Fry's affluent background and her mischievous personality as a girl, illustrated by the episode of organising her sisters to help her stop the mail coach. In the middle section of the panel her prison work in adult life and her ability to influence important committees, are contrasted with her revealing use of the quotation 'I believe; help thou my unbelief'.

There were other complex subjects to be understood and interpreted in designs. The concept of Simplicity (Panel D2) was explored by Ann Castle's study group, with no suitable story coming to mind. Ann Nichols suggested the episode of the King and his retinue visiting David Barclay in order to watch the Lord Mayor's procession. This story illustrated the remarkable contrast between the sumptuous clothes of the Court and the Quaker simplicity of dress, and David Barclay and his son provided a talking point about hat honour. After making enquiries of Friends House Librarian the full story and detailed descriptions were presented from the diaries of David Barclay's daughter, who had attended the party and was very impressed by the Queen.

Shared experience of design work

A discussion based on good research and careful selection of quotations usually created a design in my mind which I could sketch, sometimes on the back of an envelope, so I could hear the immediate reactions. Sometimes I would draw the finished design known as the cartoon; at other times I would design the layout and lettering, and an illustrator would supply the drawing. With few exceptions I compiled the children's work to make a connected design. I admired their drawings greatly and took good care not to distort them. We have had valuable help from several designers, including the architects Maurice Green and David Butler; also Margery Levy who has drawn many sensitive, complicated cartoons: her work is distinctive and requires very skilful embroidery: this can be enjoyed in 'Industrial Welfare' (Panel D11), which was embroidered by the Friends in Birmingham who also made the Elizabeth Fry panel. Not all the groups provided adequate research or thoughtful interpretations, but sent in completed cartoons, which required a lot of correction; to repeat the research and amend the panel sometimes took many months and held up the group's progress. Several times a group refused to accept the finished cartoon. 'Marriage' (Panel C8) and 'Vigils' (Panel F17), which was considered too aggressive, were both rejected by their original groups. Many times there were compromises, but if this failed and the cartoon was acceptable to the committee, it was then offered to another group who completed it most successfully.

1986 was considered to be mid-term in the making of the Tapestry. The Committee had decided to apply for charitable status to provide the Tapestry with security, simplify financial transactions and allow independence for decision-making. The constitution was accepted at the AGM during Yearly Meeting at Exeter University 1986, when the Quaker Tapestry Scheme became recognised as an educational charity. Amid the activity of the Exeter exhibition both men and women Friends settled for a quiet period of work at the embroidery frames, and were surprised at the sense of tranquility. We all answered a tremendous number of questions and felt confident that

A5. The good ship Woodhouse

people liked what they saw. Many people returned for quiet consideration, and one person explained that 'the first time you just look, the second time you consider the insights, and then return again to enjoy the embroidery'. The first time someone wept in front of an embroidery we were surprised, but now we know that the panels can speak to the deepest emotions and open the way for people to rethink, and even in some cases return to the Society.

The Tapestry as outreach

From the beginning panels have been loaned to accompany 'Meet the Quakers' exhibitions or for special celebrations. Printed words in prepared statements might not be read, but embroidery is immediately attractive and presents no threat. The craftsmanship and illustrated stories catch the imagination and the message gets through. We are told that panels open conversations: they also make it possible for Meetings to participate in ecumenical festivals of flowers and crafts. On many occasions our members have been invited to speak and show slides to other church gatherings, art societies, Women's Institutes and Embroiderers' Guilds. Although their subject is community embroidery, it is also a mirror reflecting Quakerism and an opportunity to explain some of the insights.

I have already mentioned the recurring enquiry, 'Where will it finally be exhibited?' – the omega question. The Tapestry in its entirety has so far no permanent home. Remembering that the aims of the project include education and communication, the expectation is that the embroideries and photographs will continue to serve small exhibitions, both at home and abroad. Seventy-five single subject panels allow many different exhibitions to be mounted – 'Live Adventurously' or 'Quaker Personalities' come to mind. Amongst the seventy-five panels there are at least twenty-three which are relevant to a Peace exhibition. Selecting your own imaginary exhibition is both entertaining and thought-provoking. Oak frames to display our embroideries are fixed in some Quaker buildings and the intention is to provide a changing display of panels.

The important exhibitions that have marked our progress have been planned to coincide with the residential Yearly Meetings, when approximately 2,000 Friends come together for one week and have the opportunity and time to consider new ideas. In 1989 the Tapestry was displayed for the Society and for the public in the Aberdeen City Art Gallery. The following year, 1990, when the ten-year project has reached its climax, the seventy-five panels are complete and this book is published, the embroideries will be presented to the public at a Spring Exhibition in London at the The Royal Festival Hall, and later a Summer Exhibition in France, at the Museum of William the Conqueror in Bayeux. Here the embroideries will be displayed in a beautiful, medieval, stone-pillared room, directly below the Bayeux Tapestry gallery. I am deeply grateful to everyone who has co-operated to make the new embroidery, and we all feel a tremendous satisfaction that for one month the Quaker Tapestry will be seen in the same Museum as the remarkable Bayeux Tapestry; both embroideries are outstanding examples of story-telling through craftsmanship.

Travelling with the Tapestry

The major responsibility for teaching the embroidery has been shared by three teachers: Ann Castle, Ann Nichols and myself, Anne Wynn-Wilson – often referred to as the three Anns. We each take responsibility for a number of panels: this entails travelling to visit groups. At other times we combine to serve the residential workshops and Tapestry Holidays. Each of us has undertaken major teaching journeys. Ann Castle travelled in Australia, Ann Nichols in Canada and myself in the United States.

We have succeeded in maintaining a good standard of craftsmanship by setting it high at the beginning: this has inspired all those who wished to participate. Visitors to our exhibitions often remark on the evident care and devotion of the workers and the co-ordination of style and colour throughout the whole work, whilst keeping diversity, humour and individuality. It is these qualities that transmit to the viewer of the embroideries the presence of a quiet energy.

I remember that when I wrote my final embroidery examination papers, to my surprise I answered the seemingly simple question 'What are the attributes of a good embroiderer,' by describing the many qualities of true love! Amongst these attributes are: caring deeply, integrity, awareness, respect and learning from experience: all essential when successfully sharing friendship and a community embroidery project.

The world family of Friends

The final panel in the series expresses our hopes for the future; the design was made in 1986 whilst I was attending the World Family Gathering at Waterford, Southern Ireland. I experienced the energy springing from the Seed, which inspired me to represent the Society as a great oak tree expressing the strength and diversity of its members, yet rooted in one source. I feel that religion should be spiritual; this is the root and the tree bears many fruits which include social responsibility and peacemaking. The various international sections of the Religious Society of Friends and their shared traditions are included in the spirals of energy surrounding the tree. The World as seen from the Moon has no apparent divisions; we wish to cradle and support her. I expected that children could demonstrate a unity of vision about the human family. These delightful drawings were collected by Friends from Quaker children in the countries named, during a two-year period. Drawings of 'Me and my friends' look very similar whether they come from Sweden, Japan or Canada. The embroidering of this panel has been widely shared. Samplers to decide how the World should be embroidered were made during our Tapestry holiday at Charbonnières in France, and other work has been undertaken in Switzerland, Scotland and various parts of England. 'The World Family of Friends' accompanied me across America when it was available for Friends to contribute, even if they only added a few leaves. George Fox's quotation is very apt for travellers: 'Be patterns, be examples in all countries, places, islands, nations, wherever you come, that your carriage and life may preach among all sorts of people, and to them; then you will come to walk cheerfully over the world, answering that of God in every one.'

If the last panel represents the growth and organization of the Society, the Title Panel celebrates the inspiration of Friends. 'Light' has always been used as a symbol of purity and knowledge. From the beginning of Quakerism, Friends' teaching was of belief in the 'Inward Light', in 'that of God in every man'. Early Friends could quote from St John's gospel: '. . . in whom was life, and the life was the light of men', . . . 'that was the true light, which lighteth every man that cometh into the world'.

Inspiration for our present time is not that religion should primarily be social, but that religion should be first spiritual. This is represented in the design by the intrinsic nature of the spiral, extending from the origin to infinity. The creative use of colour in the embroidery speaks of happiness and goodwill, of people reflecting the light, and speaks of the coming together of many different qualities, to become greater and more vibrant than one alone.

At the beginning of the project our intention was to explore Quaker history, but we soon found that we were discovering the insights which motivate Friends. We began to think of the Tapestry as a celebration of Quaker insights, certainly an exploration of the mystery that led early Quakers to call themselves the Children of Light.
September 1989

References

1 *The story of Quakerism* by Elfrida Vipont, reprinted by Friends United Press, 1977

2 *The journal of George Fox*, ed. John L. Nickalls, London Yearly Meeting/Cambridge University Press, 1952, rptd. 1975

3 *The Valiant Sixty* by Ernest E. Taylor, 1947, 3rd ed., Sessions, 1988

4 *Christian faith and practice in the experience of the Society of Friends*, London Yearly Meeting, 1960

A7. Conscientious objection

1. The Quaker context

John Ormerod Greenwood, the author of this book, died on 12 June 1989 in his eighty-second year. He had completed the text, shown it to various folk in draft chapters, dealt with their initial comments, and sent it to the publisher. Now, following his death, some of his friends (who are responsible for the greater part of this chapter) have had to take a look at the balance of the book as a whole and to make what changes they think Ormerod would have wished to make. In doing this we have kept in the forefront of our minds the purpose of the book as Ormerod Greenwood expressed it in his preface.

Ormerod Greenwood's preface

The book which follows is not a history of Quakerism; it is an extended commentary on the Quaker Tapestry, whose evolution has been described in Anne Wynn-Wilson's Prologue, as it grew from the inspiration of a woman and a boy into the participation of thousands.

Quakerism is a grass-roots movement, and this has been a grass-roots experience. The many groups who took part chose what they wanted to commemorate or express, some episode or insight which seemed important *to them*, which inspired *them*. Once or twice, startled by omissions, the committee sought to fill conspicuous gaps, but no attempt was made to ensure a general balance. Much is portrayed here, but much more (both of good and ill) is missing. The widest tapestry, the longest book, has limits; and now that there are Quakers in so many countries, we could not fairly claim to represent their experience; this is our gift to the rest, and to the general public who may be interested to learn a little of the Quakers through a medium far different from a formal exposition or a theological treatise. Above all, there is in the United States a great body of Quakers, grown from a common origin but with different traditions, and well able to speak for themselves.

This book is for those who have seen the Tapestry, and wish to remember it and to know more. It is also for those who cannot yet see the Tapestry, but wish they could, as a foretaste of its pleasures and a glimpse of its experience. We would like to follow the example of the good ship *Woodhouse* and its reluctant captain in panel A5, and as we leave you, to 'kindle a fire and leave it burning'.

Worship and church affairs

Thus far, Ormerod. Now his friends must take up their pen again to sketch some background pictures which will, we hope, help the reader to feel more familiar with some of the words and phrases which will occur throughout the book. And first, something about Quaker worship, a subject to which we shall return later (p.80).

At the heart of Quaker life is the meeting for worship. The early Friends, setting aside all notions of a pre-arranged service or an appointed person to 'lead the worship' met (as in Britain and various, but not all, other parts of the world they still do) in silent, expectant waiting, believing that as the spirits of the worshippers become attuned to God and to one another there will result 'a living silence' and 'a gathered meeting' out of which any one of the worshippers may be moved to offer vocal ministry or prayer.

Ormerod himself has written: 'It is important to understand that all meetings for worship are public; there is no form of outward communion or ceremony reserved to members alone. It is sometimes said that Quakers have no sacraments. What should be said is that, seeing life as sacramental, they have no distinct or separate outward sacraments; the sacramental experience may occur in or out of Meeting, depending on our readiness or integrity'.

Quakers saw, and see, their meetings for church affairs as, in essence, meetings for worship in the course of which the necessary business is transacted. It was in 1662 that Edward Burrough counselled Friends not to proceed 'as a worldly assembly . . . ., by hot contests, by seeking to outspeak and over-reach one another in discourse, as it were controversy between party and party [but] assisting one another in whatsoever ability God hath given; and to determine of things by a general mutual concord'.

Early Friends, believing that Christ was the president alike in meetings for worship and for business, appointed no man or woman to that office, and used the term *clerk* for the Friend selected to record the transactions of a meeting for church affairs. It was, and is, the responsibility of the clerk to draw up a minute recording 'the sense of the meeting' on any issue before it, to read the minute aloud to the meeting, and to amend it as may then be agreed. Friends believe that this method, based on a search for unity (which they distinguish from unanimity), leads to loyal observance of decisions where the practice of voting may tend to lead to aggrieved minorities.

To appreciate the growth of Quaker insights it is necessary to have some understanding of Quaker polity, at least as it relates to Britain. The central unit in the various meetings for church affairs was, and is, the area *monthly meeting*, though congregational meetings came to be held in connection with local meetings for worship, being known as *preparative meetings* because their function was to prepare business for the monthly meeting. The area monthly meetings were grouped together into county (later regional) *quarterly meetings* which since 1967 have, with modified functions, been renamed *general meetings*. The quarterly meetings together formed a yearly meeting which, because it consistently met in London until 1904 was, and unfortunately still is, known as London Yearly Meeting, but which is perhaps more accurately described as the Yearly Meeting of Friends in Britain.

There is no need to describe in detail the national organization which grew up in order to carry out Yearly Meeting's wishes. But we must refer to the *Meeting for Sufferings*, set up as a result of a conference in 1675 to consider how far Quakers could obtain redress from those prosecutions under the penal laws which appeared to be illegal and thus to 'stay the arm of the oppressor'. It was in origin a small committee of London Friends meeting weekly with an efficient network of correspondents appointed by the county quarterly meetings so that it rapidly became an effective instrument in what was virtually parliamentary lobbying.

Meeting for Sufferings, instituted to help protect Friends from oppression, was before long concerned about the oppression of others and its network of correspondents was effectively used, for example, in the eighteenth century campaign against the slave trade. The Meeting still retains its original name (for there is among Quakers a strong streak of conservatism in such matters) but is now composed mainly of representatives of the area monthly meetings and meets about nine times a year, being in effect the representative assembly of London Yearly Meeting, charged with acting in its name between its annual sessions.

We must return for a moment to meetings for worship. While, out of the gathered silence any one of the worshippers might speak, it was early recognized that there is a diversity of gifts and that to some the gift of the ministry of the word is entrusted in larger measure than to others. The practice grew up whereby a monthly meeting 'acknowledged' or 'recorded' the gift it discerned in a particular Friend, woman or man, and those Friends became known as *recorded ministers*. In no sense were they appointed to an office, still less were they paid, though when they were 'liberated' by their monthly meeting to 'travel in the ministry', whether in other parts of Britain or overseas, their expenses were reimbursed.

On the principle that those who are most likely to speak should sit where they can

"SWEAR NOT AT ALL" Matthew chapter 5 v.34

The right to affirm achieved by Quaker Burgesses of Aberdeen in 1714.

Friend Robert Barclay reading the minute of the Privy Council.

We regard the taking of oaths as contrary to the teaching of Christ, as setting up a double standard of truthfulness; whereas sincerity and truth should be practised in all the dealings of life. — Christian Faith and Practice 1911 & 1925.

A9. Oaths

1623 **MARY FISHER** 1698

one of the many women "publishers of the truth"

"the World, East + West, was their parish" 1657

for God's Spirit dwelt in every man.

1652 ELIZ. HOOTON

YORK GAOL

CAMBRIDGE MARKET 1653

'OLD' ANNE AUSTIN 1655

BOSTON MASS.

MARY DYER 1660

B2. Mary Fisher

best be heard the ministers sat on a raised stand or 'ministers' gallery' at one end of the meeting house. The practice of recording was discontinued by London Yearly Meeting 1924.

Monthly meetings have also since the eighteenth century appointed *elders*, initially 'to counsel ministers' but now, more positively, to nurture the spiritual life of the meeting as a whole, having the right holding of meeting for worship as their particular care. Similarly, monthly meetings have appointed *overseers* to have responsibility for the pastoral care of the meeting, ensuring the visitation of the membership and the particular care of those in need. The appointment of elders and overseers is for a three-year period, being carefully revised.

The system of meetings for church affairs which we have described is neither congregational nor hierarchical. Just as the insights of individual Friends were tested by those of the gathered group, so the insights of the monthly meeting were tested against those of the quarterly or yearly meeting. It is in this exercise of continual testing that insights are shared, judgments reached, and loyalties formed. On occasion a monthly or quarterly meeting would seek the judgment of the yearly meeting on one issue or another. The counsel offered in response was later codified into what became known as the *Book of discipline*, a work revised (with due Quakerly disregard for times and seasons) at intervals of roughly a generation.

Our meetings for church affairs used to be commonly known as *meetings for discipline*, but to modern ears that phrase may, like *Book of discipline*, sound at least austere and at worst harsh and repressive. Perhaps, through modern eyes, some of the counsel and regulations of an earlier age were pretty stringent. But, in essence, it is a 'discipline we lay upon ourselves and corporately accept', as our Yearly Meeting recorded in 1967, adding: 'It is not something imposed from without, a discipline of law, but it is a quality of the spirit. Christian discipline is the help that the group gives the individual in his search for discipleship'. If the word is encountered in the pages that follow it is in this sense that it is to be understood.

A celebration of insights

For four years Ormerod Greenwood was a member of the committee which revised that part of our *Book of discipline* entitled *Christian faith and practice* and approved by our Yearly Meeting in 1959. Some passages are recorded as drafted by the committee but, as Roger Clark of Street (he of the shoes and sandals) once wrote, 'it is not easy to compose an outstanding document by the committee method' and the revision committee wisely left virtually unaltered what we can now acknowledge as Ormerod's preamble to the first chapter, 'Spiritual experiences of Friends'. In the preamble he recalls that the chapter first formed part of the book in 1921

> after a time of theological difference, by Friends who longed not to be separated by dispute, but to share an experience which men and women had reached in diverse ways. For the Society of Friends might be thought of as a prism through which the Divine Light passes, to become visible in a spectrum of many colours; many more, in their richness, than words alone can express.

The image of the prism, the subject of the opening panel, serves to underline not only the diversity of experience and of insight but also the fact that the tapestry — and this book — sets out to be not a history but a celebration of Quaker insights over upwards of three hundred years, insights of individual men and women and insights which have been so shared and developed that they can be described as the corporate insights of Friends generally. These are what Friends often refer to as 'our testimonies'.

This theme will be developed later in the book. Here it is necessary to say only that the testimonies, while springing from a root which is universal and eternal, may find expression in forms that change from age to age. Thus, with changed legislation with regard to the state church and changed social conditions, English Friends no longer felt in the later nineteenth and twentieth centuries that they needed to maintain 'our ancient testimony against tithes' though continuing their fundamental convictions on the non-necessity of a paid and separated ministry.

A testimony develops not from a cerebral notion that it ought to exist and still less from external pressures that 'Friends ought to be doing something'. A testimony becomes real as a conviction is formed that here is a witness which must be made because it is God's will. It is likely to be a gradual process as such a conviction gradually takes hold of a whole group. Our Yearly Meeting has reminded us that:

> It does not lessen our responsibility to press the urgency of a question, if we cannot as yet unite upon the answer to it. Until we can, we may have to refrain from corporate statements implying a corporate decision, not in evasive hesitancy but in resolute patience. It is no service to the Kingdom of God if those who pray for its coming exaggerate the present clarity of their judgment or the present sufficiency of their understanding.

Quaker language

T. S. Eliot once described Quakerism as 'a distinguished but isolated culture'. On occasion the isolation of Quakers has been overstressed, not least by some Quaker historians, and it is salutary to remember that at the very time when Friends were at their most intemperate about the 'hireling priests' there existed a good and firm friendship between William Penn and Edward Stillingfleet who after 1689 was Bishop of Worcester.

Nevertheless, Quakerism is a sub-culture and like any other group with a continuing life of its own it developed a private and at times peculiar vocabulary. Some usage can be seen as part of the testimony of Friends concerning truth: Ormerod Greenwood died 'in his eighty-second year' a phrase which is true for a twelvemonth whereas 'aged 81 years' is strictly truthful for but one day. The use of 'thee' and 'thou' stemmed partly from the testimony for truth (for 'you' is not a singular pronoun) and partly from the testimony concerning social equality, for in the seventeenth century 'you' was a form of flattery to social superiors.

Or again, early Friends, testifying against the heathen names of the days of the week and (most of) the months of the year, were accustomed to use numbers instead, the day called Sunday being first-day and the day called Thursday fifth-day. With the months it is not so simple as, until 1752, the year began on Lady Day, 25 March, so that for the Quakers March was first-month (despite the 24 days that belonged to the old year). There was, of course, no objection to the use of September, October, November and December, these being Latin statements of fact. After 1752, however, September was no longer the seventh but the ninth month and it became untruthful to use the name and Friends were counselled not to do so. In the nineteenth century our Yearly Meeting began on the first third-day after the third first-day in fifth-month, but Quakers have – with the occasional exception – abandoned this testimony against the heathen names. This book, therefore, follows present rather than ancient usage, save in quotations or where the flavour of an occasion requires it.

Quakers, protesting against the superstitions which had grown up around saints, and objecting also to every title relating to the hireling priesthood, eschewed the use of 'saint' or 'bishop' or 'abbot' in place names, speaking of Albans or Petersburg, Stortford or Auckland, so that, indeed, in the middle of last century an elderly woman Friend in the city of London encountered some difficulty in finding the street she was seeking as she enquired diligently for Mary Axe.

Quaker language also became standardized through usage. Friends did not speak or pray in meetings for worship: they 'appeared in the ministry' or 'appeared in supplication'. If Friends travelling in the ministry held a meeting for worship in the course of a family visit, it was 'an opportunity'. Steeped in Biblical imagery they were, if cast down, 'as a sparrow alone upon the house top' (Psalm 102: 7). Given to understatement and caution, the Quaker replied to the enquiry after the health of his delicate wife, 'Thank thee, I think I may safely say that she is much as she sometimes is'.

Ormerod had himself joined the Society of Friends by convincement ('a received

B1. George Fox preaching on Firbank Fell

Friend' as those of the Quaker dynasties were wont to say) and there were times when he wanted to shake and even to shock Friends for what he regarded as their narrowness of outlook. But there was a strong conservative streak in him and he loved 'the ancient way'. Partly this was his literary taste savouring the unusual but telling phrase. But it was more than that: it was that in old customs and old phrases he felt that he was holding a key to the understanding of attitudes and convictions. Anxious that others, too, should hold that key, he included in this book words and phrases which may at first sight seem puzzling and even alien. But they are worth working at, for they may well help us to deeper insights.

May the light prevail

We are now almost ready to turn to the first panel and to see what we can learn from the insights of George Fox. But, before we do so, it is important to reiterate that neither the tapestry nor this book attempts more than to portray a very few Friends, a very few episodes. Let us return to Ormerod's own words in the preamble to the first chapter of *Christian faith and practice*:

> If we could have shown Rachel Metcalfe mothering her orphans from her invalid chair; or George Swan, the boy from the fairground, playing his concertina through the villages of India — if only we could have shown them all!
>
> But then in honesty we should have had to reveal also the extent of our failure; the light dimmed in narrow hearts and creeds, the baptism of grace lost in timidity and torpor, the corrosion of arrogance and self-satisfaction — for we have known these too. May the light prevail over the darkness; may those who are here speak for all the children of the Light, to the needs of other times as well as their own.

2. How Quakerism began

George Fox and the Fenny Drayton background (A1)

A weaver's cottage with its loom; a parish church and its priest in the porch. On the left of the panel, a lad tending sheep; on the right, the lad drinking with friends; in the centre that same lad, pensive, in despair. Below, the rival armies of Cavalier and Puritan. Fenny Drayton, the panel says; but 'Drayton-in-the-Clay' is what he called it; a small village in Leicestershire in the middle of England, a village with a strong Puritan tradition. George Fox was born in 1624, the son of Christopher Fox, weaver and also churchwarden, and Mary (Lago): they and their cottage are represented on the left of our panel. His father's nickname 'Righteous Christer' speaks for his character and principles; George's description of his mother as 'of the stock of the martyrs', implies that her family claimed to have been Protestants who died for their faith during the Marian persecutions. A holy background then; some of the family said he should be a priest. The key-word 'pure' which gave the Puritans their nickname continued to be on his lips: 'When I came to eleven years of age, I knew pureness and righteousness; for when I was a child I was taught to be kept pure.' He would pay heavily for that weight of purity before he had done with it. However, he did not become a priest; he would find out in time that 'priesthood' is something that all the 'members' of the 'Church' (men, women, and children) have to share.

He was sent to serve a shoemaker in a neighbouring village, who was branching out as a grazier, dealing in sheep, wool and cattle. William Penn long years after wrote of Fox: 'He was brought up in country business, and as he took most delight in sheep, so he was very skilful in them; an employment that very well suited his mind in several respects, both for its innocency and solitude, and a just emblem of his ministry and service.'

'Innocency and solitude' perhaps; George's verdict on those times is far from idyllic: 'people living in all filthiness, loving foul ways and devouring the creation; and all this in the world, in the pollutions thereof, without God.' He saw around him folk with 'mouths full of deceit and changeable words' and felt called to a life of integrity: 'The Lord taught me to be faithful in all things, and to act faithfully two ways, viz inwardly to God and outwardly to man, and to keep to "yea" and "nay" in all things'.

His faithfulness was brought to the test in a curious way. He had gone to Atherstone to the fair one day in 1643, when he was 19 years old. His cousin Bradford ('a professor and having another professor with him') asked George to share a jug of ale. As they were 'professors' (persons professing to be religious) he 'being thirsty went in with them, for I loved any that had a sense of good, and did seek after the Lord.' But it wasn't just a quiet drink but seemed set to become a rowdy party: 'They began to drink healths and called for more drink, agreeing together that he that would not drink should pay for all.' George was disgusted 'that any that made profession of religion should offer to do so'. He got up abruptly, laid a groat on the table, and said, 'If it be so, I'll leave you.' He finished his business and went home, but not to sleep. 'I did not go to bed that night, but sometimes walked up and down, and sometimes prayed and cried unto the Lord who said unto me, "Thou seest how young people go together into vanity and old people into the earth; and thou must forsake all, both young and old, and keep out of all, and be a stranger to all."'[1]

'Then, at the command of God, on the 9th day of the Seventh Month 1643, I left my relations and broke off all familiarity with young or old.' Was this teenage restlessness or was there something deeper? To understand, look at the date on the panel: 1643. The previous summer Charles I declared war on the Commons of England and raised his standard at Nottingham, calling the 'trained bands' (local militia) into service. Civil war, for the first time since the Wars of the Roses, but a different kind: not feudal lords against each other, but the King, 'God's vicegerent on earth', against his 'faithful Commons'. Less than seven years later, Charles Stuart would be led out from his own Banqueting House in Whitehall to the scaffold where the executioner was waiting, masked, to cut off his head. England would become a 'Commonwealth' (the general good of the country held in common) and Oliver Cromwell, a country gentleman from East Anglia, its 'Lord Protector'.

It was in the atmosphere of anxiety and of new and radical notions that young George Fox left home. Many thought that these were the days spoken of in the Book of Revelation: the creation of all things new, the coming of the Heavenly City, Jerusalem, when time would end and the Lamb of God reign.

Fox's search and discovery (A1)

Those years, 1643 to 1647, were years of travel and of search, years of temptations to despair and years of 'openings'. From home he went to Lutterworth, Northampton,

B3. John Bright

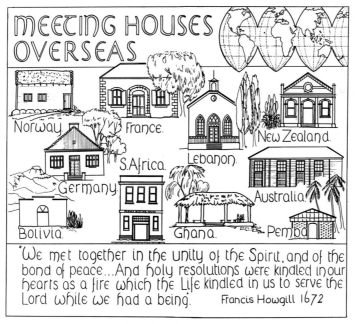

C5. Meeting houses overseas

Newport Pagnell, Barnet, and thence to London, where 'some tender people would have had me stay'. But his parents were troubled at his absence and, lest he grieve them, he returned home to Fenny Drayton.

His relatives had simplistic remedies for his troubles: he should get married or join the army, but he was 'grieved that they proffered such things to me, being a tender youth'. And he turned to many priests of the neighbourhood in search of help – to Nathaniel Stephens in his own parish and to others at Mancetter, Coventry, Atherstone. Walking with Dr Cradock of Coventry in his garden, George trod on some plants as he discoursed 'at which the man was in such a rage as if his house had been on fire'. One priest betrayed his confidence by talking to the servants 'so that it got among the milk-lasses'; and in his own parish Nathaniel Stephens used George's material for his sermons.

By now it was 1646. His relations were troubled that he would not go to church with them but would go by himself into the orchard or the fields with his Bible. He continued to travel in the neighbourhood and, in an age of growing sectarianism, he met groups of seeking folk with a variety of beliefs, some bordering on the bizarre. Then, early in 1647, he went into Derbyshire and Nottinghamshire and 'met with a tender people, and a very tender woman whose name was Elizabeth Hooton'. We shall meet her again later on: sufficient for the moment to say that she was the wife of Oliver Hooton of Skegby, near Mansfield, and that she was in her late forties, a generation older than Fox.

For the moment he still held apart and went his way: 'I was often under great temptations; and I fasted much, and walked abroad in solitary places many days, and often took my Bible and went and sat in hollow trees and lonesome places till night came on'. But the long search was to end with the discovery of the immediacy of religious experience:

> But as I had forsaken all the priests, so I left the separate preachers also . . . And when all my hopes in them and in all men were gone, so that I had nothing outwardly to help me, nor could tell what to do, then, Oh then, I heard a voice which said, 'There is one, even Christ Jesus, that can speak to thy condition', and when I heard it my heart did leap for joy.

But this experience of joy was still accompanied with many 'deep workings' of pain and suffering, an experience he could not understand until 'the Lord answered that it was needful I should have a sense of all conditions, how else should I speak to all conditions'. His central experience, however, convinced him that God enabled people to rise 'atop' (a favourite word) of the dark side of life: 'I saw also that there was an ocean of darkness and death, but an infinite ocean of light and love, which flowed over the ocean of darkness. And in that also I saw the infinite love of God'.

With these openings Fox was ready to set upon journeyings of a different nature: he was to call men and women to rely on the workings of the Inward Light of Christ in their own hearts.

We must pass rapidly over the next four years, during which Fox was preaching his new-found convictions in the midland counties. These years included convincements and opposition, an imprisonment at Derby about which we shall hear later on (see p. 183) and a strange episode at Lichfield in 1651.

George Fox at Lichfield (D1)

In the autumn of 1651 George Fox, recently freed from Derby Gaol, saw the spires of Lichfield Cathedral which, he said, 'struck at my life'. A mile from the city 'I was commanded of the Lord to pull off my shoes of a sudden' and, leaving them with some shepherds, he went up and down the streets crying 'Woe unto the bloody city of Lichfield' and it appeared to him as though there were a channel of blood in the streets.

He had been nearly a year in prison; he had suffered physically from foul prison conditions; he had suffered mentally by the sight of men and women being put to death for petty offences. He was steeped in the Bible and his mind was full of its language and images. Now, with lowered physical vitality but heightened sensitivity of mind, his horror at the inhumanity he had witnessed appears to have found expression.

He may have known, as depicted on the left hand side of our panel, that Joyce Lewis of Mancetter (the village where he had been apprenticed) had been burned at Lichfield in 1557 during the Marian persecutions; he later heard the tradition that Christians had been martyred there under Roman rule.

It is an episode which he did not attempt to edit out of his *Journal* nor more fully to explain. In our panel we have linked it to his underlying convictions about light and stillness. It had been in 1647 that he had the experience of the 'infinite ocean of light and love, which flowed over the ocean of darkness', and it would be in 1658 that he would write to Oliver Cromwell's daughter, 'she they called the Lady Claypole [who] was very sick and troubled in mind' with the words, 'Be still and cool in thy own mind and spirit from thy own thoughts, and then thou wilt feel the principle of God'.

He began in the midlands; as far as he had a 'centre' it was in Mansfield, with Elizabeth Hooton's house at Skegby as an anchor. In that area he had small and intermittent success. From there in 1651 he now went to Yorkshire, 'through

Doncaster and several other places, and then came to Balby, where Richard Farnworth was convinced and several others . . . and went into the country about Wakefield where James Nayler lived, where he and Thomas Goodaire and William Dewsbury and many more were convinced'. We must now pause in Fox's travels to find out more about Nayler, who will be an important figure in our story.

James Nayler, a Quaker from Cromwell's army (A2)

James Nayler was seven years older than Fox, and very different in background, character and experience. His family were proudly independent yeomen who owned land and gave their children a good education; Ardsley Hall, supposed to be James Nayler's birthplace, was a very substantial house. George Fox refused from the first to fight in the Civil War or any other war; James Nayler was a soldier with eight years active service for the Parliament. The war had swept up to his front door as the Royalists occupied Wakefield Castle; he volunteered at 26 and was almost certainly in action when the Parliamentary forces took the Castle in 1643. His enthusiasm, courage and resolution brought him advancement to the rank of Quartermaster in the crack regiment of Lambert's cavalry. He fought at York, at Marston Moor, at Dunbar.

After Dunbar, a cavalry officer was riding at the head of his troop when he saw a crowd and sent one of his men to investigate. The soldier didn't come back, so he sent a second, and then decided to go himself:

> When I came thither I found it was James Nayler preaching to the people, but with such power and reaching energy as I had not till then been witness of. I could not help staying a little though I was afraid to stay, for I was made a Quaker, being forced to tremble at the sight of myself. I was struck with more terror before the preaching of James Nayler than I was before the battle of Dunbar, when we had nothing else to expect but to fall a prey to the swords of our enemies.

James Nayler was not yet himself a Quaker, but was clearly preaching doctrines which were recognizably Quaker. Next year, 1651, after he had been invalided out and had become 'a member of a very sweet society of an Independent Church', he first met George Fox, who held meetings in the house of Nayler's West Ardsley neighbour and army comrade, Lieutenant Roper. Fox, as we have seen, arrived late in 1651, not so very long after his Lichfield experience, and recorded the convincement of Nayler and others. But it was at the time of barley-sowing next spring that Nayler records his own call:

> I was at the plow, meditating on the things of God, and suddenly I heard a Voice saying unto me, 'Get thee out from thy kindred and from thy Father's house'. And I had a promise

PUBLISHERS of TRUTH
The principal fountain of truth must be the Truth itself
Robert Barclay of Ury published his Apologia 1676
Others wrote Journals + letters
Edward Burrough
Isaac Penington
Benjamin Clark
Mary Westwood
John Woolman
Job Scott.
Tracts were often printed by women and distributed by travelling ministers and packmen

B4. Publishers of Truth

given with it. Whereupon I did exceeding rejoice that I had heard the Voice of that God which I had possessed from a Child, but had never known him.

Let us now leave Nayler for a few minutes while we follow once again the journeyings of Fox.

Fox travels to Sedbergh (B1)

Fox, then, had been at Balby and Wakefield in the last months of 1651. He now moved into the East Riding of Yorkshire, reaching York towards the end of December, and then going north into Cleveland, back to the East Riding and thus to Balby and Warmsworth once more. It was perhaps May 1652 when he was again at Lieutenant Roper's, where 'there were James Nayler, Thomas Goodaire and William Dewsbury that had been convinced the year before and Richard Farnworth'. We are going to meet most of these again.

Richard Farnworth of Tickhill, near Bawtry, travelled with Fox to Pendle Hill, where 'the Lord let me see atop of the hill in what places he had a great people to be gathered'. Soon after this, Fox and Farnworth parted, Fox travelling by upper Wensleydale towards Sedbergh, where it was the time of the hiring fair.

Our panel commemorates two events of 1652, Fox preaching outside Sedbergh church on Wednesday 9 June, and his great meeting on Firbank Fell the following Sunday, 13 June. But we must first reflect on one of his experiences while travelling in the midlands in 1648, of which he wrote, 'Now the Lord God hath opened to me by his invisible power how that every man was enlightened by the divine light of Christ; and I saw it shine through all'. This belief in the Inward Light of Christ, to be found in every human heart, however much hidden by worldly accretions and irrespective of knowledge of the historic Jesus, was to be central to Quaker teaching.

At the hiring fair at Sedbergh Fox declared 'the day of the Lord' and then got by a tree in the steeplehouse yard and 'declared the everlasting Truth', how that 'the Lord Christ Jesus was come to teach his people himself and bring them off all the world's ways and teachers'. And then a captain said, why would he not go into the church, for that was a fit place to preach in; but Fox 'opened to the people that the ground and house was no holier than another place, and the house was not the church, but the people which Christ is the head of'.

And so we come to the gathering on Firbank Fell where it was judged there were about 1000 people and where Fox preached for about three hours. There was a chapel on the fell and there were many old people there who 'looked out of the windows and thought it a strange thing to see a man to preach on a hill or mountain and not in their church (as they called it)'. But Fox declared that 'Christ was come, who ended the temple, and the priests, and the tithes'.

He spoke of the danger of those who have the scriptures 'and are not in that spirit which gave them forth' and called his hearers to 'come to know Christ their teacher, their counsellor, their shepherd to feed them, and their bishop to oversee them and their prophet to open to them'.

This conviction, then, that each person can be enlightened by the Inward Light of Christ was to lead Quakers to stress that religion must permeate the whole of life, that consecrated buildings were an irrelevance, and that no separated clergy could stand as mediators between God and each individual man or woman.

From Firbank, Fox travelled to Preston Patrick, Kendal, Underbarrow, and so through the Furness district of Lancashire until he came to Swarthmoor Hall, near Ulverston. But we must now go back and trace James Nayler's steps.

Nayler's call to the ministry (A2)

It was, as we have seen, at barley sowing that Nayler had heard the call, 'Get thee out from thy kindred and from thy Father's house'. In May 1652 Fox had again met him, and now came the second call:

> I began to make some Preparation as Apparel and other Necessaries, not Knowing whither I should go: but shortly afterward, going agateward with a Friend from my own House, having on an Old Suit, without any Money, Having neither taken Leave of Wife or Children, I was commanded to go into the West, not Knowing whither I should go nor what I was to do there.

What can we know of Nayler? One of his adversaries allows him 'an exceeding quick wit and sharp apprehension', granting him also 'the gift of good oritory with a very delightable melody in his utterance'. Another adversary describes him as 'a man of good complexion, brown hair which he wears of an indifferent length' and a short beard, a man with 'a melancholy aspect' and with 'his hat hanging over his brows, his clothes very plain'. He was better educated than Fox; he had all Fox's personal magnetism; but Fox's discernment of others' spirits and Fox's robust common sense he lacked.

Now he was excommunicated *in absentia* by his pastor and was travelling in different parts of Yorkshire, at some juncture returning home, where his brother William had joined the growing group of Quakers. Richard Farnworth, as we have seen, had parted with Fox soon after they had been atop of Pendle Hill. Now he and Nayler joined forces, moving north-westward until, a couple of weeks or so after Fox, they too arrived at Swarthmoor Hall.

The Swarthmoor household (C1)

Swarthmoor Hall was the home of Judge Fell and his wife, Margaret, and their family. Judge Fell was now in his early fifties, his wife some 15 years younger. He was Vice-Chancellor of the Duchy of Lancaster and Attorney for the County Palatine, Attorney-General of the North Wales Counties and Judge of Assize for the Chester and North Wales Circuit. He had supported Parliament in the Civil War but disapproved of Cromwell's increasing power.

The Fells had been married for 20 years; theirs was a hospitable home; and it was in Ulverston that Fox heard that he might be welcome there. Margaret Fell and the children (the Judge was away on circuit) had a few days earlier learned that this travelling preacher was in the neighbourhood.

It so chanced that she was away that day in late June 1652 when Fox arrived. When she got back she found that the young stranger had been in argument with William Lampitt, the minister of their church in Ulverston. Priest Lampitt came back next day and Fox 'had a great deal of discourse with him' in Margaret Fell's presence. A day or two later, Thursday 1 July, it was a lecture or fast day and Margaret Fell and her children were at Ulverston church. As the congregation were singing the psalm before the sermon George Fox came in. She recalled the subsequent course of events:

> and when they had done singing, he stood up upon a seat or form and desired that he might have liberty to speak. And he that was in the pulpit said he might.

As Fox warmed to his theme

> he went on and said, How that Christ was the Light of the world and lighteth every man that cometh into the world; and that by this Light they might be gathered to God, etc. And I stood up in my pew, and I wondered at his doctrine, for I had never heard such before.

Then Fox continued:

> You will say, Christ saith this, and the apostles say this; but what canst thou say? Art thou a child of Light and hast walked in the Light, and what thou speakest is it inwardly from God?
>
> This opened me so that it cut me to the heart; and then I saw clearly we were all wrong. So I sat me down in my pew again, and cried bitterly. And I cried in my spirit to the Lord, 'We are all thieves, we are all thieves, we have taken the Scriptures in words and know nothing of them in ourselves'.

When Fox began to apply his words to 'false prophets and priests and deceivers of the people' it was too much for one of the Justices of the Peace, John Sawrey ('a rotten professor'), who cried out, 'Take him away'. But Margaret Fell said to the officers,

B5. Stephen Grellet

'Let him alone, why may he not speak as well as any other?' so Fox 'declared a pretty while' until finally the constables removed him.

It was three weeks before Judge Fell came home. Just before he arrived he was met by a group of local dignitaries who told him that a travelling preacher had bewitched his family and household – alarming news when witchcraft was common belief. When he got home, though George Fox had not returned from his travels, the Judge was met by James Nayler and Richard Farnworth, (who had arrived in the meantime) and they spoke to him moderately and wisely, and assuaged his worst fears.

The Judge was also affected by his wife's plea, and the great change he noticed in her. At dinner time (she recalled) 'the power of the Lord seized upon me, and he was struck with amazement and knew not what to think, but was quiet and still. And the children were all quiet and still, and grown sober, and could not play on their music that they were learning: and all these things made him quiet and still. At night George Fox came . . .'

We need not follow in detail the events of the next few days, but, when Friends of the household and neighbourhood were discussing where they might worship, the Judge, overhearing them, said with remarkable tolerance: 'You may meet here, if you will'. And, until 1690, when a meeting house was built in the neighbourhood, Friends met for worship in the great hall at Swarthmoor. Judge Fell never became a Quaker: for a year or two he sat alone in the family pew at Ulverston church, but for some years before his death in 1658 he would sit in his parlour at the time of meeting, with the two doors open between his room and that in which Friends were worshipping.

We shall return to the Swarthmoor household and its place in the Quaker movement, but we must now follow George Fox and James Nayler on some of their travels.

Fox at Ulverston (E1)

The story which our panel depicts is easily told, but it may take a lifetime to assimilate the messages which it brings to us. Between June 1652, when he first arrived at Swarthmoor, and the late summer, Fox was travelling in the neighbourhood. One day in, perhaps, September, he was 'moved to go again to Ulverston steeplehouse' upon a lecture day, to find Priest Lampitt 'blustering on in his preaching'. Fox, as was to be expected, spoke, assured by John Sawrey that if he would speak according to the scriptures, he might speak:

> Then the rude people said to the Justice, 'Give him us!' and he did. So of a sudden all the
> people in the steeplehouse were in an outrage and an uproar, that they fell upon me in the

steeplehouse before his face, with staves and fists and books, and knocked me down and kicked me and trampled upon me.

Justice Sawrey finally put Fox in the custody of four officers, bidding them whip him and put him out of town. In the affray 'many friendly people' were knocked down and 'the blood ran down several people so as I never saw the like in my life' and he was dragged along, being beaten with staves and hedge stakes, holme bushes and willow rods, until they reached the common moss, about a quarter of a mile away, where he lay on the watery common:

> I lay a little still, and the power of the Lord sprang through me, and the eternal refreshings refreshed me, that I stood up again in the eternal power of God and stretched out my arms amongst them all, and said again with a loud voice, 'Strike again, here is my arms and my head and my cheeks'.

Perhaps it was inevitable that somebody should respond and 'a mason, a rude fellow' gave a blow on his outstretched hand with his rule-staff so that 'my hand and arm was so numbed and bruised that I could not draw it unto me again but it stood out as it was':

> Then the people cried out, 'He hath spoiled his hand, for ever having any use of it more'. The skin was struck off my hand and a little blood came, and I looked at it in the love of God, and I was in the love of God to all them that had persecuted me. And after a while the Lord's power sprang through me again, and through my hand and arm, that in a minute I recovered my hand and arm and strength in the face and sight of them all and it was all as well as it was before, and I never had another blow afterward.

It is comparatively easy to admire Fox's courage. It is sometimes harder to discern that he is sensitive to the evil in individuals, and in a mob, and to the good in individuals, and in a mob, and that he is sensitive to both at the same time. It is also easy to miss his tenderness and gentleness. Whether it was the mob upon the common moss at Ulverston or those whose ministry in meeting went 'beyond their measure', he bade Friends bear it: 'that is the tender'. It is this essential element in his personality, combined with his courage, his common sense, and his shrewd assessment of personality and situation, that made him, in William Penn's words, 'an original, being no man's copy'.

Nayler at Appleby

Meanwhile, James Nayler, after various journeys with George Fox, travelled north alone: late in 1652 he was arrested under an Elizabethan statute as a wandering vagabond and committed to Appleby gaol, where he was fellow-prisoner with Francis Howgill.

Seventeenth-century prisons were farmed out to gaolers who were responsible for bringing prisoners to court when required. Conditions were often dangerously unhealthy but treatment varied from the brutal to the accommodating. Privileges could be bought for money, or relatives and friends allowed access to bring food, nursing or comfort, or else debarred, according to the gaoler's whim. On occasion, 'safe' prisoners might even be allowed to go out into the town. On the other hand there was neither appeal nor redress should the gaoler or his wife be brutal. Margaret Fell wrote to her husband, absent on one of his journeys:

> We sent to my dear Brother James Nayler, and he is kept very close and cannot be suffered to have any fire. He is not free to eat of the jailor's meat, so they eat very little but bread and water. He writ to us that they are plotting again to get more false witnesses to swear against him things that he never spoke. I sent him two pounds, but he took but five [shillings].

The trial was inconclusive and Nayler returned to prison: the woman who kept the gaol became 'very tender'; and Nayler set to in writing a pamphlet to rebut the charges against him. And, after five months in the prison, he had satisfied the justices and was set free.

Nayler in London and Exeter (A2)

Released from gaol, Nayler found his way by stages to London, though he entered it as Fox had done, with 'trepidation'. He joined Howgill and young Burrough there, and these 'plain North country Plowmen' began both plowing and threshing in that stubborn field. Soon they were able to take over a part of a substantial city inn 'The Bull and Mouth' for their meetings, 'the new hired great tavern chapel' their opponents called it. Fox came and went, sometimes giving place to Nayler, as he did at a great debate in Derby in 1654 where he was at first nervous for Nayler ('I had a travail in my spirit for him, and the Lord answered me, & I was moved to bid him goe on') and in the end heard the people shout 'A Nailer, a Nailer, hath confounded them all.' When parted, they wrote each other affectionate letters; Nayler begged Fox to let him live in his heart for ever.

Circumstances now took a hand, as they always do. Nayler's success in London was heady. Outsiders saw him as the most prominent figure, and he and Fox were summoned before Cromwell when the Government received reports of great Quaker gatherings, and of more than 30 meetings settled in London itself. On the one hand

B6. Woodbrooke

there was the radicalism of the army, which touched Nayler and some other leaders; on the other the suspicion of Royalist intrigues. Cromwell seems to have been reassured and to have taken a liking to Fox, who told him: 'With the carnall weapon I do not fight, but am from those things dead' – dead to war as a corpse is dead. After the meeting Fox and Nayler parted at the gates of London city, Fox bound for the west. With a moment of doubt about Nayler's wisdom, recorded perhaps with hindsight, Fox wrote: 'As I parted from him, I cast my eye upon him, and a fear struck me concerning him.'

Nayler's success swept him into high society; he wrote a letter to Margaret Fell at Swarthmoor about a meeting at the Lady Darcy's, with 'some called Lords', divers ladies, divers officers, Sir Harry Vane and friends. Meanwhile Fox, arrested once more and in prison at Launceston in Cornwall, suffered an unbelievable degree of degradation. For thirteen days from 9 April 1656 he was put with others as a punishment into the 'Doomsdale' where excrement from the other prisoners' chamber-pots was poured on their heads: 'We were so bespattered that we could not touch ourselves or one another . . . in this manner we stood all night, for we could not sit down.' Cromwell might be lenient with these anarchists, but the Mayor of Launceston knew better. Streams of visitors made their way to Fox, some like Ann Downer walking hundreds of miles to be with him. The Quaker women were strip-searched for letters, some cast into prison. The local gentry backed the Mayor; Fox says that when 'Elizabeth Trelawney of Plymouth, a baronet's daughter, was convinced, the priests and other great persons and professors her kindred, were in a great rage concerning her and wrote letters to her, . . . and she sent her letters to me.'

In London Nayler grew desperate over Fox in Launceston, though Fox wrote from there some of his most radiant and ringing words of courage. Nayler entered a period of intense depression, like that which he had felt when he left the army; he could not sleep, and endured long fasts; his friends grew anxious for him. He was persuaded to go to Bristol where he had never been, although the 'Vision' had told him to go west. The Quakers had made great progress there with the support of substantial citizens, especially Dennis Hollister, former MP for Somerset, and owner of the best inn, the White Hart. Fanatical followers from London led by Martha Simmonds arrived; Martha fell at Nayler's feet among the crowd; the other Quakers dragged him away into a house, and when Martha persisted, threw her down the stairs. Fox earnestly and urgently summoned Nayler to Launceston.

The Bristol leaders urged Nayler to go to Fox, and he set out but never got to Launceston. At Okehampton, only 15 miles away, he and his party were arrested and taken to Exeter Gaol, where Nayler was described as quiet, and fasting for a month, 'waiting in his own way, for he is precious and dear with God, and is willing to bear reproach'.

Meanwhile the indefatigable Martha Simmonds hurried from Bristol to Launceston to tell Fox, entering the prison singing. She delivered a contentious message which Fox mistakenly thought was from Nayler and then made her way to Exeter where, entering Nayler's cell, she knelt and kissed his feet while he laid his hand on her head and blessed her. Relationships between Fox and Nayler deteriorated, certainly not helped by the rumours that Nayler had raised to life Dorcas Erbury, one of his fellow-prisoners. In September 1656 Fox was released from Launceston after an imprisonment lasting eight months: he made his way to Exeter to meet Nayler and the encounter between the two men did credit to neither. But we must remember that both must have been exhausted by their imprisonments and that Nayler must have been faint from long fasting. This estrangement is a sad prelude to the next episode in this tragic story.

Nayler's entry into Bristol and subsequent ordeal (A2)

Encouraged by Martha Simmonds and other followers, Nayler decided to demonstrate in Bristol by a symbolic act the second coming of Christ, which so many expected. The practice of 'acting a sign' was one not uncommon at that time and the Quakers were concerned to stress that the second coming of Christ was not an event to be looked for in the future but an event that had already happened, that indeed 'Christ had come to teach his people himself'. We need to understand this if we are to have any comprehension of what happened.

At Glastonbury Nayler and his followers formed up in procession and set out to walk to Bristol. Nayler was seated on a horse with a woman either side holding the bridle, splashing knee-deep through mud and water. By the time they reached the Redcliffe Gate of Bristol crowds had gathered and saw the procession throw down their wet cloaks in the road for Nayler to ride over as they sang 'Hosannah' and 'Holy, holy, holy, Lord God of Israel'. The Bristol Quakers had been warned to stay away, and they were absent.

The procession continued past the High Cross to the White Hart. There the authorities were sent to arrest them, and on Nayler they found 21 letters. Some, like that from Fox, denounced him; others praised him in the extravagant terms which (as we have seen) they all shared. Hannah Stranger had called him Son of God, the fairest in ten thousand, the Everlasting Son of Righteousness and Prince of Peace, and in one letter her husband had added a postscript: 'Thy name shall be no more James Nayler but Jesus.' Among the letters was a pass from Oliver Cromwell himself; but it no longer did Nayler any good.

The City Fathers decided that this was more than a local matter, and sent Nayler to London to be judged by Parliament, whether he should be put to death for blasphemy. The affair became known all over Europe, and Nayler, considered to be the leader of the Quakers' sect, was living proof of the awful end to which the sects were driving. It took the House of Commons nine sittings, in the midst of national and international affairs, to decide Nayler's fate, with Cromwell pressing all the time for leniency. Nayler was condemned to stand in the pillory, to be branded on the forehead with B for Blasphemer, have his tongue bored through with a hot iron, and then to be paraded and beaten through the streets of London and Bristol, before being returned to prison to repent.

Now (and this is the point of this whole tragic story) Nayler showed his Christ-like qualities. He bore the punishment with exemplary patience and dignity, and forgave and embraced the executioner. By the time he reached Bristol for the last part of the ordeal, opinion was relenting and the Bristol Quakers turned out to accompany him. He was sent back to Bridewell Prison in London and at first treated very severely but nursed back to some sort of health by an 'ancient widow' designated as his keeper, and by his wife Anne, who came to London, won the right to be with him, and petitioned Parliament to mitigate his punishment. Finally, after the death of Cromwell, he was released and went to stay with friends, when Anne went home to look after the family and the farm.

Nayler's last years (A2)

Nayler was now full of remorse, acknowledged his mistake and published pamphlets of explanation and self-defence; he showed all his old powers of persuasion, for which there is impressive tribute, for example, from the young squire Thomas Ellwood who later edited Fox's *Journal*. Nayler's last tracts contain passages of sublime beauty. He was determined to be reconciled to Fox, and went to Reading to try and see him. Fox was ill and refused to meet him, and Nayler wrote to Margaret Fell a most touching letter, saying: 'I was not permitted to come where he was . . . but my spirit was quieted, in that simplicity in which I went, in that to return; and (God) gave me his peace therein, as though I had my desire . . . and so his will is my peace.'

A reconciliation between the two men was eventually effected and at last, in October 1660, Nayler took the road home. Some miles beyond Huntingdon 'he was taken ill, being as it is said, robbed by the way, and left bound'. He was 'found in a field by a countryman toward evening' and taken to the house of a Quaker at Kings Ripton, where he died. His last words 'spoken about two hours before his departure out of this life' come straight from heaven:

B8. Quaker Peace Action Caravan

There is a spirit, which I feel, that delights to do no evil, nor to revenge any wrong, but delights to endure all things, in hope to enjoy its own in the end. Its hope is to outlive all wrath and contention, and to weary out all exaltation and cruelty, or whatever is of a nature contrary to itself. It sees to the end of all temptations. As it bears no evil in itself, so it conceives none in thoughts to any other. If it be betrayed, it bears it, for its ground and spring is the mercies and forgiveness of God. Its crown is meekness, its life is everlasting love unfeigned; it takes its kingdom with entreaty and not with contention, and keeps it by lowliness of mind.

In God alone it can rejoice, though none else regard it, or can own its life. It's conceived in sorrow, and brought forth without any to pity it, nor doth it murmur at grief and oppression. It never rejoiceth but through sufferings; for with the world's joy it is murdered. I found it alone, being forsaken. I have fellowship therein with them who lived in dens and desolate places in the earth, who through death obtained this resurrection and eternal holy life.

3. Publishers of Truth

We must return to the year 1654. George Fox recorded in his *Journal*:

> And so when the churches were settled in the north, the Lord had raised up many and sent forth into his vineyard to preach his everlasting Gospel, as Francis Howgill and Edward Burrough to London, John Camm and John Audland to Bristol through the countries, Richard Hubberthorne and George Whitehead towards Norwich, and Thomas Holme into Wales, a matter of seventy ministers did the Lord raise up and send abroad out of the north countries.

Seventy had good biblical precedent (Luke 10: 1) but when in 1694 Thomas Ellwood edited Fox's *Journal* he altered the figure with Quaker caution to sixty, and 'the Valiant Sixty' is now a phrase embedded in Quaker usage. In fact, 66 Friends have been identified as coming from the northern counties and as starting their service in or before the spring of 1654: of these, 12 were women.

Elizabeth Hooton (B2)

Our panel B2 celebrates five of these women. Elizabeth Hooton we have already met – the 'very tender woman' of Skegby, near Mansfield, whom Fox had encountered in 1647. She was then in her late forties. They had found that they were travelling on similar spiritual journeys and she may be claimed not only as the first adherent to the new movement but as the first of an impressive line of women ministering Friends. Quakers were not unique in recognizing that the gift of the ministry of the word is given to women equally with men, but it has been from the outset an essential belief which they have consistently upheld.

In 1651 Elizabeth Hooton was imprisoned at Derby for reproving a priest; the following year she was arrested at Rotherham for addressing the congregation at the close of parish worship, and taken to York Castle where, with her friend Mary Fisher (whom we shall shortly meet), she was confined for 16 months; in 1654 she was imprisoned for five months at Beckingham in Lincolnshire 'for declaring the truth in the place of public worship' and the following year she had a further three-month imprisonment in the same county.

It was in 1661 that she felt called to service in New England, but before we recount that story of great bravery we must turn to others who published Truth in New England. Before even that we must tell the story of another publisher of Truth, James Parnell, not usually reckoned among the Valiant Sixty, but valiant nonetheless. And there is a prelude to his story.

Friends visit Oxford and Cambridge (B2, D3)

It was December 1653 when Elizabeth Williams and Mary Fisher, aged respectively about 50 and 30, came to Cambridge and fell into discourse with some scholars of Sidney Sussex College, but 'observing the Froth and Levity of their Behaviour, told them they were Antichrists, and that their College was a Cage of unclean Birds, and the Synagogue of Satan'. Complaint was made to the mayor that two women were preaching and they were summoned before him: their replies to his cross-questioning having made him angry, he 'issued his Warrant to the Constable to whip them at the Market-Cross till the Blood ran down their bodies'. Our panel B2 depicts this, and though the sentence was executed 'far more cruelly than is usually done to the worst of Malefactors, so that their flesh was miserably cut and torn', yet they 'in the midst of their Punishment sang and rejoiced, saying, The Lord be blessed, the Lord be praised, who hath thus honoured us, and strengthened us thus to suffer for his Name's sake'. As they were led from their whipping they told the people that 'this was but the Beginning of the Sufferings of the People of God' and were then 'thrust out of the Town, no Man daring to shew them any Countenance'.

Next year Elizabeth Williams fared somewhat better at Oxford, whither she had gone with Thomas Castley 'crying Repentance to the People, who were Evilly Intreated by the Rude schollars & townsmen, being Hurried up & down the streets & feilds by them, untill Night drew on, & then Hurry'ed into a Poole of watter, called by the Name of Giles's Poole', for here the mayor sent his men to rescue them and deliver them to those who would care for them. But, alas, the couple gave cause to make 'the Truth evell spoaken of' and on 5 July 1654 Edward Burrough, while they were in Stafford Gaol, was driven into writing to Fox to 'call them in when they come out of prison' — a reminder indeed that 'we have this treasure in earthen vessels' (II Corinthians 4: 7).

It was later in 1654 that John Camm, of Camsgill, near Preston Patrick, came to Oxford:

comeing to this Citty, had greate servise, who kept a Meeting att Richard Bettriss house &

C1. Swarthmoor Hall

another att James Pinnells, who, with his wife, in a short time after, were Convinced of the Truth; but not being Faithfull, fell from it againe. Also the Power of the Lord reached unto Thomas Loe, whom the Lord afterward made a Minister of his Everlasting Truth.

Thomas Loe, who died in 1668, was an Oxford tradesman, but his convincement is important to us because, as we shall see later (p.94), it was he who was instrumental in the convincement of William Penn.

Before Richard Bettriss fell from Truth, meetings for worship were held at his house and it was in 1670 that he was fined £20, being distrained upon for half as much again, while Thomas Nichols, then aged about 30, was among others who had their goods distrained. He had earlier been imprisoned and in 1683 was to be again imprisoned, victim with numerous other Oxford Quakers to a couple of informers who had come to meeting with a constable. Nichols, who died in 1720, was a well-concerned Friend and was twice a representative to the Yearly Meeting in London.

James Parnell (A3)

James Parnell was born at Retford, Nottinghamshire, in September 1636. Though described as 'labourer' in an indictment, he was in fact well-educated. He was disowned by his family when, in the earliest days of the Quaker movement, he left work and sought out 'a few miles from the town where I lived' some of those 'whom the Lord was a-gathering out of the dark world, to sit down together and wait upon his name'. This was the group at Tickhill and Balby in south Yorkshire.

The 1653 episode which the children have depicted in our panel reminds us of his long journey on foot to Carlisle where Fox, whom he ardently wanted to see, was imprisoned. Though the gaoler had refused access to others, he relented and let James go in to Fox, who records the visit in his *Journal*: 'Whilst I was in the dungeon a little boy, one James Parnell, about fifteen years old, came to me, and he was convinced and came to be a very fine minister of the word of life, and turned many to Christ'.

In the summer of 1654 Parnell went to Cambridge, moved to go there because of the cruel treatment meted out to Elizabeth Williams and Mary Fisher. He was thrown into prison for publishing two papers against the corruption of the magistrates and priests. When he was tried at Quarter Sessions the jury, anxious not to convict, merely found that the papers were his. He was expelled from the town as a vagrant but returned again later and was again imprisoned, though freed next day by a friendly justice.

He went on to Colchester in the summer of 1655 and Steven Crisp, one of those convinced by his preaching, describes how:

he preached the Gospel to many thousands of people, first in his lodging; then in a steeple-house there after the sermon; then in a great meeting appointed on purpose, and after that [he] disputed with the Town-Lecturer and another priest in the French-school, all in one day.

The 'steeple-house' was St Nicholas's Church; the 'French-school' one set up for Huguenot refugees. As Parnell left the church someone in the crowd whacked him with a great staff, saying: 'There, take that for Jesus Christ's sake', to which he replied: 'Friend, I do receive it for Jesus Christ's sake'.

At Coggeshall, eight miles away, a fast day was ordered for 12 July, 'to Fast and Pray against the Errors of the Quakers'. Feeling ran high that day and the preacher, an Independent, did not spare his language. When he had done, Parnell began a reply but was arrested for causing a riot and committed to Colchester Castle. He was sent to Chelmsford for trial, chained day and night on the journey with felons and murderers. When the judge could not get a clear verdict against him, he committed Parnell for contempt of court, charging the gaoler 'to let no giddy-headed people come near him'.

All through the winter of 1655–6 Parnell lay in Colchester Castle without fire to warm him. He wrote to Essex Friends: 'As I had a time to preach the Truth amongst you, to the convincement of many, so also now I have a time to seal the same with patient suffering'. At first he was kept in 'the Hole in the Wall, which is very high from the ground, and where the ladder was too short by six foot, and when his friends would have given him a cord and a basket to have taken up his victuals in, they would not let him . . . but he must either come up and down by a rope (or else famish in the Hole) which he did for a long time'.

Eventually he 'missed the rope and fell from a very great height down upon stones'. He was 'taken up for dead [and put] in a little low Hole called the Oven . . . without the least air, hole or window for smoke'. Thomas Shortland, a Colchester Friend, offered to lie in prison for him 'body for body' while he restored his strength at a Friend's house: this was refused. At the end Shortland and another Friend were with him: 'The last Words he was heard to speak were, Now I go, and then stretching himself out, slept about an Hour, and breathed his last'.

'He died a Youth, about nineteen Years of Age, but approved himself a strong Man in Christ.' A plaque in his memory may now be seen at Colchester Castle. But let the last word rest with his friend Thomas Bayles: 'What Christianity or Holiness is that, which hurts or destroys, and thinketh thereby of doing God service?'

The first Friends in America (B2)

Near the end of 1655 Mary Fisher and Ann Austin arrived in Barbados, the first

[63]

Quakers to reach the Americas. We have already met Mary Fisher at Cambridge, but we must now say something more about her. She had been convinced of Truth when living at Pontefract and had already endured two if not three terms of imprisonment in York Castle, one, as we have seen, with Elizabeth Hooton. She had been a servant in a Quaker home at Selby and is described as having 'intellectual faculties . . . greatly adorned by the gravity of her deportment'. She was now about 32 years old. Ann Austin was already 'stricken with years', the mother of five children, and resident in London.

In July 1656 a ship from Barbados brought these two women into Boston harbour. The governor of Massachusetts Bay was absent and the deputy governor, alarmed at the possible introduction of heretical doctrines into the colony, ordered that the two Friends be detained on board ship and that their trunks be searched for any printed works they might have brought – over 100 'corrupt books' being confiscated and burnt, as shown in our panel. They were then brought ashore, confined to Boston gaol, their bodies searched for any mole or other sign of witchcraft, and, after five weeks, put on board a vessel back to Barbados.

Before they had left Barbados for Boston, Mary Fisher had written to her friends in England, 'Here is many convinced and many desire to know the way'. On their return they continued their work in Barbados and had their faith and zeal well rewarded for Lieutenant-Colonel Rous, a wealthy sugar-planter, and his son John were among those to identify themselves with Friends. John Rous came forth almost immediately in the ministry and was later to marry one of the daughters of Margaret Fell.

Mary Fisher and Ann Austin returned to England, perhaps separately, in the winter of 1656–7. We shall meet Mary Fisher again shortly. Of Ann Austin we can learn from the Kendal Fund accounts that £8.6.0. was spent on her 'passage back from Barbados' and there is an entry of £3.1.0. for 'clothes for Ann Austin when she went to keep Samuel Fisher's house'. She settled in London and in 1659 'suffered Imprisonment for preaching and declaring the Truth to the People in the publick Places of Resort and Concourse'. She died in 1665, victim to the great plague in which it is estimated that over 75,000 Londoners died.

The voyage of the 'Woodhouse' (A5)

It was in 1657 that Robert Fowler, a Quaker and mariner of Bridlington, Yorkshire, built a small ship, the *Woodhouse* (as shown on the left of our panel). As he later recalled, 'it was said within me several times, "Thou hast her not for nothing"; and also New England presented before me'. Nevertheless, 'entering into reasoning, and letting in temptations and hardships' he tried to ignore the inner voice, but the ship

C2. Margaret Fell

'contrary to my will . . . was brought to London'. Here, as our panel shows, 11 Friends were waiting for passage to America and 'Upon the 1st day of the Fourth Month called June, received I the Lord's servants aboard'.

The crew had mostly been pressganged by the navy 'so that for this long voyage we were but two men and three boys, besides myself' and once again 'reason entered upon me' to ask for a convoy; but, the wind driving the ship to Portsmouth, he secured sufficient crew. Shortly after, he found three 'pretty large ships' bound for Newfoundland, with whom he could sail the first part of the voyage.

They had sailed for a while when they saw a great ship bearing down on them, and under fear of attack the other ships took defensive measures and prepared to desert the *Woodhouse*. One of the leaders of the Quaker party, Humphrey Norton, warned Fowler early in the morning that 'they were nigh unto us that sought our lives' but added the comforting words: 'Thus saith the Lord, ye shall be carried away as in a mist'. The other ships tacked to escape the privateer but 'in the very interim the Lord God fulfilled his promise, and struck our enemies in the face with a contrary wind'. On parting from these three ships the Friends asked counsel of the Lord and heard the words: 'Cut through and steer your straightest course, and mind nothing but me'.

Their sense of divine guidance was so strong that they could testify that they saw 'the Lord leading our vessel even as it were a man leading a horse by the head; we regarding neither latitude nor longitude, but kept to our Line, which was and is our Leader, Guide, and Rule'. So, after several escapes on their two-month voyage, they came to Long Island and sat in prayer and rejoiced; and 'an irresistible word came unto us, That the seed in America shall be as the sand of the sea'.

Fowler compares his ship to Noah's Ark, 'wherein God shut up a few righteous persons and landed them safe'. New Amsterdam was then a tolerant Dutch colony and soon to be New York: in our panel the tiny houses of the Dutch settlement have behind them the skyscrapers of the city to be, and at the foot are the little company who are to become as the sand of the sea. Robert Fowler expressed himself poetically in allegory: 'Also there was a shoal of fish which pursued our vessel and followed her strangely, and along close by our rudder; and in our meeting it was shown me, these fish are to thee a figure. Thus doth the prayers of the churches proceed to the Lord for thee and the rest'.

'New England judged' (B2)

We must now say something of Mary Dyer, the remaining figure in our panel. She was living in Massachusetts when our story begins in 1637 with Anne Hutchinson arraigned before a General Court for her heretical beliefs and sentenced to be banished.

Anne Hutchinson was excommunicated by the church in Boston and as she found her way down the aisle to go forth into exile Mary Dyer stepped out from her seat, took her place by Anne Hutchinson's side and went out with her. They made their way to the new – and tolerant – colony of Rhode Island. It was for Mary Dyer the beginning of a spiritual journey that was to lead her to Quakerism and it was while on a visit to England that she was convinced of Truth.

At the end of 1658 the Massachusetts legislature, by a bare majority, enacted that every person 'of the cursed sect of Quakers' who was not an inhabitant of the colony, but was found within its jurisdiction, should be apprehended without warrant by any constable, and imprisoned, and on conviction as a Quaker should be banished upon pain of death, and that every inhabitant of the colony convicted of being a Quaker should be imprisoned for a month, and if obstinate in opinion should be banished on pain of death.

Some Friends were banished under this law, but in June 1659 William Robinson (one of the party who had crossed in the *Woodhouse*) and Marmaduke Stephenson came into the colony 'Boston's bloody laws to try'. Mary Dyer also came from her home in Rhode Island. The three were banished. They returned, and in October Governor Endicott passed sentence of death upon them.

On the day of execution, Thursday 27 October 1659, after the usual meeting day of the church in Boston, they were taken to the gallows on Boston Common. The two men had been hanged and Mary Dyer had stepped up the ladder, her face covered, and the halter round her neck, when the cry was raised, 'Stop! for she is reprieved'. She was again banished but returned in May 1660. This time there was no reprieve. After she had gone up the ladder, some said to her that if she would return home she might come down and save her life. To which she replied, 'Nay, I cannot, for in obedience to the will of God I came, and in His will I abide faithful to death'.

Quakers were not slow to recount at length the story of their sufferings and the title of three books published in these years are significant – *The New England ensign*, *The standard of the Lord lifted up in New England*, *New England judged by the Spirit of the Lord*. It was indeed the Massachusetts authorities who were judged. 'She did hang as a flag for others to take example by' jeered a member of the General Court after Mary Dyer's execution. And now in Boston there is a statue of her, so that others may take example by her stand for religious liberty.

The later years of Elizabeth Hooton (B2)

It was into this tense situation that Elizabeth Hooton felt called to travel in 1661, being accompanied by another woman Friend. They were immediately imprisoned in

Boston and, on being released, were driven from the colony into the wilderness through which 'amidst many dangers' they travelled until they arrived at Rhode Island. They then sailed for the West Indies but, believing that it was required of them to revisit New England and testify against the spirit of persecution, they soon returned to Boston. The authorities, however, bent on their expulsion, caused them to be arrested and conveyed back in the same ship in which they came. In this they returned to Virginia and soon after to their native land.

But Elizabeth Hooton had not long been at home before the duty of returning to Massachusetts revived with increased weight and clearness. She bethought her this time to avoid banishment by obtaining from the King a licence 'to buy a house for herself to live in, Friends to meet in, and ground to bury their dead in'. The authorities, however, were determined to frustrate her effort, royal licence or no. The story of her travels, being set in the stocks, imprisoned, whipped, cannot be recounted here: on one occasion, at Salem, her horse was taken away which obliged her, in order to get to Rhode Island, to travel 70 miles by foot — a woman now in her mid-sixties. 'Yea', she once observed, 'the love that I bear to the souls of men, makes me willing to undergo whatsoever can be inflicted on me'.

These journeyings occupied her several years, but when past 70 years of age she once more crossed the Atlantic, for she was among the group who accompanied George Fox when he first visited America in 1671. They came first to Barbados and then to Jamaica, but about a week after they arrived there she was taken ill, dying on the following day: 'She departed in peace, like a lamb', wrote Fox, 'bearing testimony to truth at her departure'.

Mary Fisher, the Great Turk, and other journeys (B2)

We must now go back to the 1650s and follow the travels of Mary Fisher. We have seen how she had come back from America early in 1657: she was now to set out on her most spectacular journey, which we celebrate in the main section of our panel.

In the spring or early summer of 1657 a party of six Friends, three men and three women, set out towards the Middle East. By 29 July they had reached Leghorn, where they had considerable service; and on 6 September they were at Zante, where the group divided, Mary Fisher and four others reaching Smyrna (Izmir) on 18 November and the other two joining them at the very end of the year.

When the English consul at Smyrna discovered their plan to convert the Sultan he was kind to them but, at the same time, encouraged them to return to England. They took his advice and Mary Fisher and four others took immediate ship for Venice, only

C3. Keeping the meeting

to find a strong wind forcing them once more to the Isle of Zante. Here they decided that three of the five should

> passe into the Morea againe into Turkey . . . to goe toward Adrianople (Edirne), where we heare the Turkes Emperour, lyes with his Army, being as is supposed Six days Journey from the place where they may land, as the lord makes way for their Passage.

It was decided, having crossed the Morea, to take shipping for Constantinople (Istanbul) and to try to approach the Sultan from that spot.

Sultan Mohammed IV was then a young man of 17, whose viziers had revived the military prowess of the Turks and made them again a menace to Europe. When the vizier was told that an Englishwoman had come to the camp with a message to the Sultan from the great God, he caused her to be received with state ceremony. She, now aged about 35, was brought before the Sultan with his great men about him. Bidden to speak her message she was silent, pondering what to say. The Sultan told her not to fear but to speak the word of the Lord to them, and she then spoke through an interpreter, the Turks listening with gravity and attention.

When she had ended the Sultan said that he had understood every word and that it was the truth. Though he invited her to stay in the country, saying that they felt respect for one who had come so far with a message to them from God, she 'having performed her message, departed from the camp to Constantinople, without a guard, whither she came without the least hurt or scoff. And so she returned safe to England'.

This visit, when she may have been accompanied by another woman Friend, must have been in the first half of 1658. It is only fair to say that Sir Thomas Bendish, the English ambassador at Constantinople, wrote home on 24 July 1658 that he had suffered the three Quakers 'with tenderness so long as their comportment was offenceless, but when at length becoming scandalous to our nation and religion . . . and insufferable also by reason of their disturbance of our Divine exercises and several notorious contempts of me and my authority, I friendly warned them to return'.

Mary Fisher was to live another 40 years, being twice married and widowed, and in 1697, the year before her death, nursed a Friend shipwrecked off the coast of Florida, who wrote: 'I had the good fortune to have a good nurse, one whose name you have heard of, a Yorkshire woman, born within two miles of York; her maiden name was Mary Fisher, she that spake to the great Turk'.

Swarthmoor as a home base (C1, C2)

All the travels we have described — and there were many, many more — depended on that centre of comfort, administration and inspiration, depicted in our panel C1. And the life of Swarthmoor Hall revolved, in large measure, round the practical genius and energetic personality of Margaret Fell, the subject of our panel C2. It was fortunate for the young movement that in those early days Judge Fell's local eminence and authority served to shield those at the Hall from attack. After his death in 1658 things would be different.

There was soon set up at Swarthmoor an organization best described as a secretariat, a sort of party headquarters, dealing with planning, finance and co-ordination. There still exist hundreds and hundreds of letters written to Margaret Fell from these publishers of Truth – giving news, seeking advice or, in their isolated journeyings, just needing the assurance that she was still there. Swarthmoor helped each individual to feel that he or she was part of a larger whole. And when the travellers returned, tired or bruised in body or spirit, the atmosphere of Swarthmoor provided healing and renewal for them, and Margaret Fell, the family, and the household were there to listen.

One of the early needs was to have a fund Friends could draw on for the inevitable expenses of their missionary work. This fund was known as the Kendal Fund because Margaret Fell asked two Friends of that town to act as her agents and we have seen (p.64) how it was used to pay the expenses of Ann Austin, who was one of very many to whom grants were made. By 1655 the fund was receiving substantial contributions from Yorkshire and Bishoprick (or County Durham). Several times Margaret Fell sent epistles appealing for more money 'so you may come to be one with them [the publishers of Truth] in their sufferings, in their travails, troubles, buffetings, whippings, stebings {scoffings}, prisonings, beatings'.

But collection was not always easy and she had to deal with Friends who doubted if such financial help was truly according to the teaching of Christ. The two Kendal agents did not always find life straightforward ('Truly sister, this service lies heavily sometime'); they were now and then out of purse; and there were murmurings about the administration. It was Margaret Fell's determination that won through, and the Kendal Fund gradually became the National Stock.

On ten occasions, the last when she was 84 years old, Margaret Fell visited London, the journey there and back being 500 miles. The first visit, that of 1660, deserves special mention. George Fox was at this time imprisoned in Lancaster Castle, charged with plotting against the King. In June Margaret Fell drew up a paper which was delivered into the King's hand towards the end of the month:

> We are a people that follow after those things that make for peace, love and unity; it is our desire that others' feet may walk in the same, and [we] do deny and bear our testimony against all strife and wars and contentions. . . Our weapons are not carnal, but spiritual . . . And so we desire, and also expect, to have the liberty of our consciences and just rights and

outward liberties . . . Treason, treachery and false dealing we do utterly deny; false dealing, surmising or plotting against any creature upon the face of the earth; and speak the Truth in plainness and singleness of heart; and all our desire is your good and peace and love and unity.

Margaret Fell's seven daughters all married Quakers and continued, albeit sometimes at a distance from Swarthmoor, to support her activities. Her disappointment must have been in her son, George. He was perhaps 14 years old in 1652 when Fox first arrived at Swarthmoor, and he had been 'somewhat convinced of the Truth'. But the following year he went to London as a student at Gray's Inn, and his behaviour caused increasing anxiety. In March 1657 Thomas Rawlinson of Graythwaite Hall, some miles from Swarthmoor, looked him up: 'I was with him 3 or 4 hours in his chambers. We spake of many things. The spark is not quite out'.

When Margaret Fell went to London in 1660 she found her son living in idleness and extravagance. It was in December of that year that he was married to Hannah Potter, a young widow. For political reasons George was nervous at the time of the Restoration, petitioning for a royal pardon and blaming his father as 'a great malignant', perhaps to hide his own questionable activities during 1659. And the pardon probably cost him yet more money.

From the outset, Quakers had seen that Truth required that they should refuse to take oaths, and the oath was a commonplace of contemporary life for a whole host of day-to-day transactions, as well as more major matters. It is one of the major matters, however, that concerns us here. Several Elizabethan and Jacobean statutes provided for tendering an Oath of Supremacy, or an Oath of Allegiance or Obedience: these were designed as a guard against Roman Catholic recusants. Local justices were given wide powers in tendering the Oath of Allegiance to anyone convicted, indicted, or merely suspected of failure to attend church or to take the sacrament twice in the past year. Refusal led to imprisonment and justices throughout the country (and also assize judges) had long realized that to tender it to a Quaker was a sure way to secure imprisonment.

Continued refusal led to *praemunire*, placing the offender outside the king's protection and involving forfeiture of goods and chattels, loss of all income from real property, and imprisonment for life or at the king's pleasure.

Judge Fell had left Swarthmoor Hall with 50 acres to Margaret and the rest of the estate to his daughters. George, by this time, was probably owner of two-thirds of the nearby Marsh Grange. He resented the Quaker activities at the Hall and, perhaps, saw his possession of it as a way out of his financial difficulties. For whatever reason, he was soon plotting with Margaret Fell's enemies in the neighbourhood.

C4. Meeting houses

On 14 January 1664 Daniel Fleming, a local justice, wrote to Secretary of State Williamson at Whitehall about the Quakers: 'They are a very dangerous people'; two weeks later he wrote again complaining about the activities of Margaret Fell, 'If we receive any encouragement from you herein, we'll tender her the oath, & so *praemunire* her according to law, which will be the only way to take effectual course with her, who is the chief maintainer of that party in this country'.

Justice Fleming found he had to press his fellow-justices to support him, but in February Margaret Fell was summoned. They threatened her with the Oath of Allegiance unless she promised to have no more Meetings at her house: but 'I told them I should not deny my faith and principles, for anything they could do against me; and while it pleased the Lord to let me have a house, I would endeavour to worship him in it'.

She was imprisoned in Lancaster Castle until the March assizes, and then returned to gaol until the assizes in August, when the sentence of *praemunire* was at last pronounced. 'But', she recalled many years later, 'the great God of Heaven and Earth supported my spirit under this severe sentence, that I was not terrified; but gave this answer to Judge Turner, who gave the sentence, "Although I am out of the King's Protection, yet I am not out of the protection of the Almighty God" '. For four years, from February 1664 until June 1668, she lay a prisoner in Lancaster Castle.

Meanwhile, on 1 December 1664 George Fell, as we might expect, sent the King his 'humble petition' for his mother's estate; yet though he received his request he never, in the event, gained possession of the Hall, nor was there the contemplated sale of goods. On 14 October 1670, at Marsh Grange, he died.

At Bristol, the previous year, Margaret Fell and George Fox were married in the Friars meeting house in Bristol. The children's work at the bottom of our panel C2 reflects the supportive joy of her daughters and sons-in-law and, to the right, reminds us of the dissentient George Fell who, not surprisingly, absented himself from the occasion. Margaret Fell was to live over 30 years more, active to the last and well deserving of the epithet, 'mother of Quakerism'.

Meeting for Sufferings (A3)

We have seen examples of persecution both sides of the Atlantic. Friends early took care to record their 'sufferings' and it is now time to say something more about them. There had been sporadic (but, as we have seen, sometimes severe) persecution of Quakers under the commonwealth; but after the restoration of the monarchy in 1660 a series of enactments penalized all dissenters.

Quakers were prosecuted particularly for not going to church; for holding meetings of five or more 'under the pretence or colour of worship'; for refusal to swear an oath; for refusal to pay tithes, church rates, and other customary dues; and for a variety of other offences. They could be prosecuted under common law, canon law and statute law. Among the statutes they particularly complained of were the second Conventicle Act (1670) which gave the common informer sweeping powers, and the recusancy acts of Elizabeth I and James I, for under these they were liable to fines of £20 per month and possible loss of land. We have already seen the effect of these acts when coupled with the Oath of Allegiance and can sympathize with Margaret Fell's rejoinder to the judge: 'The Lord forgive thee for what thou hast done. This Law was made for Popish Recusants, but you pass sentence but on few of them'.

Quakers publicized their sufferings in numerous tracts and broadsides and, as we have seen, they were carefully recorded centrally. But by 1672 the Yearly Meeting had to remind the county quarterly meetings to be exact in drawing up their sufferings and diligent in reporting them. It was not only a question of reporting and recording but of redress from illegal proceedings and of reform of the law. Yearly Meeting 1675 therefore decided to call a conference 'that the cruelty and oppressions (which also under pretence of Law are committed) tending to the ruine of Innocent families may not be hid but laid before those in power to redress them'.

There were those, the saintly William Dewsbury and Isaac Penington among them, who refused to set the law in motion for their own relief, assured that their persecutors could hold them in prison no longer than the determined time appointed by God. Dewsbury, who had at one time been a trumpeter in the parliamentary army, could recall long years of imprisonment at Warwick and wrote:

> For this I can say I never since played the coward, but joyfully entered prisons as palaces, telling mine enemies to hold me there as long as they could; and in the prison house I sung praises to my God and esteemed the bolts and locks put upon me as jewels; and in the name of the eternal God I alway got the victory, for they could keep me no longer than the determined time of my God.

This extreme of passivity went beyond the views of most Friends and the conference in October 1675 advised 'that Friends do not judge nor reflect upon one another in these cases, a freedom being left upon urgent occasions to take such course for relief and ease to the oppressed as may not be prejudicial to Truth's testimony'. Thus Meeting for Sufferings was established, one of its first objects being to persuade parliament to modify the recusancy laws, so that Quakers would be exempt from prosecution under those particular statutes.

We celebrate the establishment of Meeting for Sufferings, whose later history has already been described (p. 32), in the same panel which tells the story of James Parnell, and it is perhaps appropriate that his collected works, running to nearly 500 pages, should have been published in this very year 1675. It was in 1689 that the Toleration Act brought to an end the greater part of Friends' 'sufferings': by that time some 15,000 Friends had suffered various legal sentences and more than 450 are known to have died in prison.

The printed word (B4)

'Take heed of Printing any thing more, than ye are required of the Lord God' wrote George Fox in 1656. But the previous year he had written, 'Nor none stop Writing or Speaking, when ye are moved with the Spirit of the Lord God'. By the end of the seventeenth century some 4000 publications had emerged from the Quaker press, ranging from broadsides hawked about the streets to the ponderous folios of 'collected works' running to 500 pages or more. 'Who have wrote more than the Quakers' said 'our implacable adversary' Francis Bugg, and the printed output is indeed the more impressive when it is recalled that from 1662 to 1679 and 1685 to 1695 it was illegal to print a book or pamphlet without authority, authority which the Quakers were unlikely to get and did not seek.

A memorandum supplied to the government about 1664 'Concerning Printers of Seditious Books' records, for example, the pamphlets of Rebecca Travers (1609–1688): 'Rebecca Trewish in Watling streit is a wryter of books and getts them prented by Widdow Dover' and 'the said widdow is a common prenter for all scandalos pamfletts'. Our panel, therefore, properly centres round the printing press. Two of the six names recalled on the left were printers, Benjamin Clark and Mary Westwood.

Mary Westwood printed for Friends certainly between 1658 and 1660 and is perhaps the M.W. who printed 40 books more after the Restoration. She is perhaps most celebrated as having printed *These several papers were sent to the Parliament* (1659), popularly known as '7000 handmaids of the Lord' and giving as many signatures, far from all Quaker, of 'such as feels the Oppression of Tithes'. Benjamin Clark was printing by 1674 and his imprint is found on Jacob Claus's Latin edition of Robert Barclay's *Apology for the true Christian divinity*, commemorated at the top of our panel. Shortly before this Clark had got at cross-purposes with the Second Day's Morning Meeting, which vetted Quaker manuscripts for the press and which on 20 December 1675 'Ordered that the paper . . . printed by B. Clerk being a Relation of the Warr in New-England be not dispersed, but brought to John Osgoods there to lye till freinds see meet to deliver them back for waste paper & that B.C. print no bookes for the future but what are first read & approved by this Meeting'.

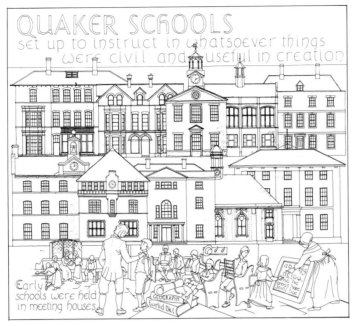

C7. Quaker schools

C11. The Leaveners

Among Clark's Quaker authors, besides Barclay, were Thomas Ellwood, Thomas Lawson and William Penn, all of whom we shall meet later in this book, and Isaac Penington, commemorated in this panel. Penington had 70 pamphlets to his credit and Burrough 75, and their folio collected works ran to 496 and 896 pages respectively.

We cannot pass from this panel without mention of Andrew Sowle (1628–1695), outstanding printer of Friends' books and founder of a firm which continued under various names until as late as 1829. He did indeed 'suffer for the Truth', 'his house being often searched, and his printing materials, as presses, letters, &c., as often broken to pieces, and taken away . . . and had at one time, by his adversaries, about a thousand reams of printed books taken from him'. In 1692 it was said that he 'is now Ancient and Dark-Sighted, but his Daughter Tace Sowle, who understands the Business very well, Carries on his imploy'. She was in fact already running the business and when she died in 1749 a newspaper described her as having printed books for Friends for near 70 years and as being the oldest printer in London.

The panel reminds us, too, of two American ministering Friends, both of whom visited Britain and both of whom spread their message through the printed word. John Woolman (1720–1772) we shall encounter in a later chapter but Job Scott (1751–1793) deserves mention. He was of Rhode Island, a man of deep spiritual experience and an impressive speaker. Much of his writing has an eternal quality and it is perhaps significant that a selection from his works, published as *Pearls from the deep (1911)*, should have brought spiritual solace to numerous conscientious objectors imprisoned during the First World War.

It is no good printing books unless they can be distributed. The government noted in 1664 the names of 44 dispersers of Quaker books, not only in Bristol and Plymouth, 'Brimmingen' and Nottingham, Lincoln and York, but at Felsted in Essex, Ross in Herefordshire, and Oakham in Rutland. And Yearly Meeting 1673, in order to 'encourage the printer', devised what might be described as a compulsory book club for Quakers. There would be a print run of 600 for each approved book and paper, and county quarterly meetings were told the number they were expected to buy, either for their libraries or for sale.

Yearly Meeting's plan was not popular and had frequently to be modified. Berkshire in 1675 complained of 'the great Charge of Books & many that Remaine upon our hands & of little service' and more pointedly in 1700 'that how through the avarice of the printer books are become burthensome & a generall grievance'. And Berkshire was far from being alone.

But, over the years, books and pamphlets were widely distributed, in royal palaces and rural cottages. The bottom of our panel shows a typical Orkney wagon, its bright cover made from reused sailcloth from fishing boats. This may serve as a reminder that there were few places untouched, at one time or another, by the printed word.

The Leaveners (C11)

The Quaker Youth Theatre ('The Leaveners') began its work during Yearly Meeting 1978 under Alec Davison, a professional director of youth theatre, driven by his passion for peace and justice into creating a special vehicle for Quaker Youth to express itself in the fields of drama, music and art, which the Quaker movement has conspicuously lacked. A series of music dramas, some allegorical, some based on Quaker history or contemporary world history, have been produced, as well as satirical reviews. Some have taken place at Yearly Meetings, some in local centres, at Quaker schools and in public halls; in the age of glasnost a fraternal exchange with Russian Youth Theatres has begun. Choirs and orchestras, singers and dancers, have made an impact of a kind quite new to Quaker experience – always in association with the practice of worship of a deep and reverent kind.

4. 'Keep up your Meetings'

Quaker worship experienced by three newcomers

We have already (p.31) briefly described Quaker worship, based on silent expectant waiting upon God. Let us now see how three meetings for worship in three different centuries appeared to strangers. First Robert Barclay (1648–1690):

> Not by strength of arguments or by a particular disquisition of each doctrine . . . came [I] to receive and bear witness of the Truth, but by being secretly reached by [the] Life. For, when I came into the silent assemblies of God's people, I felt a secret power among them, which touched my heart; and as I gave way unto it I found the evil weakening in me and the good raised up; and so I became thus knit and united unto them, hungering more and more after the increase of this power and life.

Or we may turn to Caroline Stephen (1834–1909) two centuries later:

> On one never-to-be-forgotten Sunday morning, I found myself one of a small company of silent worshippers who were content to sit down together without words, that each one might feel after and draw near to the Divine Presence, unhindered at least, if not helped, by any human utterance. Utterance I knew was free, should the words be given; and, before the meeting was over, a sentence or two were uttered in great simplicity by an old and apparently untaught man, rising in his place amongst the rest of us . . . My whole soul was filled with the unutterable peace of the undisturbed opportunity for communion with God, with the sense that at last I had found a place where I might, without the faintest suspicion of insincerity, join with others in simply seeking His presence.

That was at Falmouth in 1872. Somewhat different was the experience of Edgar Castle (1897–1973) when he attended Golders Green meeting in the 1920s:

> I went in a mood of curiosity rather than in a reverent spirit; and therein lay my failure . . . [I] waited for something to happen – to happen not to me, but in the meeting. I found it most difficult to sit still. But still I waited, in a nervous expectancy, for someone to speak, for something to happen. And then something quite startling did happen. A man rose to his feet and, with the fluency we tend to associate with the ranting preacher, spoke to his

C8. Quaker weddings

own home-made text, 'Three per cent of salt', likening the Society of Friends to the salt that gives savour to the sea.

But he had not proceeded far with his adulatory discourse before a white-haired woman rose to her feet and said in a clear firm voice, 'I hope our friend will sit down. We are not gathered here to listen to the praises of the Society of Friends: we are here waiting upon God'. Our friend sat down with some protest, much discomforted. He too, it seemed, like me, was an intruder . . .

I was at this meeting to wait upon God, and for no other purpose. I relaxed; and waited. But waiting was very difficult because I did not know what I was waiting for, nor how to wait, nor how to focus my attention on an idea for more than a few minutes . . . And yet I came away from that hour of very amateur silent worship with a dim awareness that here was an experience of some significance, too important to neglect lest there might be discovered one day, in the stillness, something rich and strange.

Quaker worship is, as Edgar Castle discovered, fraught with risks, risks that have to be taken if the rewards are to be found. Those who gather together, whether five or fifty or some larger number, are likely to be folk of different temperaments and different gifts. Each worshipper is a participant, even if the participation extends no more than a silent offering simply of a sense of need. Worship 'stands neither in forms nor in the formal disuse of forms, and may be without words as well as with them, but *must* be "in spirit and in truth" (John 4: 23)'. Despite our many failures, our form of worship is very precious to us. It depends, under God, on the faithfulness of each worshipper and it is natural that our panel should be entitled 'Keeping the meeting'.

'Keeping the meeting' (C3)

The second Conventicle Act (see p.75) came into force on 10 May 1670. 'And Friends asked me' recalled George Fox, 'to what meeting I would go and I told them, into the fields to Gracious Street meeting where I expected the storm was most likely to begin'. And on 2 January 1671 he wrote to Friends at Bristol to 'encourage Friends to keep up their Meetings as usual there-away; so that none faint in the time of Trial; but that all may be encouraged, both small and great, to stand faithful'.

The temptation to meet in secret must often have been great, but Friends consistently (with, admittedly, a few renegades) held their meetings openly. The Independent minister, Richard Baxter, wrote:

. . . the fanatics called Quakers did greatly relieve the sober people for a time: for they were so resolute, and gloried in their constancy and sufferings, that they assembled openly . . . and were dragged away daily to the Common Gaol, and yet desisted not, but the rest came the next day nevertheless. . . Yea, many turned Quakers, because the Quakers kept their meetings openly and went to prison for it cheerfully.

We can now look in detail at the episodes portrayed in our panel.

Christopher Wren at Horsleydown (C3)

The centre of our panel depicts the time in the summer of 1670 when the government's fear and suspicion fell heavily on Friends in Southwark. Information having been laid of 'Conventicles and Seditious Meetings, under Pretence of Religious Worship at a House, or Building in Horsleydown' an order in council was promulgated commanding 'That Christopher Wren, Esq., Surveyor General of his Majesty's Works, do cause the said House, or Building to be pulled down, and demolished' so that nobody could henceforth meet there for unlawful assemblies.

This was done, the meeting house pulled down, and the boards, windows and benches removed and sold. Southwark Friends, however, 'as obliged in Conscience towards Almighty God, resolved to keep their Solemn Meetings'. They lived up to that resolution and suffered for it severely. Week after week, as they gathered at the site of destruction, they were set upon by soldiers, and week by week accounts are given of the brutal treatment meted out to them. Let one such account speak for all:

> On the 9th of the 8th Month [October], the Soldiers, Horse and Foot, came to the Meeting, and one of them having a Shovel, threw Dirt and Mire upon both Men and Women, in a shameful Manner: After him, both Horse and Foot furiously fell upon them, striking and knocking down, without regard to Age or Sex, in a very cruel Manner . . . and when some of the Inhabitants, in Pitty took them into their Houses, to save their Lives, the Soldiers forced open the Doors, and haled them out again into the Street . . . insomuch that many had their Heads broken in a grievous Manner.

'And thus they continued for some time', says the account, and 'The Number of those sorely bruised, and that had of their Blood shed that Day, were above fifty Persons'.

Southwark Friends, bruised and battered, remained faithful. They needed no consecrated building for their worship, nor did they lose their experience of the presence of God, who 'restrained the Remainder of our Adversaries Wrath, frustrated their evil Purposes, and disappointed their mischievous Designs. And in him we have trusted, who has helped and delivered us out of many troubles'.

Children keep the meeting (C3)

The bottom of our panel celebrates those children who kept the meeting while their elders were in gaol. This is remembered most in relation to Reading and Bristol, but is perhaps true also of other places. By the summer of 1682 most of the adult members of Bristol meeting were in prison, and on 7 July the authorities disperst the Meeting which then consisted chiefly of Children [who] kept up their Meetings regularly, and with a remarkable Gravity and Composure: It was surprising to see the manly Courage and Constancy with which some of the Boys behaved on this Occasion, keeping close to Meetings in the Absence of their Parents, and undergoing on that Account many Abuses with Patience.

It is tempting to wonder whether any of these were the same as those who the previous year 'who usually sitt in the front of the gallery in our meeting house [who] have been of late rude and disorderly', a complaint made not once but many times.

Throughout August the story was the same. On the 3rd, 'Tilly, with a small Faggot-stick, beat many of the Children, but they bore it patiently and cheerfully'. On the 6th some were beaten with a whalebone stick, and four boys were sent to Bridewell with threats of whipping if they met together again; on the 13th 11 boys and four girls were sent to Bridewell, being mostly from 10 to 12 years of age. And so one could continue. The object of our panel is to remember not the violence of the authorities but the faithfulness of Friends under daunting circumstances.

'Despise not the day of small things'

Quakers of the eighteenth century were constant in their reference to Zechariah 4: 10, 'For who hath despised the day of small things?', for faithfulness in keeping the meeting depends, for most of us, on the minor incidents of life rather than on the dramatic persecutions which have been depicted. 'Shall a cloudy sky', wrote Yearly Meeting 1765 in its epistle to all Meetings, 'a little wet, a little cold, a little ease to the flesh, a view to a little earthly gain, or any common incident, furnish an excuse for declining this duty, and thereby depriving ourselves of the blessed advantage . . . of enjoying heavenly communion together in spirit with the Lord of life and glory?'

Or take Mary Ann Cash (1819–1916), born in Coventry and a member of the family associated in many people's minds with name-tapes. The meeting had been a large one in her youth but it 'declined in numbers until [she] was the only regular attender. However, possessed of "faithfulness" (a grace often mentioned by early Friends), she caused the meeting house to be kept open and so gave opportunity in 1892 when other Friends came into the city to organise again the work of our Society here'.

With these reminders, whether of precept or example, let us turn to Quaker meeting houses.

Meeting houses (C4)

We have seen (p. 50) how in 1652 the Friends at Swarthmoor Hall were discussing how they and others in the district could meet to worship as they wished, and how

QUAKER PILGRIMAGES
who knows on what far mountain
of the spirit a vision awaits us
the Kingdom of Heaven
did gather us
and catch us all as in a net
We came to know
a place to stand in and what to wait in

C9. Quaker pilgrimages

Judge Fell, overhearing them, at once and with a remarkable tolerance, said 'You may meet here, if you will'. And we have also seen (p.46) how Fox, preaching at Sedbergh a few weeks earlier, 'opened to the people that the ground and house was no holier than another place, and that the house was not the church, but the people which Christ is the head of'.

Early Friends, therefore, met wherever it was convenient – in the great hall at Swarthmoor, or in a farmhouse kitchen, or, less comfortably, 'they met without Doors, for many years, on a place called Pardshow Cragg'. But complications arose and 'It was agreed to remove the meeting at Uffington from John Steevens's his house: but for no other cause but the Littleness of his room'.

So, now as then, though it is true that God needs no house, it is often equally true that human beings do. A new Quaker Meeting may begin in a private house or a hired room but it is likely that it will soon hope and plan to get a place of its own, a meeting house converted from an existing house or other building or designed by an architect. The meeting house may run its course of 30 years or 300 but if it stays there long enough it will acquire the same kind of interest, ambience, patina, awe, which attaches to a village church, a place where prayer has been valid.

The particular quality of good Quaker meeting houses, old or new, is the beauty of plainness and simplicity. Everything is stripped to the bare essentials, but the essentials are lovely in their proportions. In older buildings there may be scrubbed benches, windows set high in the wall, and, at one end, a low gallery or stand with one or two steps and a rail, facing the rows of benches. On the first step, during the eighteenth and nineteenth centuries, sat the elders of the meeting, charged with the right holding of the worship; they were divided, like the rest of the congregation, by sex, men to one side, women to the other. Behind them, one step higher and behind a wooden rail, sat the ministers recorded by the monthly meeting (see p.32), or coming from elsewhere on their 'travels in the ministry'.

Older meeting houses may have stairs to a gallery or loft above (not to be confused with the ministers' gallery): this could often be closed off from the main room by shutters. In the days, long since past, when there were separate business meetings for men and women, this gallery or loft was often used for women to conduct their business, while on large or special occasions the shutters could be opened. In some meeting houses the main room might have shutters which could divide it into two portions for business meetings.

Things have changed. There are no longer any recorded ministers; there are no longer separate men's and women's business meetings; the sexes are no longer segregated in meetings for worship; the benches may have been replaced by chairs;

and the arrangement is more likely to be in a hollow square or circle than a series of benches facing the ministers' gallery.

Let us look at the meeting houses depicted in our panel. On the top row are Mount Street, Manchester (1830), Jordans (1688), Hertford (1670), Broad Campden (1663) and Burlington, New Jersey (1686), with, behind it, Blackheath (1972). The middle section shows, to the left, Swarthmoor Hall, and then – with Friends House, London (1926) as a background – Come-to-Good (1709), Brigflatts (1675) and Drapers, Margate (1710). What can we say to bring these meetings to life?

We have chosen to illustrate meeting-houses famous for their history, their significance or their charm. Many of the most venerable are in New England, but one of the oldest at Burlington, New Jersey (topright of C4), was built in the shape of the Abbot's Kitchen at Glastonbury which had been used by Somerset Quakers. Believed to be the oldest purpose-built meeting-house still in use in England is in the centre of the top row (C4) – Hertford (1670) with a splendid king-post in the middle of the floor. Next to it on the left as we look is Jordans in Buckinghamshire in its beautiful graveyard, where the Penns, Peningtons, and Ellwoods are buried together. The Meetings there were originally held in Thomas Russell's farmhouse up the hill, scene of many stirring episodes under Charles II, and now a guest-house. Depicted immediately below Jordans in the panel is the thatched roof of the charmingly named 'Come-to-Good', remote as Jordans used to be, beautiful and still in service. There are other thatched meeting-houses at Portishead, near Bristol, and Pales in former Radnorshire. All meeting houses have had their ups and downs: Jordans in the nineteenth century had only occasional Meetings; Broad Campden was sold in 1930 and became derelict, but was restored between 1961–4 by Charles Tyson and is once more beautiful and in use.

Some meeting-houses like Mount Street in Manchester, proud product of the industrial age, are built in the classic style. The imposing facade of Friends House serves to remind us that it is the administrative centre of the Society, opened in 1926 opposite Euston Station in London, and successor to Old Devonshire House in the City of London. The top row is completed by Blackheath Meeting, a handsome modern building thriving in a London suburb. Both these latter, so different architecturally, and yet so much a product of their times, won architectural awards. On the left in the second row we have Margaret Fell's old home, Swarthmoor Hall, which in the early days was effectively the centre of the movement. On the other side of thatched Come-to-Good is Cumbria's Brigflatts with its pen for the sheepdogs of the fells who came with their masters; still a Meeting and a great place for Quaker pilgrims (C9) for no place more vividly represents the spirit of early Quakerism.

Finally, in the bottom corner of panel C4 is 'Draper's' with its clock-tower, the picturesque alms-house founded by Michael Yoakley (1631–1708). He began as a farmer's boy; turned fisherman in Margate on one of the 'hoys' which carried fish and farm produce to London; graduated to be captain, then owner, of a fleet of hoys; and a London merchant. In 1701 he purchased the 'Draper's' Estate (hence the name) and set up 'Yoakley's Charity' under trustees who have mainly been Quaker.

Quaker marriage (C8)

Quakers have one form of Meeting which, by its nature, is inevitably more structured than the rest: the Quaker wedding, with its seventeenth-century flavour. The structure centres round a public declaration of intent in a form which is legally necessary. This declaration is based on a form of words originally provided by the 'Directory' of 1644 and ordained by a law of the Commonwealth Government in 1655, whose object was to provide a form of *civil marriage for all*. This law provided that:

> all persons intending to marry shall come before a Justice of the Peace . . . then the marriage shall proceed in this manner, viz. the man shall take the woman by the hand, and distinctly pronounce these words:
>
> I, A. B. do here in the presence of God the searcher of all hearts, take thee, C. D. for my wedded wife, and do also in the presence of God and before these witnesses promise to be to thee a loving and faithful husband.

Then the woman:

> I, C. D. (as before) promise to be to thee a loving, faithful, and obedient wife.

The Quaker form which appears on our panel C8 (some minor variations in the wording are allowed by the *Book of discipline*) is notable for two variations from the Commonwealth form. It omits the requirement for the wife to obey her husband; and it adds, what the Commonwealth strangely omits, a life-long commitment: 'So long as we both on earth shall live' (an older variant says more sternly: 'Until it shall please the Lord by death to separate us'). Fox's pronouncement in 1669 echoes Catholic doctrine:

> It is God's ordinance and not man's; and therefore Friends cannot consent that they should join them together: for we marry none; it is the Lord's work, and we are but witnesses.

So there is no presiding priest, but there is a Quaker-appointed, unpaid, Registering Officer in each Monthly Meeting and recognized by the State, who deals with the necessary preliminaries and records the marriage in the registers required by statute law. Since there are usually many present who are unfamiliar with Quaker procedure, a Friend is sometimes asked to introduce the meeting with some words of explanation.

"TURN from DARKNESS to LIGHT + know
the SPIRIT of GOD in your heart." G.Fox.
Repent. Rethink.
Be still + cool in thy own mind
Woe to the Bloody City of Lichfield
I saw an ocean of darkness +
death, but an infinite ocean of
light + love, which flowed
over the ocean of darkness.

D1. George Fox, the visionary

The bride and groom make their declaration when they feel it right, without prompting; and they are free if they wish, to exchange rings; but there is no place for the ring in the ceremony, and most Quaker brides in the past did not wear one (some still do not). A further element of structure is found in the 'Certificate of Marriage' illustrated in our panel. From the outset, long before there were state registers, Quakers kept careful records of births, marriages and deaths. The traditional 'Certificate' is retained, and is read in the meeting after the declarations have been made and the parties have signed it, with all present subsequently signing as witness; in just the same way as George Fox and Margaret Fell, or William Penn and Gulielma Springett or Thomas Ellwood and Mary Ellis in the scene depicted in our panel.

The example chosen by our embroiderers, however, is especially dear to Quaker hearts because of the story that lies behind it, a double story of loyal friendship, love and renunciation uniting Penn, Gulielma, Ellwood and Mary in one band. Thomas Ellwood (1639–1713) was the youngest son of an Oxfordshire squire with Parliamentary sympathies, from Crowell near Thame in Oxfordshire, who removed to London for safety at the beginning of the Civil War when Thomas was two years old. They became intimate with the family of Lady Springett, whose husband Sir William had perished at the siege of Arundel at the beginning of the war; his wife seven months pregnant made a heroic journey to be with him at the end; and the baby born after his death was named Gulielma Maria Postuma Springett. She was Tom's companion 'almost from our cradles' as he wrote later, 'being admitted to ride with her in her little coach, drawn by her footman about Lincoln's Inn Fields'. Mary Proude, a Lord Mayor's daughter before she married William Springett, now made a second marriage with a Lord Mayor's son, Isaac Penington the younger (1616–1679) whose father had been a notable republican, fortunate to die in 1660 before Cavalier retribution could reach him.

Isaac and Mary Penington went to live at Chalfont St Peter in Buckinghamshire, called Peter's Chalfont by the Quakers to avoid the word 'Saint'. After long pilgrimages in the spiritual desert as the Commonwealth collapsed, they had turned Quaker. It was to them that the young squire Thomas Ellwood looked for advice and support when he too became interested in the new Quaker movement; and at their house he met again his childhood playmate, now a teen-age heiress. He found Gulielma, like a heroine of medieval romance, 'gathering flowers in the garden attended by her maid'. She did not recognize in this athletic young man the boy who had played with her in childhood. He was so coolly received that he became abashed: 'I found myself not so much master of myself as to pursue any further discourse with her.'

They got over this bad beginning; for Tom's father treated him so harshly over his interest in the Quakers that, penniless, Tom took refuge with the Peningtons and became tutor to Guli and the children. Seven years of toil and turmoil ensued, during which Penington and Ellwood went in and out of gaol, and Mary finally had the house taken away from her. During this time Tom, when not in prison, became Guli's unofficial guardian, always at her side, accompanying her on visits to relatives and later, on business with her tenants, for she was a substantial heiress.

At twenty Gulielma Springett was a prize: rich, beautiful, intelligent, a fine musician, a girl with a heart for the poor and sick. Her person, her wealth, her talents and her temperament put her in great danger in the atmosphere of Charles II's England, where immorality was counted virtue and to abduct a rich heiress and force her through a form of marriage made a man master of her person and her money. Her adherence to a hated, despised and persecuted sect made her fair game. Thomas Ellwood, like any gentleman of his time, was an accomplished swordsman; but when he went to Meeting wearing his sword he was ashamed, and could no longer carry it. It is clear that, like everybody else, Tom was in love with Guli; but it was hard to be accused of having ingratiated himself into the Penington household in order to marry her.

> For she having now arrived to a marriageable age, and being in all respects a very desirable woman (whether regard was had to her outward person, which wanted nothing to render her completely comely; or to the endowments of her mind, which were every way extraordinary and highly obliging; or to her outward fortune, which was fair and with some hath not the last nor the least place in consideration, she was openly and secretly sought and solicited by many, and some of them almost of every rank and condition; good and bad, rich and poor, friend and foe. To them, in their respective turns (*till he came for whom she was reserved*) she carried herself with so much evenness of temper, such courteous freedom, guarded with the strictest modesty, that, as it gave encouragement or grounds of hope to none, so neither did it administer any matter of offence, or just cause of complaint to any.

'No encouragement or grounds of hope to any' – and that included Thomas Ellwood. 'He for whom she was reserved' was William Penn; released from the Tower, he had come to Bury Farm, Amersham, home of the Peningtons, on 16 September 1669, a visit after which he and Guli considered themselves betrothed. They were married in 1672. Ten years later, as he wrote to her before leaving her for the first journey to America – dangerous and perhaps fatal:

> My dear wife, Remember thou wast the love of my youth, and much the joy of my life; the most beloved, as well as the most worthy of my earthly comforts: and the reason of that love was more thy inward than thy outward excellencies, which yet were many. God knows, and thou knowest it, I can say it was a match of Providence's making.

It was perhaps only when Tom at last recognized, well before the Bury Farm meeting, that Guli was not for him, that he turned elsewhere. There was a Friend several years older than himself, a neighbour whom he had known some time 'in common friendship only' and for whom he had done 'a small piece of service' to whom Thomas Ellwood found his heart 'secretly drawn and inclining'; her name was Mary Ellis, and she is the bride of our panel. Isaac and Mary Penington approved, but Tom still hesitated until, sitting alone, it was as if a voice said to him: 'Go, and prevail'. He went to Mary's home and 'after some little Time spent in common Conversation . . . solemnly opened my Mind unto her'. He soon, however, perceived that this 'was a great Surprisal to her, for she had taken in an Apprehension, as others also had done, that mine Eye had been fixed elsewhere and nearer home.' He went on a journey for two weeks and on his return found that his concern had prospered. And so 'on the 28th day of the eighth month, called October, in the year 1669' they were married.

> We took each other in a select meeting, of the ancient and grave friends of that country, *holden in a friend's house* where in those times not only the Monthly-Meeting for business but also the Publick Meeting for Worship was sometimes kept. A very solemn meeting it was, and in a weighty frame of spirit we were, in which we sensibly felt the Lord with us, and joining us; the sense whereof remained with us all our lifetime, and was of good service, and very comfortable to us on all occasions.

This is the Meeting which we attend on the panel; and by the way, remember that since 1860 Quaker weddings have not been restricted to Quakers; quite often nowadays, neither party is a Friend.

D2. Quaker simplicity

5. Two Quaker thinkers

William Penn's early years

On 14 October 1644 William Penn was born at Tower Hill: his father, then Captain Penn, had the previous year married a young Dutch widow. The son was educated at Chigwell, in Essex, and then sent to Oxford University, but he got into trouble there so his father (now an Admiral) shipped him off to the continent where he had the best part of his education in France.

His father had grants of lands in Ireland and it was at Shanagarry, near Cork, in 1658, that he unwittingly settled his son's future when out of curiosity he invited a travelling preacher from the new sect of Quakers to his home. The preacher was Thomas Loe, he who had been convinced at Oxford by John Camm (see p.62). That day at Macroom Castle Loe reduced both the Admiral and his black servant Jack to tears, and made the fourteen-year-old William wonder, 'What if we all become Quakers?'

For the moment it was but a passing incident. The Admiral returned to active service after a period of disgrace which had landed him in the Tower, and William went off to college. But, returned from his travels on the continent, he was sent back to Ireland in 1666 to look after the family concerns there. One day he went into a shop in Cork where he used to go as a boy, and across the counter chatted of old days: he would ride a hundred miles, he said, to hear Thomas Loe again. 'No need of that', said the Quaker shopkeeper, 'Thomas Loe is in Cork and will be at meeting tomorrow'.

So Penn went to meeting in his fine clothes, 'a finch among the sparrows'. He did not yet know the Quaker way, that in Meeting no one is appointed to speak, and that Loe might not speak at all. So he was disappointed when 'another appearing first, he was not affected by his testimony; but when Thomas Loe stood up he was exceedingly reached'. All we have of Loe's words are the first, based on I John 5: 4–5, 'There is a faith that overcometh the world, and there is a faith that is overcome by the world'.

Penn was much affected by Thomas Loe's words, 'so that he wept much, and it seemed to him as if a voice said, "Stand upon thy feet, How dost thou know but somebody may be reached by thy tears?" So he stood up that he might be seen'.

At a subsequent Meeting a soldier came in and began to cause trouble, so young William Penn (still not knowing the Quaker way) took him by the collar to throw him out, until the Quakers begged him to stop. The soldier went to the magistrate to complain and returned with a squad to make arrests. Penn and others were brought before the magistrate, who thought the young gentleman was there by mistake, but Penn insisted on going to prison with the rest. His father sent on 22 October 1667 a peremptory letter: 'Sonne William: The cause of this writing is to charge you to repair to me with all possible speed . . . and not to make any stay . . . untill it please God ye see mee (unless for necessary rest and refreshment)'.

Another Friend accompanied young William to enable him better to face his father, who retained his temper though both men remained with their heads covered (for Quakers removed the hat only during vocal prayer, and never as a sign of deference to any human being). But when father and son were alone the whole conflict burst forth: why did he say 'thee' and 'thou' Sir William demanded. His son explained that the Quakers recognized no rank and considered all men equal. Sir William tried to compromise: his son might thee and thou anyone except the King, the Duke of York, and his own father. But no compromise was possible; and it was the same over hat honour. The evening ended in impasse.

Next day they went by coach into the park, and then repaired to a tavern for a glass of wine; but it was no better. Had it not been tragic the situation might have seemed melodramatic when there was a knock on the door and a nobleman entered for, having seen Sir William's coach outside, he thought to pass a friendly moment. With that apparent tactlessness which sometimes rescues tense situations the nobleman told the Admiral 'that he might think himself happy in having a son who despised the grandeur of the world'.

And now we have set the scene for the first of our two panels on William Penn, commemorating an event three years later than these conversations.

The Penn–Meade trial (F2)

We have already seen the effect of successive acts of Parliament in the 1660s on all dissenters, and in particular we have noticed how the second Conventicle Act gave wider powers to those engaged in suppressing conventicles, and was thus an incentive to renewed zeal.

On 14 August 1670 William Penn, William Meade and their fellow-Quakers found the meeting-house in White Hart Court, in the City of London, locked against them:

they therefore proceeded to hold their Meeting in the adjacent Gracechurch Street. Penn and Meade were arrested and sent for trial almost immediately but, in their haste, the officers indicted them not under the new Act, which did not require a jury, but under the common law offences of making a riot and a breach of the peace, which did.

The trial was held from 1 to 5 September. The jury returned verdicts of 'Not guilty' against Meade, who was merely standing by. He had been a captain and he said in court:

> I am accused that I met *Vi et Armis, Illicite & Tumultose* [with force and arms, illegally and riotously]. Time was, when I had freedom to use a carnal weapon, and then I thought I feared no man, but now I fear the living God, and dare not make use thereof, nor hurt any man; nor do I know I demeaned myself as a tumultuous person.

As for Penn, the jury found him 'guilty of speaking in Gracious Street' for the witnesses had admitted that they could not hear what he said, because of the noise. They knew their verdict in effect pronounced Penn guilty of something which was no offence, and they would not withdraw it.

The Recorder grew more and more angry, finally declaring, 'It will never be well with us, till something like the Spanish Inquisition be in England'. The jury were locked up 'without meat, drink, fire or tobacco . . . they had not so much as a Chamber-pot, though desired' but they finally brought in both prisoners 'Not guilty'. They were fined forty marks apiece and sent to prison until the fines were paid. But the following year a conclave of judges agreed that 'no jury could be fined for its verdict', thus establishing a principle of English law, celebrated alike in our panel and in a plaque in the Old Bailey itself.

Penn and Pennsylvania (F11)

Our second episode shows Penn on the world stage. Engravings of Benjamin West's picture of Penn and the Indian sachems under the elm tree used to hang in every good Quaker home. West shows Penn as he appeared later, a corpulent ageing man; whereas at the time he was 38, active and athletic. The encounter under the great elm tree at Shackamaxon, 'the Place of Kings', may have been a legendary occasion or the fusion of several meetings; the treaty roll which Penn is supposed to have given to the Indians has never been seen since 1720. Yet the essential truth is there, and other documents have survived. The lower part of our panel attempts to reproduce some of the Indian signatures. There is Tamanen, chief sachem of the Lenni Lenapé, who according to the story presided at Shackamaxon, 'placing on his head a small chaplet

Quakers were evilly treated+abused
by students + townspeople
OXFORD 1654-70
Thomas Nichols shoemaker
for attendance at Meeting
was fined three times and
his goods
distrained

Love wisdom and patience
will overcome all
that is not of God
George Fox

D3. Personal devotion

into which was twisted a small horn . . . it proclaimed the place sacred, and the persons of all present inviolable' (Thomas Clarkson's account). Other signatures in the two rows are of Malebone, Maughheughsin, Peridanoughas, Neshannock, and in the lower row Tangours, Secane, Noneshikken, Kekelappen, and Icquoquehan. These are taken from authentic Penn documents; and Penn's own signature from his letter to the Indians sent from London in 1681 before he set out.

The central vignette in our panel does not copy but echoes West: Penn is shown as he was, a man in the prime of life, but without the blue sash which was his only badge of office. Authentic touches are the gifts being offered, and the presence of women and children. An oral version recalled the famous treaty which, as Voltaire said, was never sworn to and never broken, as beginning that all the people of Onas (the Indian word for pen or quill) and all the native Americans 'should be as brethren, as the children of one father, joined together as with one heart, one head and one body;' that their houses should be open to each other; that they should not believe false rumours against each other; that offenders should be brought to justice, but when satisfaction had been made, 'the injury or wrong should be forgot, and be buried as in a bottomless pit', and finally that this accord should be taught by one generation to the next so that it should be 'kept bright and clear without rust or spot, between our children and children's children, while the creeks and rivers run, and while the sun, moon and stars endure'.

In our panel we have set this incident within the wider questions of Penn's 'Frame of Government' and the issue as pertinent to our day as his, the connection of religion and politics, in which his view was unequivocal: 'Government is a part of religion itself, a thing sacred in its institution and end.' Pennsylvania's Constitution provided freedom for all who believed in one God, if they could live 'peaceably and justly under the civil government' and were ready to accept one day of rest in seven, 'to the end that looseness of religion, and atheism, may not creep in under pretence of conscience'. There was to be no arbitrary taxation; trial was to be by jury, with no oaths required, and claimants might plead in person or by counsel. Felons must make satisfaction to those they wronged; prisons were intended to reform, for 'they weakly err who think that there is no other use of government than correction, which is the coarsest part of it'. The death penalty was to be for murder alone (treason was added later, but none of the two hundred capital crimes then part of British law).

Let us place Penn's plans for his own colony within the frame of his *Essay towards the present and future peace of Europe* published anonymously in 1693 while England was fighting France. Europe had already suffered the Thirty Years War (1618–48) which devastated central Europe, and now 'the bloody tragedies of this war in

Hungary, Germany, Flanders, Ireland and at sea' drove Penn to try and think of something better. His scheme was for 'deputies' from 'the sovereign states of Europe' to meet in a 'general Diet, Estates or Parliament, and there establish rules of justice for sovereign princes to observe' so that the whole, 'united as one strength', could compel 'the submission and performance of the sentence'.

To this parliament Germany was to send 12 delegates, France and Spain 10, Italy 8, England 6, and so on. To avoid quarrels over precedence, the Assembly Room should be round and have plenty of doors; and decisions should be by two-thirds majority and by secret ballot, like the Venetians. Penn denied that such a scheme would mean a loss of sovereignty or that it would make peoples effeminate, for nations could introduce schemes for the training and discipline of their youth. Its advantages would be to prevent the spilling of blood, save vast sums of money and preserve cities and towns; once more, as in Roman times, people would travel securely wherever they wished; princes could become friends and finally, would be able 'to choose wives for themselves such as they love, and not by proxy merely to gratify interest'.

Penn's creed has become part of the Quaker way: 'True godliness don't turn men out of the world, but enables them to live better in it, and excites their endeavours to mend it.'

The witness of John Bellers (E2)

John Bellers (1654–1725) was called by William Charles Braithwaite 'by far the greatest of the early Quaker social reformers' and 'the first of the long line of great Quaker philanthropists, and the pioneer of modern Christian Socialism'. Karl Marx, in *Das Kapital* called him 'a real phenomenon in the history of political economy'.

He was born in London, the son of Quaker parents who may have been convinced among those influenced by those Publishers of Truth, Edward Burrough and Francis Howgill, in 1654–5. His father became a wealthy merchant, and was active and trusted in his services for London Friends; and John Bellers, widely educated and deeply concerned, was well equipped to enter into a similar service. He also was a hard-working and influential Friend, serving on Meeting for Sufferings and other important committees, some of which necessitated travelling and deputation work, and he was diligent in his service for his local and regional Meetings. He was twice arrested and imprisoned, in 1684 and 1685, for 'Riotous Assembly'.

Seventeenth century England saw an energetic surge in trade and its ventures, both at home and overseas, a success story which brought money, and what money could obtain in power and possessions, into the hands of those who could achieve it. But for all those who could not do so their plight became so stricken in poverty, disease and despair that it is hard for us to imagine it and to comprehend how much it was regarded as natural — and even by some as necessary — in the economics of money-making. Nor did the conditions improve in the eighteenth century.

John Bellers was never able to accept that such things should be. In London, whither the destitute flocked in the forlorn hope of work or help, wealth and poverty lived almost side by side, and he saw it, and did not either harden his heart or withdraw his mind from what burdened his conscience. He could not bear the waste of human resources, of human personalities, as our panel shows: 'The poor without employment are as rough diamonds, their worth is unknown'. His religion was a living reality which had to have active expression in what he did and thought, and for the rest of his life he wrote papers, suggested plans, petitioned Parliament for the improvement of conditions for the 'labouring poor', and even more for the poor who had not even the meagre wages of labour.

The panel gives some of his ideas which he urged to be put into practice; though the range of his plans are even wider than those which are shown. He saw the despair and the deaths of those who are dependent on the haphazard benefits of charity, and on the all-too-often callousness of local officers of relief. He saw the purpose of the State as the good of all its people, without exception, and therefore much of his work was towards State provision of essential services: education, employment schemes, a free health service, the care of all those unable to care for themselves.

To him it was people who mattered — 'as God's handiwork and therefore as brethren' as Fox had written. Of the gangs of destitute children, the 'Black Guards', he wrote;

> They are our Neighbours, our Flesh and Blood, our Relations, our Children, however mean and contemptible they may now appear . . . It is not he that dwells nearest us that is our Neighbour, but he that wants our help also claims that name.

He wanted the abolition of the death penalty for felons, at a time when some 2,000 people were hanged a year — and for prisons to try to be places of reformation, not merely of retribution. And, looking beyond English matters, he gave in 1710 *Some reasons for an European state*. Written during the war with France, this is a reasoned effort towards mutual co-operation between the European states. He suggests means of achieving a central senate with representation. It is a determined effort to show the benefits of a lasting peace as well as the moral and Christian duty to inaugurate and maintain one.

His constant writing and his efforts to obtain State responsibility for improvement of appalling conditions does not mean that he despised or rejected his personal help or that of others. In this, as in his public work, his concerns were wide. In 1685 he

D4. Coalbrookdale

purchased 5,000 acres of land in Pennsylvania for the settlement of Huguenot refugees from France, and in 1709 he proposed to Parliament a plan for help to 'the poor Palatines' – Rhenish Protestants fleeing from religious persecution. And from the distant distressed to the near at hand his thought and money are ready. In a letter near the end of his life he wrote:

> Persuance to my advice of treating the poor Prisnors with Baked Beefe I yesterday treated 58 of my Poorer neighbours with the same fare much to their Sattisfaction & but about 3d head cost.

And in the bottom left hand corner of the panel we see some of the 58 waiting to begin on that Beefe. Between the Huguenots and his poorer neighbours lay countless acts of help.

In all his works, both in writing, petitioning and action, he demonstrated his unwavering sense of responsibility, a responsibility upon individuals and on the State to love their neighbour. Each of us matters to God, and therefore we matter to one another, and are answerable for what we do and do not do. He did not cease to use his capacity, his influence, his wealth, to persuade people and authorities of their humane, their Christian duty.

In 1711 he sent a paper to the clergy of the Province of Canterbury, following their Convocation. May some words from that speak for all he did:

> One Consideration that offered to me upon Reading those Prayers was, that what is Prayed for of God above, Man must be Instrumental to accomplish here below; there being but few, if any, who believe he will make Angels visible to do it.

6. John Woolman and the slave question

Slavery, it is clear, is deeply rooted in human societies. This is not the place to go back to ancient Greece or to Rome where the system was, more than anywhere else in the ancient world, 'extended in its operations and methodized in its details'. Our concern here is with the enslavement of Africans and with the institution of colonial slavery, a development starting in the mid-fifteenth century. It was, however, in the late seventeenth century that the slave trade became a free-for-all in Britain, and it has been estimated that between 1680 and 1786 over two million blacks were imported into the British colonies on the American mainland and into the West Indies. Indeed, it was in the years immediately before the War of Independence that the trade reached its peak, being carried on chiefly from Liverpool, but also from London, Bristol and Lancaster.

Early Friends and slavery (F3)

It is against this background that we must look at Quaker attitudes to slavery, and it should not surprise us unduly that the earliest Friends, many of them already slave-owners in the West Indies when they were convinced, should have accepted the institution as part of the natural order of things. It was the Independent, Richard Baxter, who in 1673 had declared that the African slavers were 'pirates' engaged in the 'worst kinds of thievery in the world', criticizing also those colonists who purchased blacks, to use them 'as beasts, for their mere commodity, and betray, or destroy, or neglect their souls'.

A decade and a half earlier – in 1657 – George Fox, with characteristic clarity of insight, had seen the danger in the master–slave relationship and had written an epistle 'To Friends beyond sea, that have blacks and Indian slaves', reminding them that God 'hath made of all nations of one blood to dwell upon the face of the earth' (*cf* Acts 17: 26) and that 'the Gospel is preached to every creature under heaven', finally exhorting them 'to be merciful, as your heavenly Father is merciful'.

Fox's visit to America in 1671 led him to increased concern for the welfare of slaves and in a tract in 1676 he declared that Christ 'died for the tawnies and for the blacks as well as for you that are called whites . . . [and] hath enlightened them as well as he hath enlightened you; and his grace hath appeared unto them as well as it hath appeared unto you'. From this fundamental idea of the Inward Light in every person Fox reasoned that the servitude of negroes should end in freedom, just as the Mosaic law provided that bondsmen should be set free after a limited time: and, Fox added, 'when they go, and are made free, let them not go away empty-handed'.

The non-Quaker slaveholders of Barbados quickly recognized the peril to their social and economic system in Fox's plan to teach negroes that they were of one blood with the whites and in 1675 a law was passed prohibiting 'the people called Quakers from bringing Negroes to their meetings' and from allowing slaves to attend Quaker schools. In 1680 Friends were forbidden to hold religious meetings of any kind. But, as yet, the issue was the right of blacks to be taught Christianity, not their right to freedom. This was to come much later – and not in Barbados.

William Edmundson, an Irish Quaker, companion of Fox in his 1671 visit, revisited the West Indies and mainland America some four years later and gradually became convinced that a Christian should not be a slaveholder, for 'perpetual slavery is an aggravation, and an oppression upon the mind, and hath a ground; and Truth is that which works the remedy, and breaks the yoke, and removes the ground'. These words he wrote in a letter in 1676, adding as a postscript: 'And many of you count it unlawful to make slaves of the Indians: and if so, then why the Negroes?'

William Penn, as we have seen, began the 'holy experiment' of Pennsylvania in 1681, and though he tried to provide that blacks imported by the Free Society of Traders should be regarded as servants and released after 14 years, in the event Pennsylvania became a colony in which slavery was regarded as part of the natural order of things. One small group of Pennsylvanians alone had difficulty in reconciling slavery with their religious principles, a company of Rhineland artisans – German, Swiss and Dutch – who in 1684 had founded Germantown. In 1688 this group drew up a formal remonstrance against slavery and the slave trade and forwarded it to their monthly meeting, which in turn felt it too weighty to meddle with and referred it to the quarterly meeting which likewise found it 'a thing of too great a weight' to determine, and charged the Germantown Friends to bring it before the Yearly Meeting which, not surprisingly when one considers how many Friends were slaveholders, quietly abandoned the subject.

By 1696 the Yearly Meeting for Pennsylvania, New Jersey and Delaware took a small step against the slave trade and advised 'that Friends be careful not to encourage

Rural industry develops into urban factory

INNOCENT TRADES

flourished with caring support
of closely linked friends

Lead Silver+
Coal mining
Iron Smelting
Brass Founding
Metal Casting
Boot+Shoe Making

Weaving Printing
Food Production
Canning Brush+
Pottery making
Pharmacy

D5. Innocent trades

the bringing in of any more Negroes' and two years later Robert Pyle, an active Friend, suggested that quarterly meetings ought to assume responsibility for arranging with Quaker slaveholders a definite date for liberating their negroes, and, further, that meetings should require a settlement between Friends and their ex-slaves to compensate them for their labour while they had been in bondage.

The Quaker-dominated Pennsylvania Assembly now began to take action to prevent the import of slaves only to find itself overruled by the Privy Council in London. Three colourful figures – William Southeby, John Farmer and Ralph Sandiford – now took up the cause and lost no opportunity for confrontation. Sandiford's *A brief examination of the practice of the times* (1729) was reissued the following year with the more stirring title, *The mystery of iniquity*, and Philadelphia Yearly Meeting 1730 issued the guarded statement that 'Friends ought to be very cautious of making such purchases [of negroes] for the future, it being disagreeable to the sense of this Meeting'.

It was a step forward, albeit a small one. Sandiford did not live to see the results for, broken in health, he retired to a small farm where, in 1733, he died at the age of 40. During his last illness he had received visits from the yet more colourful and yet more confrontational abolitionist, Benjamin Lay. To him we must now turn.

Benjamin Lay (F3)

Benjamin and Sarah Lay had arrived in Philadelphia in 1731, less than two years before Sandiford's death. Benjamin was then aged 50, his wife some five years older. He was an Essex man who had had a varied life – farmer, glovemaker, sailor, storekeeper, bookseller and farmer again. He had visited the Holy Land, seen the spot where Christ talked to the woman of Samaria and drunk from Jacob's well; he had had a personal interview with George II; and he had had protracted quarrels with two Quaker meetings in England. Benjamin and Sarah Lay, both diminutive and hunchbacked, had gone to Barbados, where he had kept a store. That was where he had seen some of the worst evils of slavery and by the time the couple came to Philadelphia the subject had become almost an obsession with him.

He was vegetarian, would not wear the wool of any animal, and dashed his wife's teacups to the ground in protest against the evils of that beverage. They lived in a cave-like dwelling just outside Philadelphia, raising vegetables for food and flax for clothing. And he went from meeting to meeting to testify, in season and too often out of season, against slavery. Once he stood before a meeting-house gateway, with one bare foot in the snow, to show how slaves suffered in winter without shoes. On another occasion he lay down in a rainstorm at the door of a meeting house from which exasperated Friends had expelled him, forcing them to step over him in order to leave.

His most notorious exploit, the 'bladder of blood' prank, occurred at the Yearly Meeting at Burlington, New Jersey, in 1738. There he appeared with a bladder of red liquid – probably pokeberry juice – hidden in a hollowed-out book, which he concealed, together with a military cloak and a sword, under a great, plain, Quaker overcoat.

At a well-judged moment he got up and began to speak against slavery: 'All you negro masters who are contentedly holding your fellow creatures in a state of slavery, you might as well throw off the plain coat as I do' – and, discarding his overcoat, he disclosed his military trappings to the astonished Quakers. 'It would be as justifiable in the sight of the Almighty', he went on, 'if you should thrust a sword through their hearts as I do through this book!' And with that he drew his sword, pierced the book and the bladder, and sprinkled the 'blood' over the Friends who sat near him.

It was undoubtedly a colourful episode, but it is scarcely surprising that it tended to antagonise those who might have been persuaded by a less confrontational approach. Lay lived on for another 20 years after this episode. His wife had died in 1735. He gradually quieted down, but kept up his acquaintance with Benjamin Franklin and other eminent Philadelphians. Shortly before his death in 1759 he heard of the momentous decision of Philadelphia Yearly Meeting 1758 finally to disown members who bought or sold negroes, and to encourage those who held slaves to set them free. 'Thanksgiving and praise be rendered unto the Lord God', Lay exclaimed, 'I can now die in peace'.

The Philadelphia decision of 1758 was the result of a groundswell of antislavery feeling which had begun to show itself among Quakers on both sides of the Atlantic by the middle of the century. It represented the convictions of a new generation of Friends, led by new, gentler and more persuasive leaders than Benjamin Lay or Ralph Sandiford. Foremost among those we remember among those leaders, but very far from alone, was John Woolman. Let us take a look at another panel.

John Woolman's early years (A6)

Isolated events, sometimes insignificant to others, may be decisive in the life of an individual. Thus it was with Fox when, at the age of 19, he was with his Cousin Bradford in the alehouse. Thus it was with John Woolman when he killed a nesting robin in his childhood, and, later, when his employer asked him to write a bill of sale for a slave. We must look at both incidents but, first, let us find out something about him.

John Woolman (1720–1772) was the fourth of the 13 children of a Quaker farmer and fruit grower in Burlington County, New Jersey, less than 20 miles from Philadelphia. The family was not wealthy, nor was it poor, and his father's friends included some of the leading businessmen and entrepreneurs of Philadelphia. Leaving the farm when he was 21, Woolman moved to Mount Holly, five miles away, where he was employed in a retail store. The rest of his life can wait for the present.

In his childhood, on his way to a neighbour's house, he saw a robin sitting on her nest

> and as I came near she went off, but having young ones, flew about and with many cries expressed her concern for them. I stood and threw stones at her, till one striking her, she fell down dead. At first I was pleased with the exploit, but after a few minutes was seized with horror, as having in a sportive way killed an innocent creature while she was careful for her young. I beheld her lying dead and thought those young ones for which she was so careful must now perish for want of their dam to nourish them; and after some painful considerations on the subject, I climbed up the tree, took all the young birds and killed them, supposing that better than to pine away and die miserably.

He faced — as we do not all — the consequences of his rash act. He also concluded that 'he whose tender mercies are over all his works hath placed a principle in the human mind which incites to exercise goodness toward every living creature' and that it is the rejection of that principle which is disastrous to tenderheartedness and sympathy at every level.

It was during his employment in the store at Mount Holly that the second experience occurred. His employer had decided to sell his woman slave; the purchaser was there waiting; and Woolman was instructed to draw up the bill of sale.

> The thing was sudden, and though the thoughts of writing an instrument of slavery for one of my fellow creatures felt uneasy, yet I remembered I was hired by the year, that it was my master who directed me to do it, and that it was an elderly man, a member of our Society, who bought her; so through weakness I gave way and wrote it, but at the executing it, I was so afflicted in my mind that I said before my master and the Friend that I believed slavekeeping to be a practice inconsistent with the Christian religion.

He was now in his early twenties and decided he would not do the same again, so that when, some time after, a young man (also a Quaker) spoke to him about drawing up an instrument for a slave he had taken into his house, 'I told him I was not easy to write it, for though many kept slaves in our Society, as in others, I still believed the practice was not right'. He spoke 'in good will' and the young man responded that slaveholding 'was not altogether agreeable to his mind' but that, as the slave was a gift to his wife, he had accepted her.

It was during his early twenties that Woolman set up shop for himself. Sales grew

D6. Quaker merchants

and he began to prosper; success and affluence were before him; but so were the demands of commerce upon his time. He reflected that 'though my natural inclination was toward merchandise, yet I believed Truth required me to live more free from outward cumbers'. He married, just before his twenty-ninth birthday, and there were two children, only one of whom survived infancy. He and his wife were prepared, perhaps eager, to live simply, and at first Woolman cut back his trade, but then, when he was about 36, gave up merchandise altogether in favour of a business as a tailor, which he could control more easily. He supplemented this income by surveying, drawing up such legal documents as wills and deeds, and in tending 'a nursery of apple trees, in which I employed some of my time – hoeing, grafting, trimming and inoculating'.

He wished to control his getting and spending so that he could be more free for his Quaker concerns. To these we must now turn.

Woolman's travels in the ministry (A6)

Woolman had 'kept steady' to Quaker meetings for worship and one day (would he have been about 20 at the time?) he 'stood up and said some words' but, as has happened both before and since in Quaker worship, 'not keeping close to the divine opening, I said more than was required of me' and felt afflicted in mind in consequence. Some six weeks later, 'feeling the spring of divine love opened and a concern to speak, I said a few words in a meeting, in which I found peace'. He had the gift of the ministry of the word, which he was to exercise for the remaining 30 years of his life. During that time he 'travelled in the ministry' on some 30 occasions, ranging through the colonies from New England to the Carolinas, averaging perhaps a month a year away from home. He did it because it was required of him: being away from home was a great trial to him, as well as to his wife. What of these journeys?

The first religious journey, in company with another ministering Friend (as was customary) was in 1743, of about a fortnight's duration, and to local Quaker meetings. It was the first southern journey in 1746 that was significant, for it lasted three months and the travellers covered some 1500 miles (it was, incidentally, before his marriage). This brought him face to face with aspects of slavery which he had not encountered back home.

He did not fall into the trap (one so easy to fall into) of assuming that all slaveholders were alike. Where he 'eat, drank and lodged free-cost with people who lived in ease on the hard labour of their slaves, I felt uneasy', but where 'the masters bore a good share of the burden and lived frugal, so that their servants were well provided for and their labour moderate, I felt more easy'. On this visit, as later, he frequently had private conversations with these Quaker slaveholders.

It was gradually borne in upon him that by accepting this traditional hospitality he was implicating himself in the system, and in later journeys, particularly his second southern journey of 1757, so as to avoid 'the gain of oppression' he insisted on paying his hosts, or the slaves themselves, for services rendered. This cannot have been easy either for them or him. And, though his friendly but urgent conversations with slaveholding Friends were sometimes 'hard labour', yet the spirit of his approach was such that it often led to a deeper experience of the 'nearness of true gospel fellowship'.

Let us give a specific example to illustrate the effect of his persuasive personality. Woolman was at New England Yearly Meeting in 1760 and, after it was over, he felt impelled to seek out and talk with prominent Quaker slaveowners. He conferred with 'two ancient Friends who came out of the country' and who shared his concern and then, with one of them, went to one of the most noted slaveholding elders in Newport, Rhode Island, who 'in a respectful manner encouraged me to proceed to clear myself of what lay upon me', suggesting the names of some further slaveowning Friends besides those Woolman already had in mind. This is not the action of one who has been antagonized by a confrontational approach.

The fact is that, though his primary concern was the plight of the slaves, yet he also entered into the state, the spiritual plight, of the slaveholders, believing that to treat a person as a slave dimmed the owner's vision and sensitivity. His belief that the Light was in every being meant that the slaveholders needed liberation (though of a markedly different kind) as well as the slaves.

In 1750 Woolman's father, on his deathbed, had urged his son to put into print his views on slavery. By 1753 Woolman was ready and sent his essay to the Overseers of the Press of Philadelphia Yearly Meeting, who not only approved it but published it at the Yearly Meeting's expense as *Some considerations on the keeping of negroes*. One of the Overseers of the Press was Anthony Benezet (1713–1784), the son of a French Protestant who on account of persecution had been taken first to Holland and then to London where, at the age of 14, he became a Quaker. The family had moved to Philadelphia in 1731 (the same year as Benjamin and Sarah Lay) and about 1750 Anthony's interest in slavery was aroused, an interest that was to be stoutly maintained until his death.

In 1756 Quakers, after a number of years of unhappy compromise, withdrew from the government of Pennsylvania. Two years later, in September 1758, Philadelphia Yearly Meeting took the decisive step, as we have seen, of removing from positions of authority all slaveowning members, disowning those who bought or sold negroes, and encouraging all its members to set free such slaves as they held. It appointed five Friends, Woolman among them, to visit all members who were slave-holders and to labour with them. Benezet came to the committee's aid with a series of forceful pamphlets. His 1766 pamphlet, *A caution and warning to Great Britain and her colonies*, was to be effective in later campaigns. It was not until after Woolman's death, not until 1776, that Philadelphia Friends were entirely free of slaveowning. It had been a slow process of persuasion, but because it had been persuasion the successive decisions had been loyally accepted.

But we must turn to another journey, that of 1763 to the Indians. William Penn had believed in a land where settler and native Indian might be at amity. Those days had now gone. Woolman had for many years felt drawn 'toward the natives of this land who dwell far back in the wilderness, whose ancestors were the owners and possessors of the land where we dwell, and who for a very small consideration assigned their inheritance to us'. In 1761, while in Philadelphia, he met a group of Indians from Wyalusing, some 200 miles away. Gradually a concern grew in him ('I cannot form a concern, but when a concern cometh I endeavour to be obedient') to visit these Indians. In the spring of 1763 he was ready, with the support of his Meeting.

Then he was awoken in the night to go and meet some Friends who had come in haste from Philadelphia with the news 'that the Indians had taken a fort from the English westward and slain and scalped English people in divers places'. Understandably, they thought he ought to know before he left home. Characteristically, Woolman returned to bed and did not tell his wife the dire news until morning. When he did so 'she appeared to be deeply concerned about it, but in a few hours time my mind became settled in a belief that it was my duty to proceed on my journey, and she bore it with a good degree of resignation'.

Woolman was also concerned for his companion, 'for as the journey appeared perilous, I thought if he went chiefly to bear me company and we should be taken captive, my having been the means of drawing him into these difficulties would add to my own affliction'. But his companion would not leave him, and the two Quakers had the comfort of some Indian guides. It was wet and the way was at times rough and stony, at others swampy. On 12 June he wrote:

> It being a rainy day we continued in our tent, and here I was led to think on the nature of the exercise which hath attended me. Love was the first motion, and then a concern arose to spend some time with the Indians, that I might feel and understand their life, and the spirit they live in, if haply I might receive some instruction from them, or they be in any degree helped forward by my following the leadings of Truth amongst them.

When they reached an Indian settlement on the way the news was far from reassuring. And, more immediately, an Indian 'taking his hatchet in his hand at the instant I

D7. Railways

D8. Botanists and gardeners

drew near him had a disagreeable appearance'. Woolman, however, spoke to him in a friendly way 'and then he, going into the house with us and talking with our pilots, soon appeared friendly and sat down and smoked his pipe'.

And, after visiting all the Indians they could meet with in that neighbourhood, they pressed on toward Wyalusing, where they were told to sit waiting on a log. They heard a conch shell blow three times and were then invited into a house where they found about 60 Indians sitting in silence. Woolman, after a short time, 'in some tenderness of spirit acquainted them with the nature of my visit and that a concern for their good had made me willing to come thus far to see them'. And the following day, when he felt moved to pray 'and expressed my willingness for them to omit interpreting', he was to learn that Chief Papunehang had afterwards said, 'I love to feel where words come from'.

We must now move on nearly nine years to Woolman's last journey.

John Woolman in England (A6)

Before we travel with Woolman to England we must understand how he came to wear clothes of undyed cloth. He had given up the use of food which came from slave plantations and in 1761 realized that the same taint applied to the dyes used in colouring cloth, so that as each of his garments wore out he replaced it with one of natural colour. He had a second reason, believing that dyes were 'invented partly to please the eye and partly to hide dirt' and that to 'hide dirt in our garments appears opposite to the real cleanliness'. It was not an easy decision for him and he noted that some Friends 'grew shy of me'. It was to happen again in England.

He took passage on 1 May 1772 in the steerage of a small vessel. On 8 June he 'Landed at London and went straightway to the Yearly Meeting of Ministers and Elders which had been gathered about (I suppose) half an hour. In this meeting my mind was humbly contrite'. That is what Woolman says, and it is all he says.

But a story has long been current that he was rebuffed at this meeting. 'This simple disciple', the story goes, 'arriving late in the meeting unannounced, and very peculiar in his appearance, was likely, at first sight, to be regarded as some itinerant enthusiast'. His certificate was presented whereupon, the story continues, 'some one remarked, that perhaps the dedication of the Friend might be accepted, and he might feel himself easy to return to his native land'.

This account then describes Woolman's lack of resentment; his freely flowing tears; and his saying, after some pause, that he could not travel in Truth's service while the unity of Friends was withheld and that he would meanwhile maintain himself, being acquainted with the trades of shoemaker and tailor. Following this 'tears flowed freely from many eyes' until 'in the pure openings of truth, John Woolman spoke a few words in the ministry'. These words so impressed the Meeting that all sense of obstruction was removed and 'the flow of unity (first expressed by the Friend who had before spoken his doubts) became "a river to swim in"'.

If the story is true it does credit to Woolman, alike for his humility and his conviction that he still had a duty to perform. It also in fact does credit to the Meeting in general and to the Friend who first voiced doubts and then retracted them (not always something easy to do gracefully).

But the story first appears in print in 1865, 93 years after the occasion it describes – though it is said to derive from an oral tradition which could have originated in personal recollection. On the other hand, the only Friend known to have described that Meeting at the time wrote that 'All seemed to be connected in a beautiful harmony and the meeting conducted with a becoming solemnity' without so much as a mention of Woolman (though he does report his contributions later in the Yearly Meeting).

There is the minor difficulty that all the evidence is against Woolman being a shoemaker. More serious, he was not 'a simple disciple' or 'unannounced' in any real sense. It was known that he was on his way; he was well-known in his own Yearly Meeting; he was not only a sensitive minister but a competent administrator; and there were six other American Friends at London Yearly Meeting, one, indeed, having travelled on the same ship but arriving earlier by posting from Dover.

That said, there is no doubt that the undyed cloth took some getting used to, and there may have been – probably were – some conversations with the raised eyebrow. John Fothergill, the doctor and botanist who we shall later meet, wrote during the Yearly Meeting to his brother: 'John Woolman is solid and weighty in his remarks. I wish he could be cured of some singularitys. But his real worth outweighs the —'. And then, as so often in the handwriting of doctors, there is an illegible word. Later writers have deciphered it as 'trash' and as 'husk', but it might be almost anything. But, whatever it was, his real worth was recognized by a fastidious Quaker to outweigh it. And so Woolman set out from London on his journeyings. Woolman would not use stagecoaches, nor send letter by them:

> Stagecoaches frequently go upwards of a hundred miles in 24 hours, and I have heard Friends say in several places that it is common for horses to be killed with hard driving, and many others driven till they grow blind. These coaches running chief part of the night do often run over foot people in the dark. Postboys pursue their business, each one to his stage, all night through the winter. Some boys who ride long stages suffer greatly in winter nights, and at several places I have heard of their being froze to death. So great is the hurry in the spirit of this world that in aiming to do business quick and to gain wealth the creation at this day do loudly groan!

It was therefore largely on foot that he travelled through Hertfordshire, Northampton-shire and north Oxfordshire to Birmingham; then on to Nottingham, Sheffield, Settle, and into Westmorland; and so down Wensleydale, where he learned that his kinsman William Hunt, from Carolina, had four days earlier died of smallpox at Newcastle upon Tyne. Perhaps, even then, Woolman was sickening for the dread disease.

It was now September and he was purposing to be at the Quarterly Meeting at York. He travelled south by Thirsk and Huby to Towthorp, whence, next day, he was guided into the city by the 17-year-old Henry Tuke who, in later life, frequently spoke 'of the indescribable sweetness of this walk, and of the satisfaction which he felt in the remembrance of it'. We shall later meet Henry's father, the tea-merchant William Tuke: Woolman was to stay at their house but the noise of the city he found oppressive and he was therefore moved to a quieter house outside the city walls, the home of Thomas and Sarah Priestman in Almery Garth. It was to be the house where he died, and a plaque on the house is there to commemorate him.

He attended most of the Quarterly Meeting but returned to the Priestman home on Thursday 24 September, before the parting meeting for worship. He was already ill and never left the house and scarcely the room or the bed. By the Saturday the undoubted spots of smallpox had appeared. The Tukes and the Priestmans shared the task of nursing him for nearly a fortnight until his death. One episode alone we shall recount. One night he had consented to take a medicine with a view to settle his stomach, but repeatedly without effect: 'the Friend then waiting on him said, through distress, "What shall I do now?" He answered with great composure, "Rejoice evermore, and in everything give thanks", but added a little after, "This is sometimes hard to come at" '.

He had been scrupulously truthful to the last.

British abolitionists (F3)

The London Yearly Meeting epistle of 1772 expressed the hope that the slave trade might be 'utterly abolished'. American Quakers now made strenuous efforts to get Friends in Britain to give political aid to achieve this. From Virginia Yearly Meeting in 1772, Carolina in 1773, Philadelphia the same year these appeals came. But the tension between Britain and the colonies now seemed to preclude action and though there was continued pressure from American Friends the Meeting for Sufferings in London was in 1780 distancing political action: 'To lead a quiet and peaceable life in all Godliness and honesty, is our Christian and incumbent duty'.

Finally, in the summer of 1782, the Philadelphia Meeting for Sufferings, perhaps

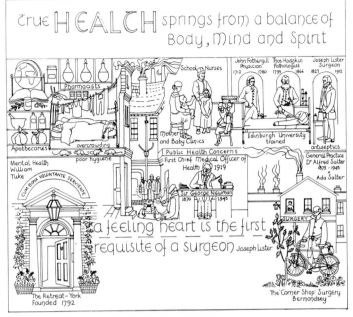

D9. Quaker doctors

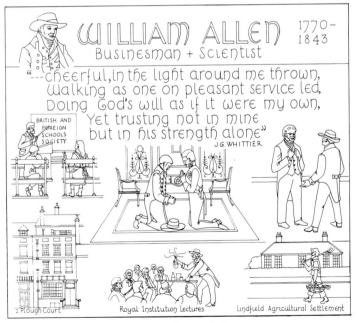

E12. William Allen

exasperated that successive pretty strong hints had been ignored, decided to write plainly:

> The Trade to the Africa Coast is still supported by Authority on your side; while this continues to be the Case, Great Britain cannot be clear of a pollution, the Effects whereof are so justly to be dreaded. We therefore beseech you Brethren that a Consideration of this Crying Enormity may have such weight on your minds, as to engage you to embrace all opportunities of promoting the discouragement of it.

And thus the matter came before Yearly Meeting 1783, our Meeting for Sufferings having already recognized that 'we must expect to meet with the greatest opposition of the combination of interested parties'.

British Quakers may have moved slowly and cautiously for a decade. Now they were ready to act, and act they did. On 13 June our Yearly Meeting considered the Philadelphia minute 'in a very weighty and solemn manner'; on 16 June it seized the opportunity of a bill then before Parliament to petition it, urging that to engage in the slave trade be forbidden absolutely. The petition was signed by 273 members of the Yearly Meeting and read aloud in the Commons next day. It is not to be wondered at that Lord North, while saying that the petition 'did credit to the feelings of the most mild and humane set of Christians in the world', declared that the abolition of the slave trade was an impossibility.

By 20 June Meeting for Sufferings had appointed 23 Friends as a Slave Trade Committee, which immediately decided that a short address to the public should be prepared. The drafting was entrusted to John Lloyd (1751–1811) and William Dillwyn (1743–1824). Lloyd, who had been for five years in America, landing there in the midst of the War of Independence, was a tobacco merchant in London and was beginning to take an interest in the family bank. Dillwyn was a Philadelphian, his schoolmaster having been Anthony Benezet, whom we have already met, and 'who took pains very early to interest his feelings on the subject of slavery and the slave trade'. Dillwyn had visited England in 1774 and settled here in 1777, the year in which Lloyd returned to London.

By October Dillwyn and Lloyd had completed *The case of our fellow-creatures, the oppressed Africans* and Meeting for Sufferings printed an initial 2000 copies. The following May, with the appointment of the new Parliament, copies were sent to all MPs and personally delivered to all members of the Cabinet. Another 10,000 copies were ordered, to be distributed 'as generally as may be throughout the nation'. This was not a random matter, but to carefully selected people who might be expected to take some action.

London & Middlesex Quarterly Meeting, for example, delivered copies to the mayor, aldermen and Common Council of the City, to the justices in Middlesex and Southwark, to the clergy, the directors of the corporations, West Indian and African merchants, and 'some persons in the law'; and later to many more, including the directors of the Bank of England and underwriters at Lloyds. And Oxfordshire asked for 40 more copies to give to Heads of Houses in the University – a request which led to similar action at Cambridge.

In 1785 it was decided to reprint Benezet's *Caution to Great Britain and her colonies*: by the end of the year the heads of a number of influential schools had been visited and given copies – Charterhouse, St Paul's (whose head agreed to forward copies personally to others), Merchant Taylors, among others, copies later being sent to Eton and Winchester. And so one could go on.

When in May 1787 the Society for the Abolition of the Slave Trade was established the need for a separate Quaker committee came to an end, but many Friends, including John Lloyd and William Dillwyn, continued to take a large share in this new body until on 25 March 1807 the bill to end the British slave trade received the Royal Assent. The campaign against the slave trade was to be followed by the campaign against slavery in the British dominions, an arduous undertaking in which a new generation of Quakers was involved. And the Emancipation Act of 1833 was followed by a further fight against slavery elsewhere, a fight which is still a continuing one.

We must not suggest that Quakers were the sole voices. Far from it. If we remember Clarkson and Wilberforce in connection with the campaign leading to the 1807 Act, and Wilberforce and Fowell Buxton in that leading to the Act of 1833, they are but three of a whole company of names. But this book is about Quaker life and Quaker insights. We have seen throughout this chapter a Quaker caution as Friends waited to be persuaded, waited for the right moment, the God-given moment: 'For the vision is yet for an appointed time, but at the end it shall speak, and not lie: though it tarry, wait for it; because it will surely come, it will not tarry' (Habakkuk 2: 3).

Quakers sometimes speak as though between the Toleration Act of 1689 and (shall we say) the Manchester Conference of 1895, there were – with the possible exception of Elizabeth Fry – two centuries of inactivity. The story of the campaign against the slave trade is only one episode which seems to suggest that the idea springs from inherited myth rather than from disciplined understanding.

The Underground Railroad (F10)

In a letter of 1786 George Washington mentioned a group of Quakers in Philadelphia who had attempted to help an escaping negro slave. The passing of a Fugitive Slave

Law by Congress in 1793 shows that escapes were sufficiently successful to worry both slave-owners and the authorities, and no doubt there were various individuals and groups such as the Philadelphia one who assisted as best they could to help runaways – probably on to ships to England.

After the Act of 1807 by which the slave trade was abolished in England and her colonies, Canada became a comparatively safe haven, and after the Emancipation Act of 1833 a really safe one, and it was towards that goal that the Underground Railroad worked its developing network of 'stations' and 'lines', by which single fugitives or groups were taken or directed from one 'safe house' to another. Many Quakers were deeply involved in the organisation, and some were among the leaders.

Several northern states refused to co-operate with the 1793 Fugitive Slave Law or that of 1850, so that the Ohio River and the Mason-Dixon Line were the first crossings into comparative safety – Eliza jumping the breaking ice on the Ohio in *Uncle Tom's Cabin* – before the Railroad conductors got them to the Canadian border. These conductors had to be brave, calm, quick-witted and resourceful, be completely discreet and trustworthy, and be sure also who could be trusted. It was a well-organized yet also a simple system. Many adventures are told, of hair-breadth escapes and of the outwitting of the slave-hunters.

The panel shows a map of the main lines of the Railroad, which reached from Kentucky and Virginia across Ohio, and from Maryland across Pennsylvania, New York and New England. There must have been many branch lines. Estimates of those who reached liberty by means of the Railroad vary from 40,000 to 100,000.

Of the names mentioned in the panel, Lucretia Mott (1793–1880), Levi Coffin (1798–1877) and Thomas Garrett (1789–1871) were Quakers: the last-named is said to have helped some 2,700 slaves to freedom before slavery was abolished in the States in 1863. Harriet Tubman and William Still were both negroes, the latter free-born and the secretary of an organizing committee; the former herself an escaped slave who made courageous journeys to collect fugitives, and was known as 'Moses' because she led so many to freedom.

D10. Quaker scientists

7 · Quakers in industry

The journals which Friends kept do not talk about daily work or business activities or the price of grain, but about fidelity to Truth, travels and spiritual experiences, philanthropic needs and achievements, courage and suffering. Sometimes you cannot even find a man's trade without looking at marriage certificates, rate books, or other outside sources. Yet what Friends achieved in their daily work, with its mixture of good and ill, is quite as much part of their spiritual pilgrimage as their vocal ministry, or their part in founding a hospital or a school.

Like other dissenters, Quakers were unable until 1871 to enter the universities of Oxford and Cambridge. They were, for the most part, debarred from the professions and other activities where the taking of an oath was an essential part of entry. Their energies, questioning minds and inventive genius were therefore largely channelled into industry and commerce.

The conviction that they should keep to 'yea' and 'nay' in all things led them to reject the current practice of haggling, for it was contrary to Truth to ask more than you were in fact prepared to accept. 'You Tradesmen,' wrote Fox, 'Merchantmen of all sorts whatsoever, Buyers and Sellers, set no more upon the thing you sell or exchange, than what you will have; is it not better and more easy to have done at a word, than to ask double or more?'

This insistence on a fixed price was, Quakers found, 'a great stumbling-block to most sorts of people, and made them stand at a distance from buying for some time'; but in the event, when people realized that they would not be cozened or cheated in Quaker shops

at last they might send any child and be as well used as themselves, so that all the inquiry was where there was a draper or shopkeeper or tailor or shoemaker that was a Quaker . . . and if there was any trading they had it, insomuch that then the cry was of all the professors and others, If we let these people alone they will take the trading of the nation out of our hands.

[122]

The trades had to be 'innocent'. Friends had from the outset testified against those 'vain superfluities' in dress and furniture which were the result of pride. Thus Thomas Ellwood on becoming a Quaker 'took off from my Apparel of those unnecessary Trimmings, of Lace Ribbands and useless Buttons, which had no real Service, but were set on only for what was, by Mistake, called Ornament'. And another Friend wrote of a couple who had been convinced: 'they have formerly lived very high and very rich in apparel, but are stripped of all: he hath ripped off his gold buttons and his wife her jewels and rich attire'.

But if one cannot wear vain superfluities, no more can one in conscience make them; and this was to cause problems. Thus at Upperside Monthly Meeting, Buckingham-shire, on 3 June 1674, 'Edward Hoar acquainted friends that, Susan Tod of great Missenden, having conscienciously left her former imployment of making Bone lace, is in some strait for want of a smal stock to enter into & carry on a trade of weaving silk laces, & therefore desired the assistance of freinds therein, who agreed to lend her five pounds'. Thus the Meeting helped her to abandon the ornamental use of lace while still retaining her skills for those aspects of the trade which were useful and everyday.

The Quaker testimony against all war meant that Friends who were ironfounders could not make guns and cannon, but they were to find that there was an almost insatiable domestic market for cast iron pans, smoothing irons, pokers, sickles and other goods that they could in conscience manufacture. And thus it often chanced that the very restrictions placed upon Friends in commerce and industry by Quaker testimonies proved, in the end, to be advantageous.

If Quakers testified against pride, they testified also against covetousness, and in this sense, too, trade had to be innocent. 'A faithful man shall abound with blessings: but he that maketh haste to be rich shall not be innocent' (Proverbs 28: 20). Thus, Steven Crisp, a Colchester weaver, he who had been convinced by the ministry of James Parnell, could write in 1680, 'Take heed of enlarging your trades and traffics beyond your ability and beyond your capacity; for both these evils have been the ruin of some'. And the Yearly Meeting in 1688 counselled Friends not 'to launch forth into trading and worldly business beyond what they can manage honourably, and with reputation among the sons of men, and so they may keep their word with all men, and that their yea may prove yea indeed, and their nay may be nay indeed'.

Friends in their meetings for church affairs watched carefully over any of their number who seemed to be enlarging their trades beyond their abilities or capacities. It is said sometimes that Quakers were harsh in their treatment of their members who became bankrupt, 'hitting a man when he was down'. It is true that monthly meetings were quick to examine any case of bankruptcy, but, by and large, a distinction was made between those whose bankruptcy was the result of unforeseeable trade cycles and those whose bankruptcy was the result of overreaching themselves in business through imprudence and who, moreover, had adopted a style of living beyond their means. It was towards this latter group that sternness was shown.

Meetings for church affairs were themselves relevant to the development of businesses. Attendance at monthly meeting and, even more, at quarterly meeting might well involve an overnight stay, and the Quaker host on such occasions might well have guests from a variety of callings – perhaps a farmer, an ironmaster, a weaver, a schoolmaster, a pharmacist (and, of course, their wives whose interest in business might be as great as their husbands'). The interaction of discussion cannot but have been stimulating, enabling Friends to get out of the groove of preoccupation with their own trade only.

There was another result. Because meetings for church affairs were social events, and because the young, or at least the sober young, were encouraged to participate from an early age, monthly and quarterly meetings, and, indeed, the Yearly Meeting, were occasions when friendships were formed, friendships which often ripened into marriages. Quaker marriage was not implicitly recognized in statute law until 1753 and not explicitly until 1836, and it was not until the Marriage (Society of Friends) Acts of 1860 and 1872 that Quakers could marry non-Quakers according to Friends' usage. Moreover, Friends considered that II Corinthians 6: 14 ('Be ye not unequally yoked together with unbelievers') precluded their marriage to any of 'the world's people'. There might be, and was, a good deal of local intermarriage, but the Society's system of church government resulted in the establishment of Quaker dynasties geographically spread throughout the kingdom. And this had profound effects on Quaker businesses. But let us now look at some of the panels.

Darbys of Coalbrookdale (D4)

In 1708 the 30-year-old Abraham Darby, a Bristol brass-founder, took over the leases of some furnaces in Coalbrookdale, specialising in cast-iron pots, kettles and other small ware. The fuel problem for the iron industry was acute. Even 100 years earlier the spoliation of woods by charcoal burners had been a menace, and the seventeenth century saw several attempts to smelt iron with coal or coke instead of charcoal. It was Darby between 1708 and 1711 who was successful.

Coke-smelting, however, was suitable only for iron immediately to be cast: for pigs later to be forged into bar iron, charcoal-smelting remained essential until about 1750, when Abraham Darby II 'conceived this happy thought, that it might be possible to make bar iron from pit coal pigs'. Being successful, he declined to get a patent, for

D11. Industrial welfare

'he would not deprive the public of Such an Acquisition which he was Satisfyed it would be'.

Throughout the eighteenth century the Coalbrookdale Company maintained its vigour, flexibility, and pioneering spirit. It is significant that of the six managers between 1708 and 1803 none was over 30 years old on taking office. Despite one or two lapses, such as involvement in the gun trade between 1739 and 1748, their management shows the application of Quaker principles to industrial life.

And, while other industrialists were engaging in the ambition (and expense) of social climbing, the Darbys were living in comfortable simplicity, close to 'the stupendous Bellows and mighty Cylinders' of the works, close to their workpeople. Their profits were reinvested in the business, or devoted to welfare of workpeople, or used in philanthropy. They left no large mansion and no derelict areas.

Our panel commemorates the Iron Bridge over the River Severn. It was in 1775 that a group of subscribers met to consider the erection of a bridge, Abraham Darby III being perhaps the most influential. It was cast in 1778–9 and was formally opened to the public on 1 January 1781, remaining a monument to a bold conception of a bridge in a new medium, prudently and diligently executed. Abraham Darby had 15 shares in the venture, John Wilkinson 12. It is time to turn to him, for he is commemorated at the bottom of our panel. He had established the first blast-furnaces at Bilston, Staffordshire, before settling in the late 1750s at Broseley, on the opposite side of the Severn from Coalbrookdale, where he took over the New Willey Company, early entering into a price agreement with Abraham Darby. It was Wilkinson's invention of an improved boring-mill that enabled the Boulton & Watt engine to become a practical and commercial proposition; and it was natural as the iron industry grew on either side of the river that Abraham Darby III should turn first to Wilkinson with his ideas of a bridge.

The other two names we commemorate are Richard Reynolds (1735–1816) and his son William (1758–1803). Richard had been born in Bristol and, though apprenticed to a grocer, had many contacts with Quaker families involved in the iron trade. Among these was Thomas Goldney who, in 1756, sent him to Coalbrookdale as an intermediary in business transactions with Abraham Darby II. The following year he married Abraham's daughter Hannah. It was a marriage of short duration for Hannah Reynolds died in 1762, Abraham II dying the very next year. Richard Reynolds now became manager at Coalbrookdale during the minority of Abraham III. It was he who pushed forward the development of railways for the transport of goods about the works and who in the late 1760s substituted iron rails for wood; it was he, too, who was concerned to build houses for the workpeople as well as a large weekday school and two Sunday schools. At a time of scarcity, flour, rice and grain were bought in bulk in Liverpool and sold at cost price to the employees. In 1804, the year after his son's too early death, Richard Reynolds retired to Bristol and devoted his last years to the welfare of his native city.

Quaker merchants (D6)

Let us turn from iron to wool and cloth. In many cases farmers would begin to sell their surplus goods by shipping ventures and, at the time when the Quaker movement began, the chief industry, the one regarded as the true 'staple', was that of wool and the clothier. The trade was beginning to be concentrated in a few particular areas, one of which was the country round Kendal and the Yorkshire-Westmorland border. It gradually during the next century concentrated in the West Riding of Yorkshire, and our panel is mostly about Leeds and Bradford Quakers.

But first we must turn to Norwich, for our panel recalls John Gurney (1688–1741), 'the weavers' friend'. His father, another John, had become a Quaker in 1683: he was a wool merchant, buying wool and putting it out to spin and weave. Our John, John II, was in partnership with his brother Joseph in the business: his son Henry and Joseph's sons John and Samuel continued the business, which, indeed, extended to yet a fifth generation. Meanwhile, Henry (who married Elizabeth Bartlett, daughter of a Bradford Quaker apothecary) had in 1770 founded Gurney's Bank, to which we shall recur later in this chapter. Our John is best remembered for the part he took in the House of Lords pleadings over the threat to the wool trade from imported calicos and cottons, describing the trade in smuggled goods and movingly depicting the consequent plight of the impoverished and unemployed weavers.

At Leeds and Bradford, as elsewhere, the clothiers put out the wool to cottagers to spin and weave, and our panel shows a pack horse train bringing in the woven undyed cloth. In Yorkshire towns one might expect cloth halls and the Coloured (left) and White Cloth Halls are depicted in our panel – the latter hall now being in process of restoration. In the foreground two cloth merchants are displaying their wares and the background represents the factories and warehouses which replaced the old domestic system in the West Riding.

Gervase Elam (1681–1771) was a Leeds clothier with several sons who were wool merchants, engaging in a large trade with the Americas, cloth being exported via Hull. It is not surprising that John Hustler (1715–1790), a Bradford woolstapler, should have taken a large share in the promotion of the Leeds & Liverpool Canal, thus enabling a more rapid export. The canal was promoted in 1768 and Brindley chosen as the engineer: here again, the choice was perhaps on the recommendation of other

Quakers, for Brindley had already worked with the Darbys at Coalbrookdale and with the London Lead Company in Derbyshire.

Nor should it surprise us that Edmund Peckover, another Bradford woolstapler closely associated with John Hustler in the canal project, should be among those who started the Old Bradford Bank, nor that Peckover's two brothers should be founding country banks in Fakenham and at Wisbech. Nor, finally, should we be surprised to learn of the close friendship between John Hustler and John Fothergill (1712–1780), the London doctor and botanist whom we shall shortly meet. Hustler was on nearly a score of occasions representative of Yorkshire Quarterly Meeting to the Yearly Meeting in London; Fothergill, seized of the importance of fuller facilities for the transit of merchandize, had a plan for bringing new canals to London and for a central terminal basin, so as to link up with the northern system. And the two men worked together for the foundation of Ackworth School (1779).

Newman Cash (1792–1866), the last name we commemorate, belongs to a different generation, but it is not surprising that this eminent Leeds merchant – who, incidentally, sprang from the Cashes of Coventry, whom many will still associate with name tapes – should have been among the original promoters of the Leeds & Selby Railway, and a director of the Leeds Northern until it became a part of the North Eastern Railway, of which he was a director until his death. It is part of the same story that effective trade involves ever more efficient transport.

Some other manufacturers (D5)

If we now turn to our panel headed, appropriately, 'Innocent trades', we are reminded of a whole range of trades in which Quakers were involved, and we cannot even begin to look for a representative of each of them. In the bottom section, however, we represent a butcher, a clockmaker, and a grocer.

Let Luke Cock (1657–1740) stand for the butchers. He had practised this trade in the fishing village of Staithes on the North Riding coast, north of Whitby. In 1721 he described his convincement many years earlier and his reaction when his inward Guide told him that 'I was to speak the truth from my heart – and before I used to swear and lie too for gain'. ' "Nay then," said I to my Guide, "I mun leave Thee here: if Thou leads me up that lane I can never follow; I'se be ruined of this butchering trade, if I mun not lie for gain" '.

So Luke Cock left the inward Guide, but was brought to sorrow and the Weeping Cross, so that he said to himself that if he found his Guide again he would follow him whither he should be led. 'So here I found my Guide again, and began to follow Him up this lane and tell the truth from my heart. I had been nought but beggary and

D12. Query 19

poverty before; and now I began to thrive at my trade, and got to the end of this lane, though with some difficulty'.

But there were harder lanes to come – first, the plain language, and, after that, to bear his testimony against tithes. His wife was not convinced of Truth and was downright in her comment: 'We'se all be ruined. What! Is tha ganging stark mad to follow t'silly Qua-akers?' But presently she was convinced: ' "Well," says she, "now follow thy Guide, let come what will. The Lord has done abundance for us: we will trust in Him" '.

There could be more of Luke Cock, but we must turn to Daniel Quare (1648–1724), the clockmaker. We cannot catalogue his achievements, but we can remember that in 1676 he invented and made a repeating movement for watches and, four years later, perfected his design, so that the watch chimed the hours by the movement of a single pin. In 1687 he made a unified drive for the minute and hour hands on clocks for, before that, they were independent of one another. In 1695 he turned his attention to barometers and brought out a portable instrument which was unspillable, however carried.

The popularity and excellence of his workmanship is shown, for example, by the Earl of Portland's accounts, he having paid Quare £64.10.0. for a gold repeater watch in 1691–2. And at the marriage of his daughter Anne in 1705 the certificate was signed not only by many eminent Friends but by the Venetian Ambassador, the Envoy of Florence, Envoys of Hanover, Portugal, Prussia, Germany, Sweden and Denmark, the Countess of Strafford, and many others of the Court circle.

But when, in 1714, he was offered a pension of £300 p.a. to be the King's watch maker, he refused for he found that an oath would be required, and 'thanked him for his Gracious Intentions to me, and at the same time tould him, I did not refuse to swear out of the Principle of Nonjurats But because I believed that Jesus Christ had Prohibited all Oaths in the 5th of Matthew'.

Daniel Quare suffered continued distraints for his testimony against tithes and against war ('two Clocks and two Watches worth £11.5.0.'; 'Plate worth £3.0.11½.'); he was a member of Meeting for Sufferings and was given considerable responsibility in the work of its Parliamentary Committee; and he maintained to the end his Quaker simplicity and integrity though he was known in all the courts of Europe and was frequently in and out of palaces and in conference with kings, princes and ambassadors.

Now to grocers. The 'Fry's cocoa' advertisement reminds us that we are in the later nineteenth century, but all the same, let us go back to the early eighteenth, and to Mary Tuke (1695–1752) of York. Her father, who died before she was ten, had been a blacksmith, and her mother continued the business of stabling horses. When her mother died in 1723 she and her brother Samuel were left on their own, and he was still in his apprenticeship. In 1725 she enterprisingly established a small grocer's shop in Walmgate and for seven years fought a long battle with the Merchant Adventurers Company, who tried again and again to stop her trading — for a woman who was neither the widow nor the daughter of a member of the Company was deemed ineligible for membership herself. She was several times fined heavily, but persisted and at last, in 1732, was given permission to trade.

The following year she married and the same year the shop was moved to Castlegate, the business being inherited on her death by her nephew William Tuke (1733–1822). In turn it passed to his son Henry (1755–1814) and to his son Samuel (1784–1857). Besides the grocery business the firm built up a considerable reputation as tea merchants and in 1849 opened a London office which in 1857 became the head office, thus leading to the firm which became Tuke, Mennell & Co.

And in 1862 Henry Isaac Rowntree of York bought the cocoa, chocolate and chicory workshop at the back of the Castlegate shop, the whole tea business being then transferred to London. Seven years later, with his elder brother Joseph, this cocoa business was moved to Tanners Moat on the other side of the river. There were then some dozen employees. The story of the development of this firm, within Joseph's lifetime, to become Rowntree & Co., with a staff of more than 7000, is a fascinating one which we have not space to recount. But we shall return to Joseph when we look at industrial welfare.

Quaker enterprise and the early railways (D7)

We have already seen (p. 126) how the Darbys constructed rail roads to carry their goods more easily about the works. The same was happening elsewhere, and it was only a matter of time before the idea grew that they might carry merchandise for greater distances. It is not to be wondered at that coal owners like Edward Pease (1767–1858) of Darlington began to think that a horse-drawn rail road might be more effective to transport coal to the coast than a canal.

And this is the origin of the Stockton & Darlington Railway, depicted at the top of our panel. As early as 1810 a committee had been set up to consider the practicability of a railway or canal to run from the Durham coalfields to Stockton; eight years later steps were taken to promote a railway, but two successive bills failed before the Stockton & Darlington Railway Act received the royal assent on 19 April 1821.

It was at just this moment that the rising engineer George Stephenson became acquainted with Edward Pease, and persuaded him that steam traction was to be preferred to horses. Stephenson was from Killingworth Colliery in Northumberland. It was as long ago as 1767 that the Coalbrookdale Darbys had supplied a steam engine for the Killingworth High Pit, and it was this engine which Stephenson tended as a young man, and which he improved in such a way as to draw the attention of his employer and secure that promotion which was to set him on his future career. He and Brindley are two engineers, neither of them Quakers, whose careers and activities were to be affected by the Quaker network.

Our panel represents, top left, Stephenson in more domestic occupation. A painting, exhibited at the Society of Arts exhibition in 1861, shows him teaching two of Edward Pease's daughters a new stitch of embroidery as they sit before the frame, their father looking on. The story is recounted by Edward Pease's daughter-in-law and is a reminder of the way in which business and personal relationships naturally mingled.

As for the Stockton & Darlington Railway, Edward Pease and his sons were among those to take part in a trial run on 26 September 1825 but they were unable to share in the opening celebrations on the following day for, during the night, Edward Pease's 20-year-old son Isaac had died: all his long life Henry Pease, the youngest of the children, felt most acutely 'the mixture that attends all earthly things' as he recalled 'this day of victory and rejoicing, and sore sorrow and bereavement'.

Turning to the bottom of our panel, we have already met John Wilkinson in relation to Coalbrookdale, but we must remember him for his engines and his cast-iron rails which led the way to the establishment of railways, though he did not live to see these fruits of his labours. But we must say something of the other figures.

It was in 1789 that Robert Ransome (1753–1830), a Quaker ironmaster from Norwich, started a foundry in a disused maltings in the middle of Ipswich with a capital of £200 and a single workman. The patenting in 1803 of his chilled plough-share and in 1808 of a method of interchangeable plough parts laid the foundations of a business important in British agricultural engineering history. It was in 1836 that Charles May (1801–1860) joined the firm: he came of a family of clockmakers and was now to be responsible for work arising from the railway building boom, concentrating on chairs and fastenings in rail laying, for which a patent was taken out in 1841. In the firm's balance sheet for 1851 agricultural work is valued at £35,000 and railway and other work at £87,000.

Thomas Clarke Worsdell (1788–1862) was a coach-builder who had joined Friends about 1815 and who in 1827 set up business in Liverpool. It was through the influence of James Cropper, another Liverpool Friend, an India and China merchant and a director of the Liverpool & Manchester Railway, that he was entrusted with the construction of the first passenger coaches for the new line, earning the praise of George

The embroidery reads:

'a very phenomenon in the history of political economy'~Karl Marx

JOHN BELLERS 1654~1725

To the Lords + Commons in Parliament Assembled

proposals
1695 a colledge of industry
1697 education of children
1699, 1714 and 1723 protection of poor and no death penalty for fellons
1710 an European State and Council of Christian persuasion
1712 ease of elections
1714 improvement of physick 1702 1714 Queen Anne

the poor without imployment are as rough diamonds

their worth is unknown

E2. John Bellers

Stephenson, who later described him as 'the best coach-builder I ever knew'.

His son Nathaniel (1809–1886) was for over 50 years with the Grand Junction and London & North Western Railways, and two of his sons, T. W. Worsdell (1838–1916) and Wilson Worsdell (1850–1920) were successively Chief Mechanical Engineer to the North Eastern Railway, while a third, Edwin Worsdell (1845–1930) was with the LNWR and, at the time of his retirement in 1910, manager of its permanent way works at Garston. And this does not exhaust the railway links of this family.

It was in 1836 that Thomas Edmondson (1792–1851), then in his late forties, was appointed station master at Milton (now Brampton) station on the Newcastle & Carlisle Railway. He found stage coach practice still in operation: the waybill was supplied to the guard of the train and a roll call held at every station. Edmondson was uneasy that the passengers handed money to him without a receipt, and perhaps still more uneasy that the fare money he collected was handed to the guard without a receipt. He therefore started writing numbered receipts for the journey money and in 1838 moved from paper to card and a simple form of printing press. In 1841 he set up in Manchester as an independent printer of railway tickets, a business carried on by his son John Beeby Edmondson (1831–1887) and continued until as recently as 1960.

George Bradshaw (1801–1853) was also a Manchester Friend, having joined the Society there in his twenties. An engraver and printer by trade, he published some canal maps before his first railway timetable in 1839. With the steady income which his business gave him, he was able to devote time to his other interests and, in particular, to the establishment of schools 'for the poorer classes' and to work for international peace; and it was, indeed, at an international peace congress at Oslo in 1853 that he was taken ill with Asiatic cholera, dying within a few hours.

Industrial welfare (D11)

By 1704 several mining and smelting companies had been consolidated in the 'Quaker Company' or 'London Lead Company': its title notwithstanding, its mining activities were around Alston Moor, extended later into adjacent areas of Northumberland, and into Weardale and Teesdale. Quakers had had an interest in one of the constituent companies since 1696 and with the amalgamation must have acquired a major control in the Court of Assistants. Thus, when the expansion of the workings brought hundreds of miners and their families into an area almost unprovided with houses, villages, and the necessities of a community, there was full scope for all operations of social welfare.

The period of greatest social activity was during the nineteenth century, following the period of greatest expansion during the eighteenth. Of all the work of improvement of living conditions – of house-building, road and bridge-making; of allotments and shops provided; of day and Sunday schools for children; of health care and sports facilities – our panel shows one.

Towards the end of the eighteenth century there was a marked upward movement in prices, with resulting poverty and hardship among labouring classes; about 1795 the shortage of food had become acute, causing widespread distress among the miners in the north, as to others. The Court of the Company decided to by-pass the corn-millers and flour-dealers, bought a property to use as a mill, bought corn in bulk, and sold the flour to its workpeople at cost price. The Company soon felt that to restrict this benefit to its own workpeople and families was unfair and likely to cause ill-feeling and therefore enlarged the scheme and threw it open to everyone in the district.

In the 'hungry forties' the Court urged men to form their own corn associations, promising help as required. These associations had considerable success, and were in effect pioneer co-operative societies. The sense of responsibility and interdependence thus encouraged had a profound effect on the whole district.

Our panel goes on to remind us that Huntley & Palmers in Reading had in 1849 established a breakfast room for its workers and had seen its responsibility for providing work clothes. We shall next turn to Rowntrees of York, represented in the top right corner of the panel. But before that let us reflect on the way many Quaker businesses had grown up.

Friends had been consistently encouraged to take young Quakers as apprentices and to recognize their moral and religious responsibilities 'by protecting them from harm, and strengthening their best resolutions'. Thus the elder Joseph Rowntree of York, writing a memorandum in 1852 for would-be apprentices, expressed his 'earnest desire that the household may in all respects maintain those habits and practices in regard to dress, language, etc., which distinguish the religious Society of Friends'. Though the conditions – and hours – may now seem daunting, and though he stressed that the 'place is *not* suitable for the indolent and the wayward', it was natural that there should be provision for apprentices to attend mid-week meeting for worship alternate weeks, and that it should be stressed that meal-times 'should be of a social and uniting character'. The life was, indeed, sufficiently uniting for the apprentices, their term completed, to keep in close touch with one another and to form the York Band of Brothers.

It was as businesses grew, as the sense of 'family' disappeared, that worries began to arise. It is all too easy, from a century or more later, to dismiss some welfare schemes as paternalistic; but the grocer with the group of apprentices in his household had been *in loco parentis* and it was but natural that he should still feel this to be his role. But how to express it?

By 1902 Rowntrees had over 2000 employees and the head of the firm, the younger Joseph (he was now approaching 70), was worried. He had spent all his early life working with small units, knowing the sense of purpose that can bind a small group together as they wrestle with a common task. He feared that this was now in danger of being lost. Long before house magazines became a commonplace he instituted the *Cocoa-Works magazine* to try to make real to everyone the interdependence of departments. And in an early issue was his 'suggestions scheme', mild and unromantic but an innovation in the industrial world of that time.

In 1901 he had bought 123 acres to create the village that became New Earswick. It was not to be a philanthropic enterprise, nor was it intended that the cottages should be let only to the firm's employees: it was, first and foremost, a challenge to bad housing, and Rowntree's hopes for it were realized as he saw it develop into a living community with a strong, enthusiastic village council.

Cadburys had appointed a works doctor in 1902 and Rowntrees did the same in 1904, following it rapidly by a works dentist. In 1905 they started a domestic school for the girls and in 1907 Swedish physical training for the boys, followed a few years later by 'continuation classes' in practical mathematics, English and woodwork. And in 1904, several years before state pensions, Joseph Rowntree started to explore the question, expensive though it might be, of a works pension scheme.

Our panel reminds us of similar developments at Bournville, begun by George and Richard Cadbury in 1895, close to the factory established there 16 years earlier. They envisaged tree-lined roads, parks, libraries, football fields, cricket pitches and swimming pools, as well as good housing. Bournville was on a larger scale than New Earswick and on the edge of a vaster city. Housing reformers rushed to inspect it and to point morals – the infant mortality rate in Bournville, for example, was half that of Birmingham as a whole. And, to obviate the dangers of paternalism, the Bournville Village Trust was established in 1900 and the Village Trust (now the Joseph Rowntree Memorial Trust) four years later.

Joseph Rowntree's eldest son, John Wilhelm, used to recur to the theme that 'the gospel must be social'. 'God is social', he wrote, 'man is social, because God is Love, and because love expresses itself through personal relationships'. And, without this underlying conviction of the importance of personal relationships, any scheme of industrial welfare will become arid.

The Quaker Trade of

BANKERING

Many Quaker Banks merged to form the core of well known Companies

BANK

Jonathan Backhouse balances the cash 1819

Honesty in business and the payment in full of debts justly incurred

JONATHAN BACKHOUSE & CO

E3. Banking

'Bankering' (E3)

The old name for the business of a banker was 'bankering'. Thus Child's *Dictionary of Trade* (1694): 'Before this way of private bankering came up . . .' Quaker 'bankering' had more than one source. In the seventeenth century some Quaker families were already engaged in the trade of goldsmiths, the 'bankers before the banks'. The Freames, Barclays, Goulds and Hoares had not only money available for borrowing, but were diversifying into metals and textiles and mining, thereby increasing their resources. Other Quaker family businesses as they prospered up and down the country, began to follow suit and even to exchange their original trade for the more lucrative business of bankering. It began, often, as a courtesy to staff, customers, other Quakers and neighbours, and became systematized and solidified; with Quaker kindliness, Quaker thrift, and Quaker business sense nicely balancing each other. Since it was both dangerous and inconvenient to carry large sums in coin, with highwaymen on the road, the banks began to issue their own promissory notes, which could (when the bearer wished) be exchanged for current coin of the realm. The system worked well enough except when, in time of bad trade or war, there was a 'run on the banks' and all the customers at once decided to present their notes for cash. In such emergencies large sums in bullion were essential.

The history of Quaker banks is full of stories of the way in which such emergencies were met. Our panel illustrates just one of them from the days when transport by canal and railway was beginning. Lord Darlington was a great 'canal' man; but the Quakers had frustrated his dream of cutting a canal in the North-East, by promoting the Stockton & Darlington Railway with the support of Backhouse's Bank. To get his revenge, his Lordship in 1819 ordered his tenants to pay their rent in Backhouse notes, with the object of presenting them all together and 'breaking the bank'. However, Jonathan Backhouse got wind of this, and departed to London to raise enough gold to foil the plot.

All went well, if hurriedly, until the return journey; when, as they passed over Croft Bridge, a fore-wheel fell off. No time for repairs! Jonathan Backhouse 'balanced the cash' by piling the gold in the opposite corner, and reached Darlington on three wheels. When Lord Darlington's agent came in with the notes, they were promptly and politely cashed.

The evolution of Backhouse's Bank is typical. The family were originally woollen dealers who diversified into flax dressing and linen manufacture, and in the mid-eighteenth century into insurance as agents for the Royal Exchange Assurance Company. The woollen and flax trades involved much extended credit to small suppliers before the days of large firms and large factories, which led in 1774 to the beginning of a family partnership in J. & J. Backhouse's Bank, which subsequently became Jonathan Backhouse & Company. Marriage connections with the Gurney, Fox and Pease families and later with Lloyds, Hustlers (D6) and Weres made for stability, with many small banking enterprises interlocking and marriages within the small closed society operating, whatever the intention, much as medieval princes operated to extend their estates.

The Lloyds of Dolobran were a Welsh family originally concerned in the iron trade. One branch of the family moved to Birmingham, partly to escape the rigours of persecution which continued much more harshly in Wales than in England, and partly to benefit from the rise of Birmingham with its multitude of small enterprises employing iron, and again like the Backhouses they found the same hunger for credit among the small traders there. Accordingly in 1765 Sampson Lloyd, second of that name, went into partnership with a button-moulder called John Taylor and raised capital of £6,000 in four equal shares to start a bank, to be run by Sampson's son, Sampson Lloyd, junior (the third of that name; Quaker families were incredibly economical of names). They accepted deposits and issued notes of five guineas, one pound, and seven shillings with the smallest denomination being especially popular. Within six years they had made more than £10,000 profit, and the iron business was left far behind. In 1770 young Sampson (III) turned his eyes to London, like many of the other Quaker country bankers; but instead of accepting an agency he formed a new partnership with a Lombard Street firm, under the style of Taylor, Lloyd, Hanbury & Bowman. Soon the process of association with other small country banks began.

The straightforward business of lending to customers and neighbours had by now become international and sophisticated; to know this we need no more than to know how easily travelling Quaker ministers financed their journeys, or how widely Quaker businesses dealt with North and South America, the British colonies and the continent of Europe. But banking has its dangers, as Quakers and the rest of the banking world learnt from the spectacular collapse of the Quaker discounting firm of Overend Gurney & Co. The firm was the inspiration of John Overend, born in Settle in 1769 and originally apprenticed in the woollen trade to a firm with banking connections, like so many. Overend travelled regularly with bankers' parcels to Norwich and got to know John Gurney. He suggested a scheme for a single charge on discounting bills which with Gurney's encouragement and eventually the participation of Gurney's son Samuel, enabled him to set up a small firm of bill brokers which grew like a mushroom, and then broke, bringing ruin and consternation in its wake (involving among others Elizabeth Fry's husband Joseph). Then began the large-scale amalgamations which went on into the twentieth century to produce the great 'High Street' banks, two of which have Quaker origins, Lloyds and Barclays.

The Society of Friends still keeps its central accounts with Barclays Bank; but though there are still Quaker names in the great banks, they have long ceased to be Quaker-led.

Friends Provident Institution (E11)

We quote in our panel some words from the annual Swarthmore Lecture, delivered in 1949: 'The true "concern" [emerges as] a gift from God, a leading of his spirit which may not be denied'. The formation of the Friends Provident Institution is the result of just such a concern. And it came about like this.

At Ackworth School in 1828 there was a bad fever epidemic, which smote 183 members of the school family: among the five deaths was a 30-year-old master. The needs of his widow and posthumous child weighed heavily on Friends and at London Yearly Meeting next year 'it was proposed that a subscription should be entered into for the Widow and Child'. That dealt with the immediate problem, but Samuel Tuke and Joseph Rowntree senior of York (tea dealer and grocer respectively, and depicted in the centre of our panel) believed that something more fundamental should be done rather than relying on response to a series of *ad hoc* emergencies. It was with them a concern.

In June 1831 they laid their proposals for a system of life insurance before Yorkshire Quarterly Meeting's Committee on Money Matters; these proposals were thrashed out in a series of discussions; and on 28 September 1831 a committee met to form the Friends Provident Institution and approve a draft prospectus, the rules and regulations being approved the next year.

There was then, of course, no system of social benefits or security, and it had been Friends' practice throughout their history to support their own poor. But provident institutions were 'in the air' and the proposals were timely, though some Friends needed reassurance that the scheme did not imply a distrust of Providence and was not in the nature of a lottery.

Among the first directors, besides Joseph Rowntree and Samuel Tuke, were John Hustler (1768–1842) of Bradford, son of that John whom we have met in connection with the Leeds & Liverpool Canal; Benjamin Seebohm (1798–1871), also of Bradford, he who as a young boy had been Stephen Grellet's interpreter at Pyrmont (pp. 162–3); and Newman Cash (1792–1866) of Leeds, director of the Leeds Northern and North Eastern Railways. And from 1908 to 1917 the chairman of FPI was to be Henry Brady Priestman, grandson of the master who had died in that fever epidemic of 1828.

E5. Elizabeth Fry

From 1832 to 1862 the FPI offices (depicted bottom left in our panel) were those of the secretary, a Bradford conveyancer, over a confectioner's shop at 67/69 Market Street: the FPI then moved to more imposing buildings in Darley Street, Bradford, until 1919 when it moved to London until its final move to Dorking (depicted bottom right in our panel) in 1958. Gradually the number of Quaker directors dwindled until the time came when it was no longer realistic for the rules to provide for a minimum number of Friends on the board. We must celebrate FPI, however, as an early effort to see beyond philanthropic response to individual crises to a businesslike plan which would systematically provide for emergencies.

8. Quaker scientists and doctors

In 1667 George Fox recommended the setting up of two boarding schools near London where youth might be instructed 'in all things civil and useful in creation', that for boys being established at Waltham and that for girls at Shacklewell. Early in 1675, while he was in London recovering from his imprisonment at Worcester, he suggested that a school should be founded to teach not only languages but the nature of herbs, roots, plants and trees. And he destined the land allotted to him in Philadelphia for a meeting house and school 'and to inclose another part for a garden, and to plant it with all sorts of physical plants for lads and lasses to learn simples there, and the uses to convert them to — distilled waters, oils, ointments, &c'.

Neither the 'Garden School-house' near London nor the herb garden at Philadelphia came to fruition, but both serve to remind us that botany has long been a Quaker tradition. A modern Friend has written that 'it is part of the large faith in the inner light, the belief that as man looks humbly and faithfully with his own eyes instead of learning dogmas out of books, he is learning to look with the eyes of God'. It is to be expected, therefore, that in Quaker family life the cultivation of gardens has fulfilled a need for aesthetic self-expression as well as giving a simple form of outdoor exercise and fostering appreciation and disciplined understanding of natural history.

The stress which Quaker educationists consistently laid on natural history and an experimental approach to science is important, for the 'essential revolution in thought which gave rise to the scientific era consisted in an acceptance of first-hand knowledge, checked by repeated experiment, instead of trust in any dogmatic authority'. With these thoughts in mind, we shall now turn to panels commemorating a number of Quaker botanists, doctors and scientists.

Quaker botanists (D8)

Among the 'hireling priests' convinced of Truth in 1652 was Thomas Lawson of Rampside, in the Furness district of Lancashire, south-west from Swarthmoor Hall towards Walney Island. Lawson became, a couple of years later, one of the Valiant Sixty, travelling with the Quaker message in Sussex and later elsewhere. By 1660 he had settled at Great Strickland in Westmorland and had opened a school. Perhaps it was the publication of John Ray's *Catalogus plantarum Angliae* (1670) that fostered his devotion to botany, but certainly by July 1674 the Swarthmoor account book records the reimbursement of 10s to Thomas Lower, one of Margaret Fox's sons-in-law, 'that hee gave Thomas Lawson for comeinge over hither to Instruct him and his sisters in the knowledge of herbs'. He must have recorded between 400 and 500 different species, and this in a day when systematic botany was in its infancy.

With the eighteenth century we move into an Anglo-American world of Quaker botanists. For 35 years, for example, there was frequent exchange of correspondence between John Bartram (1699–1777) in Philadelphia and Peter Collinson (1693–1768) in London. They never met, but the exchange was not only of letters but of seeds, roots, cuttings or pictures of their new discoveries. Bartram carried out at intervals indefatigable search of the American backwoods, crossing unbridged rivers, prying among rattlesnakes, or obliged to follow the tracks of wild beasts through dense thickets.

To obtain the cones of rare pines at the proper season for Collinson he had, he explained, 'a grievous bad time', climbing trees in the rain to lop the boughs, and then standing up to his knees in the snow to pluck off the cones. It was in 1743 that he found the large magnolia (*acuminata*) growing 100 feet high, and Collinson could write 20 years later of the seed he had received, 'I am in high delight, my two mountain magnolias are pyramids of flowers'.

A man of natural religion, Bartram disliked theology and was disowned by his monthly meeting in 1758 for his liberal views. He continued to attend meetings for worship but was never reinstated: 'It is through the telescope', he said in one of his letters, 'I see God in his glory'.

When John Fothergill (1712–1780) came to London in 1740 he soon met Peter Collinson, the woollen draper of Gracechurch Street, Fellow of the Royal Society and correspondent and friend of folk like Linnaeus and Sir Hans Sloane. Fothergill, whom we shall encounter again shortly as a doctor, bought in 1762 an estate at Upton in Essex, containing at first 30 acres but afterwards enlarged. In order to enrich this garden Fothergill entered into correspondence with persons in far countries and enlisted the aid of sea-captains and travellers, acquiring plants and seeds from China, Hindustan and other of the East Indies, the West Indies and even Siberia. Through Collinson he came to know John Bartram and, through him, Bartram's son William (1739–1823) and Humphrey Marshall (1722–1801), a cousin of the Bartrams and one

E6. Elizabeth Fry and the patchwork quilts

of the best of the early botanists of America. In this country it was inevitable that he should be in close touch with his fellow-Quaker Philip Miller (1691–1771) at the Chelsea Botanical Garden.

We may now raise our eyebrows at some of the methods used for obtaining seeds and plants but we cannot blame our predecessors that their methods were not ours: we can but rejoice at their enthusiasm, their zeal to learn, and their open willingness to share what they had discovered.

We could go on to William Curtis (1746–1799), founder in 1781 of the celebrated *Botanical magazine* (though he had ceased to be a Quaker by that time); or to the Maddock family, florists at Walworth Marsh; or to James Backhouse, (1794–1869), the York seedsman, whom we shall later meet in Van Diemans Land; or J. Gilbert Baker (1834–1920) and Daniel Oliver (1830–1916) at the Herbarium at Kew; or Sir Thomas Hanbury (1832–1907) and his famed garden at La Mortola. They would but stand for many, many more, and we turn, in conclusion to Sarah Martha Baker, whose words form the text to our panel.

Sarah Baker was born in 1887 and was for nearly the whole of her life a member of Willesden Meeting. She came of two gifted families. Her father's side ran to engineers and her uncle, J. Allen Baker, was a MP and chairman of the LCC Tramways Committee. On her mother's side the grandfather was J. Bevan Braithwaite (1818–1905), a conveyancing barrister and a Greek and Hebrew scholar. She, as a child, had an intense love of flowers but her early ideals were to become a medical missionary in the South Sea Islands. Her parents demurred and she took an honours degree in chemistry at University College, London, subsequently becoming a lecturer there. The biochemistry of plants particularly interested her, but her range was wide, from the ecology of seaweeds to the bread–making properties of possible substitutes for wheaten flour.

Her lectures to adult schools, study circles and the like were marked by clarity and simplicity and her death at the early age of 29 came as a particular blow. But the children of her Sunday School class at Willesden were to recall her teaching 'that the universe is always singing, while only man is silent; and that man must learn to listen, so that his heart may join the universal chorus'.

Quaker doctors (D9)

Let us return to John Fothergill, arrived in London in 1740 after studying medicine at Edinburgh University. For 40 years he was to be a well-known figure, with an extensive practice; and, following his death on 26 December 1780, mourned, it has been said, 'by all London', more than 70 coaches and carriages followed the hearse to the Friends burial ground at Winchmore Hill. We must be prompted to wonder what sort of a man he was.

Clearly, from his correspondence as a botanist, he was a man of great energy. He was businesslike, orderly and dispatchful. He had a keen intellect and rapid insight. He soon made up his mind — and, it may be added, he was not apt to change it. But if at times he appeared unduly brisk, or tenacious in his views, and if at times his face seemed severe, then the saving grace was a disposition of great kindness, and his smile commanded confidence and called forth in his patients new efforts towards recovery.

As a young man he had followed carefully what he had been taught, and he prescribed the reputed specifics for various disorders. But·as he went on he watched nature's ways and learned the working of the human body, and came to rely less on the maxims of authority and more on the results of his own observation. He came to put more and more stress on diet and regular habits of life, including fresh air and exercise. He saw patients in his own house in the early morning and on two afternoons in the week. He went out soon after 9 in his coach to see patients, coming in briefly about five o'clock to dine, then returning late in the evening to sit down writing until 11 o'clock or midnight.

We cannot stay to consider all his other activities — his preoccupation with medical education; his other scientific interests; his conciliation proposals in hopes of averting the American War of Independence; his Quaker activities; his use of his money, for he acquired considerable wealth but continued to live simply; his part with David Barclay and others in the establishment of Ackworth School. At his funeral a Friend quoted Isaiah 54: 10: 'For the mountains shall depart, and the hills be removed; but my kindness shall not depart from thee'.

In the bottom left corner of our panel is The Retreat, York, and we must now turn to William Tuke (1733–1822), whom we have already met (p. 131) when he inherited his aunt's business in York: we have seen how the grocery business became concentrated on tea. William had married in 1754, and it was after the death of his first wife in 1760 that he began to take an interest in Quaker affairs, often finding that it was 'his duty to oppose the course which the principal members of the Meeting were disposed to adopt'.

In 1765 he married again, his wife, Esther, being 'lively and spirited' but at the same time with 'a dignity of mien which gave her an invincible influence over the minds of young persons'. She had five step-children to deal with, and three of her own, one of whom died in infancy. It was she who, at Yearly Meeting 1784, led with dignity a deputation of women Friends asking that the annual gathering they had long since held should henceforth have administrative status; in the same year she took the lead in promoting the opening of a boarding school for girls in Trinity Lane, York, forerunner of the present Mount School.

William Tuke, meanwhile, had been concerned with John Fothergill, John Hustler and David Barclay in the foundation of Ackworth School (1779). But it was in 1790, when he was already 58 years old, that his most memorable work had its inception. That year a woman Friend, Hannah Mills, died in York Asylum in distressing if not doubtful circumstances. It may well have been Tuke's daughter Ann who first put the idea into his mind that Friends might set up alternative facilities, but William certainly took the matter up and Yorkshire Quarterly Meeting in June 1792 approved the establishment of 'A Friends Institute for the Mentally Afflicted'. It was William's daughter-in-law who suggested the name which was adopted, The Retreat.

The Retreat was opened on 11 May 1796, the first superintendent being Timothy Maud, younger brother of Esther Tuke (who had not lived to see her husband's plans come to fruition), and a friend of John Fothergill. A new chapter in the history of mental health had begun.

The bottom of our panel shows Beale's Bathing Machine. Benjamin Beale was a Margate Friend who, in the mid-eighteenth century, invented several varieties of bathing machine, from which 'the pleasure and advantages of sea–bathing may be enjoyed in a manner consistent with the most refined delicacy' for the 'umbrella' at the back of the machine was raised when it was drawn up at the steps of the bathing house, but lowered when the machine had reached the sea, thus ensuring the bather complete seclusion during immersion. Benjamin Beale was also the inventor of a light carriage for the conveyance of passengers from Canterbury to Margate. He cannot, however, have been easy in his mind when the bathing houses were improved so that the visitors were able to entertain themselves of an evening 'with playing, dancing, singing, etc.', perhaps the more so as his wife was a recorded minister.

There are yet more doctors on our panel, but we must pause at this juncture.

William Allen (E12)

William Allen (1770–1843) was the son of a Spitalfields silk weaver and it was originally intended that he should follow that trade, but at an early age his scientific bent was shown by his construction of a telescope through which he observed the satellites of Jupiter. Astronomy remained an interest all his life. His interest in chemistry aroused the attention of Joseph Gurney Bevan of the Plough Court pharmacy, and he took Allen into that business in 1792, retiring himself two years

E7. First-day schools

later. The business, which ultimately became Allen & Hanbury, is commemorated in the bottom left hand corner of our panel.

From 1802 until 1826 William Allen lectured in chemistry at Guy's Hospital; in 1804 he began lecturing at the Royal Institution; and in 1807 he was elected a Fellow of the Royal Society. But these activities are but the fringe of his life. He was, for instance, a founder member of the Geological Society, the Mineralogical Society and the Pharmaceutical Society, being the first president of this last. And he was involved in a wide range of philanthropic activity.

In 1798, for example, he joined the Society for Bettering the Conditions and Increasing the Comforts of the Poor ('I am in a strait about it, as many of the members are of the nobility, and I am fearful that I might not keep my place as a Friend') but it was no benevolence at a distance ('The soup scheme goes well – one thousand nine hundred quarts were served on sixth day') and in 1812 he was largely instrumental in a full survey of 1504 families, so that the roots of poverty might be understood.

In 1804 he became a member of the new British & Foreign Bible Society; in 1807 he was largely responsible for establishing the African Institution; and the following year 'a little society whose object was to endeavour to diminish the number of capital punishments'; and in 1808, too, beginning to take part actively in the system of schools promoted by Joseph Lancaster, whose vision, alas, was not matched by his financial acumen (the British & Foreign Schools Society was formally instituted in 1813).

At the age of 19 he saw that his opposition to slavery must be matched by 'disusing those commodities procured by the labour of slaves', deciding that 'as sugar is undoubtedly one of the chief, I resolve, through divine assistance, to persevere in the disuse of it until the Slave Trade shall be abolished'. In 1811 he began a periodical, *The Philanthropist*, and in 1821 began the 'agricultural colony' at Lindfield, Sussex, a project particularly dear to him, so that he spent much of his time among the people there, working out details of housing and gardens for the colony and in creating training schools for the children.

He was an active Friend and his 'travels in the ministry' extensive – in 1816 to Holland, Belgium, France, Germany and Switzerland; the following year to France; in 1818 on a lengthened journey with Stephen Grellet, which we shall shortly recount (p. 163); in 1822 again to the continent ('My mind is, within this day or two, pretty powerfully impressed with the feeling that it may possibly be right for me to go to meet the Emperor of Russia at Vienna'); in 1832 to Berlin; in 1833 to Spain; in 1839 to Holland, Belgium, Germany and Switzerland.

No wonder that a young Frenchwoman, staying with him in 1820, could write,

'The part of the week which was spent at Plough Court was very amusing to me by its bustle'. She recalled that 'he rose early and lighted his own fire. The early hours were generally devoted to his correspondence, and during the time he was shaving &c his daughter used to read to him in Latin from Livy, and immediately after breakfast he would hear his sister, Anna Hanbury, read French — he seemed literally to have time for everything'.

It was not only causes which preoccupied him; it was people. That same French-woman a few years later recalled that his house 'to its full extent and often beyond it, was ever open to receive all the strangers who required his aid and protection; and as memory glances over the scenes of that period I feel bewildered at the motley assemblage which presents itself. I see men of all countries and of all shades of colour; Russians, Germans, Frenchmen, Swedes, Greeks, Italians, and Spaniards, North American Indians, West Indians, and many of the suffering sons of Africa partaking of that hospitality which he knew so well how to bestow without the least ostentation'.

More Quaker doctors (D9)

We return to our panel and to Thomas Hodgkin (1798–1866), whose period with William Allen at Plough Court had not been a marked success. Hodgkin qualified in medicine at Edinburgh and, after a period in Paris, had accepted an appointment at the London Dispensary and, from 1825, a number of appointments at Guy's Hospital. His paper, 'On some morbid appearances of the adsorbent glands and spleen' had been published in 1832, and it is on this study that much of his medical reputation (and the use of the term 'Hodgkin's disease') rests.

In 1818, when he was 20 years old, he had written an essay 'on the promotion of civilization' running to upwards of 100 pages and concerned with the plight and circumstances of aborigines following the settlement of lands by Europeans, arguing that 'in the last 500 years those under the name of Christians have done far more to degrade, corrupt and exterminate their uncivilized fellow creatures than all the heathen world since the creation of man'. In the 1830s this attitude led him to be seriously critical of the activities of the Hudson's Bay Company. As, however, the Treasurer of Guy's had long been a member of that Company's Grand Committee a rupture was inevitable and in 1837 Hodgkin resigned all his appointments at Guy's.

That year he took an active part in the establishment of the Aborigines Protection Society — 'the protector of those who have no power to protect themselves' — and from 1847 to 1856 he edited *The colonial intelligencer and aborigines friend*. As early as 1823 he had met the Jewish stockbroker brothers, Abraham and Moses Montefiore: it was with the latter that he became most closely associated, from 1857 onwards accompanying Sir Moses and his wife on several overseas missions – to the Holy Land, to Rome, to Constantinople, to Morocco. On a journey with Sir Moses in the spring of 1866 Hodgkin was taken seriously ill at Alexandria and, by the time the party had reached Jaffa, was unable to proceed further. There he died on 4 April, and there he is buried; but a plaque over his house in Bedford Square commemorates him as a Londoner.

Hodgkin was a friend of Joseph Jackson Lister (1786–1869), a Quaker wine merchant with a passion for optical instruments. Lister was a founder member of the Microscopical Society and his researches, on the nature of red corpuscles in mammalian blood for example, give him a significant place in his own right. But he remains in memory as father of a more famous son, Joseph Lister (1827–1912), the next figure in our panel.

Lord Lister is best known as the founder of antiseptic surgery. He had in fact ceased to be a member of the Society of Friends at the time of his marriage in 1856, but perhaps had been increasingly distancing himself from formal association before that. He went in 1844 to the new University College, London, the 'godless institution in Gower Street' where there were no religious 'tests'. One of his fellow-students was a nephew of Dr Thomas Hodgkin, another Thomas (1831–1913), later to be a banker at Newcastle upon Tyne and author of the monumental *Italy and her invaders*. He has left us this vignette of Joseph Lister as an intensely introverted twenty-year-old medical student:

> He was not one who loved strife or debate – not even when I knew him the friendliest discussion or the brightest repartee. His friends always felt his power, but it was silently exerted power. He lived in the world of his thoughts, modest, unmasterful, unassuming, but it was not – at least as I remember him – in his nature to lay his mind along side of yours in order that you and he might beat out truth together.

In later days, honours fell thick upon Lister, including the Presidency of the Royal Society, a peerage, and the Order of Merit. But an article in 1927 recalled him as 'a man of simple habits – extremely modest and forgetful of himself, with a devotion to truth, a passionate love for humanity, and a remarkable serenity of character'. The man who wrote those words was Alfred Salter (1873–1945), the next figure in our panel.

Salter in 1889 began daily journeys from his home in south east London to Guy's Hospital. He was a young man with a crusading passion for service and he made medicine a mission. He read the lives of the great pioneers of medicine and about the works of those still living. No adventure inspired him more than Lister's battle against

E8. The Great Hunger

gangrene. Salter learned of Lister's Quaker upbringing and this first interested him in the Society of Friends, which he was to join in 1900.

When little more than a child, Alfred Salter developed an interest in politics and at one time Mazzini was his greatest hero. At Guy's, Salter's brilliant mind, hard work, and extraordinary memory and powers of concentration – he acquired fluent reading in German textbooks in six weeks – singled him out for an outstanding career as a research worker or a specialist. It was his political affinities which led him in a different direction. He was appalled at the slums he knew and particularly those of Bermondsey which he saw so often in his daily journeys.

From 1897 to 1900 he was bacteriologist at the Lister Institute, invited to that post by Lister himself, but he was becoming more and more involved in the Bermondsey Settlement and was drawn to see his future work for and among the slum dwellers of that district. At the Settlement he met Ada Brown, whom he married in 1900, the year in which he emerged from a period of agnosticism to embrace Quakerism.

Impulsively, on seeing a vacant corner shop, he rented it as his surgery, setting up a medical practice where he could carry out his ideals of service. He had long seen that medical treatment did little when housing conditions were so bad: overcrowding (a family of five living in one room); one water-closet for 25 houses; inadequate water supplies; families so poor that they had no heating and no furniture.

In 1903 he was elected to the borough council and for the rest of his life he worked, both locally and after 1922 in Parliament, for improved conditions and for better health care for those who had no means to do it themselves.

Better housing was a priority, but that was only a beginning in the revolution he inspired for Bermondsey – a garden city, trees in every street, flowers in every open space and on waste grounds. He saw it all as part of the people's health, their well-being, their self-respect, and their feeling of responsibility for their community. Not only did Ada Salter support him in all his work, but had her own active life in the betterment of Bermondsey, becoming mayor in 1922 and the first woman mayor in London. Fittingly, the Old English Garden and Rosery in Southwark Park was named 'The Ada Salter Garden' in her memory.

Finally we come to George Newman (1870–1948), whose public service is impressive – Medical Officer of Health for Finsbury from 1900 to 1907; then Chief Medical Officer at the Board of Education until 1919; finally Chief Medical Officer at the Ministry of Health until his retirement in 1935. And two major institutions – the London School of Hygiene & Tropical Medicine and the Royal Postgraduate Medical School – owe their existence to his practical vision.

But we should not remember him as an administrator at his desk but, for instance, in his Finsbury days, when a particularly black spot of overcrowding and rack-renting had to be tackled. He would go with a selected staff on inspection, lasting from midnight, when the pubs had shut, until 5 am, winter and summer, to find out the real number of men, women and children sleeping under incredibly horrible conditions. Faced by an appalling rate of infantile mortality, he sought and gained support for one of the first infant milk depots. And his books *Infant mortality* (1906) and *The health of the state* (1907) record the magnitude of some of the evils which he was trying to combat.

Two of his major interests, both of which will be mentioned later in this book, were the Friends Ambulance Unit and adult schools. When he entered the Westminster adult school there were but few members: he it largely was who attracted and held the working men who came from the neighbourhood so that there was an attendance of 80 each Sunday morning at his class: 'He was G.N. to them all. They argued with him; contradicted him; but his patience and tact never failed — for he led, and never domineered'.

Quaker scientists (D10)

Our panel has chosen three eminent Quaker scientists of three generations and one of them, A. S. Eddington, may speak for them all.

> In its early days our Society owed much to a people who called themselves Seekers. I think that the spirit of seeking is still the prevailing one in our faith, which for that reason is not embodied in any creed or formula. It would be a shock to come across a university where it was the practice of the students to recite adherence to Newton's laws of motion, to Maxwell's equations and to the electro-magnetic theory of light. We should not deplore it the less if our own pet theory happened to be included, or if the list were brought up to date every few years. Rejection of creed is not inconsistent with being possessed by a living belief. We have no creed in science, but we are not lukewarm in our beliefs. If so-called facts are changing shadows, they are shadows cast by the light of constant truth.

John Dalton (1766–1844), father of the 'atomic theory', and Arthur Stanley Eddington (1882–1944) have much in common besides their Quaker faith and their north-country origins. Dalton was born at Eaglesfield in Cumberland, his father a poor weaver; Eddington at Kendal, where his father, headmaster of the Quaker school there, died of typhoid when the boy was two. As so often happens, though they were brought up in poverty, both their mothers were exceptional people. Neither Dalton nor Eddington married, and neither of them had social graces. Dalton's fame spread throughout Europe; when he travelled abroad he relaxed his simple Quaker ways, ate and drank with the great and went to the opera, for like many scientists he had a passion for music, and even petitioned Yearly Meeting in his youth for its value and virtues to be recognized and allowed to Friends. But Dalton always wore Quaker dress and the broadbrimmed hat, knee-breeches and collarless coat and used the 'plain language'; he rose every morning to clean his own lab and light the fire; and a distinguished visitor was astonished to find him giving a lesson in mathematics to a small boy. Both Dalton and Eddington were deluged with honours by the universities and academies of Europe, and remained as unassuming as ever.

His neighbours got used to his daily routine by which they could set their watches; his abrupt and direct Quaker ways; his tall gaunt figure and hoarse voice; his fundamental kindliness which in the end made him Manchester's favourite son. When he died his body lay in state in Manchester Town Hall for four days; 40,000 people passed the coffin, and nearly a hundred carriages followed him to the cemetery – surely a unique Quaker farewell. His memorial took the form of scholarships to Owens College in Manchester.

Half a century later A. S. Eddington had there the excellent education which Dalton had missed. From Owens College he went on to become Senior Wrangler in the Cambridge Tripos examination, and went straight from the University to be a chief assistant to the Astronomer Royal at Greenwich. In 1913 he was made Plumian Professor of Astronomy at Cambridge; he became secretary and subsequently president of the Royal Society. In the Dictionary of National Biography he is called 'the modern Archimedes'; before the end of the First World War he had mastered Einstein's Theory of Relativity, helped to confirm it and began to apply it in further discoveries which 'made possible the modern theory of Stellar evolution'; his book *The internal constitution of the stars* was called at the time 'the most important work ever written on the subject'. His dream was to 'determine by theoretical methods the structure of nature' using quantum mechanics and relativity, and his final work, published after his death, bore the title of *Fundamental theory* (1946); he remains a pioneer whose personal reputation stands higher than ever.

The third scientist on our panel is Kathleen Lonsdale (1903–1971). Like the other two she had a distinguished record in the Royal Society, being one of the first two women to be elected a Fellow, and was subsequently Vice-President; she also served as President of the British Association (1967–8) and was made a Dame of the British Empire in 1956. Like the other two she had a humble beginning, in Ireland, the youngest of ten children; and she began her education in an elementary school from which she went with a county scholarship to Ilford County School and thence to Bedford College, London, where she was one of a group of only two students! However, in the B.Sc exams of 1927 she had the highest marks in the University; joined Sir

E9. Mary Hughes

William Bragg's team and went with him to the Royal Institution. At 26, in 1929, she completed her D.Sc.

As unassuming in manner and as plain in lifestyle as Dalton or Eddington (she relished the simple joys of life such as riding pillion on her husband's motorbike) Kathleen Lonsdale had perhaps wider interests than either, although just as profoundly absorbed by her work as a physicist and crystallographer. Her marriage to Thomas Lonsdale and their three children gave her a family environment unlike the solitude of the other two. Her radical pacifism gave her a lively interest in world affairs, and she was one of the first party of Quakers during the 'cold war' to go to Russia in 1953; and later she went in a similar party to China. She had been imprisoned in Holloway in 1943 because of her pacifist convictions and this experience made the traditional Quaker concern for penal reform native territory for her. She and Thomas Lonsdale were constant and faithful attenders at Quaker meetings at every level, from the little meetings where they worshipped week by week, up to Yearly Meeting where in 1953 she gave the annual public 'Swarthmore Lecture' characteristically choosing a peace theme.

9. Newgate, Muscovy and the South Seas

From Étienne de Grellet to Stephen Grellet (B5)

Étienne de Grellet du Mabillier (1773–1855) was one of several young French aristocrats attracted to Quakerism during the French Revolution. He was born in Limoges, where his wealthy father owned ironworks as well as one of the famous porcelain factories, and served Louis XVI at court, and as Comptroller of the Mint. Stephen's aristocratic background is reflected in the group shown on the left-hand side of our panel.

Grellet's family were devoutly Roman Catholic: his mother was a truly pious woman, and two of his sisters became nuns. He had an excellent education in Lyon with the Oratorians. Pleasure and agnosticism beckoned the young man in those years before the Revolution: 'I sought after happiness in the world. I expected to find it. I went in pursuit of it from one party of pleasure to another; but I did not find it, and I wondered that the name of pleasure could be given to anything of the kind'.

In 1789 the storm broke. Stephen and his brother Joseph fled to join the army of the Princes at Coblenz; but at Mont-Midi they faced a threatening crowd who promised to hang them from the lamppost. They never saw their father again. They succeeded in escaping first to Brussels and then to Holland; and as there was no hope of rejoining their parents they decided to go to South America, leaving there in 1795 for New York.

There they were taken in and sheltered by a Presbyterian family called Corsa, and the daughter of the house gave them lessons in English. She recommended Stephen to try William Penn, of whom he already knew from his favourite philosopher, Voltaire. With his dictionary he sat down to struggle through *No cross, no crown,* the title that 'reached his heart'. He read it twice and then went on to the Bible, which he had never read:

One evening as I was walking in the fields alone, my mind being under no kind of religious concern, or in the least excited by anything I had read or thought of, I was suddenly arrested by what seemed to be an awful voice proclaiming the words 'Eternity! Eternity! Eternity!' It reached my very soul — my whole man shook — it brought me like Saul to the ground.

At Colonel Corsa's there was talk of two English women on a religious visit to American Quakers and Stephen and Joseph decided to go and hear them. Joseph found the silent meeting tedious but Stephen felt a secret joy, though he understood very little of what was said. The women Friends were Rebecca Young and Deborah Darby, whom we shall meet again shortly when we describe the life of Elizabeth Fry. They were invited to dinner at Colonel Corsa's and at the end of the meal everyone fell silent. Out of the silence the visitors began to speak:

> I could hardly understand a word of what was said, but as Deborah Darby began to address my brother and myself, it seemed as if the Lord opened my outward ear and my heart . . . I was like one introduced into a new world; the creation and all things around me bore a different aspect — my heart glowed with love to all.

Stephen did not immediately join the Quakers; his friends tried to dissuade him, but still he went to Meeting. He joined the Society at the end of 1796, when he was 23; and in March 1798 he was 'recorded' as a minister.

Stephen Grellet's early travels (B5)

The year that he was recorded as a minister, 1798, was the year of the terrible yellow fever epidemic in Philadelphia. Grellet was in New Jersey at the time, and was begged to stay away from the city; but he insisted on returning, going out daily to tend the sick and dying. In due course he felt the onset of fever. All this he received with calm. He turned on his side to die more easily, but heard 'a secret and powerful language: "Thou shalt not die, but live — thy work is not yet done". . . . Then the corners of the earth, over seas and lands, were opened to me, where I should have to labour in the service of the gospel of Christ . . . I saw and felt what cannot be written. From that time the disorder subsided'.

After his recovery he was sitting in Meeting when:

> Arthur Howell, in the course of his testimony, mentioned me by name, and said that the Lord had raised me up, having a service for me in the isles and nations afar off, to the east and the west, the north and the south. I had been careful to keep to myself the view I had of these things on what seemed to me a death-bed. I knew therefore that this was a confirmation of the word of the Lord.

Further confirmation came with the arrival of an English ministering Friend, John Hall, who during the voyage across the Atlantic had 'seen' Grellet as his companion

E10. Unemployment

during travel among Friends in America. So began Grellet's missionary journeys; twice with John Hall for thousands of miles in the United States, and in 1804 into Canada where he could preach in French.

In that year he married Rebecca Collins of New York, whither he had recently moved. His father had now died and in 1807 he was able to revisit France to see his widowed mother: 'It was a solemn parting between my beloved wife and myself; but the Lord gave strength, in humble submission, to be resigned to His will'. Even before he went to his mother, Stephen visited the group of Quakers in the district round Nîmes, who had suffered severely. After a nine months' absence he returned home.

It was in 1811 that he felt called to his second visit to Europe, labouring for the first time in Great Britain. During the next two years he spoke to large audiences throughout England, Scotland, Ireland and Wales; to the nobility, the colliers, to 6000 French prisoners at Stilton Barracks in Huntingdonshire; to Jews at the Quaker headquarters in Devonshire House, London; to thieves and prostitutes at Westminster meeting-house in St Martin's Lane; to felons under sentence of death in Newgate, and to the women there. On this last visit, in January 1813, he was accompanied by William Forster and Peter Bedford.

It was on leaving Newgate, 'that abode of wretchedness and misery', one day in early 1813 that Grellet

> went to Mildred's Court to my much valued friend, Elizabeth J. Fry, to whom I described, out of the fulness of my heart, what I had just beheld, stating also that something must be done immediately for those poor suffering children.

We shall shortly see what immense effects resulted from that visit to Mildred's Court.

His own face now turned towards the continent. He crossed the Channel with a party of repatriated French prisoners. Once more he visited the Quakers of the Vaunage, and then made his way through Switzerland to the German Quakers of Pyrmont and Minden. A lame young boy belonging to the Pyrmont group had set out for a morning's sledging, one of the sports not prevented by his lameness. As he reached the top of the hill he saw his uncle Dietrich coming with the news that Stephen Grellet was coming to pay them a religious visit. Young Ben wondered 'what could be the inducement of the stranger to come all that distance, in the depth of a most inclement winter, to visit a few scattered sheep of so insignificant a flock'.

He went to Meeting to see the visitor, curious but uneasy. Grellet 'noticed me with the utmost kindness' and 'soon pressed me into the service of interpreter, young as I was': in family visits in the meeting he addressed the members with 'a tenderness and love, that seemed to come home to every heart. His words were very striking, almost prophetic. My soul bowed before the message of peace through Jesus Christ'. That young boy, Benjamin Seebohm, was later to settle in England and, beyond the claims of business, to devote his life to writing and to religious and philanthropic work.

Grellet feelingly describes the state of war-torn Europe:

> Who that has seen the horrors of war, its accompanying cruelties and vices, can plead for it? Or who that has only heard of the wickedness and misery that attend, but must bitterly deplore it? From my observations I may say, that the sight of the bloody field of battle conveys but one part, and perhaps the smallest part, of the woes that attend this horrible scourge.

It was on 1 April 1814 that he landed at Harwich and in June he was engaged, with William Allen, in conversations with the Emperor Alexander I of Russia and other allied leaders. He then returned to America, but four years later he had returned for his third European visit.

Grellet's third visit to Europe 1818–1820 (B5)

When Stephen Grellet arrived in London in July 1818 he took up residence at William Allen's at Plough Court, and was comforted when he found that he was prepared to accompany him on what would prove an extensive and arduous journey. They travelled through Norway, Sweden and Finland to Russia, where they remained six months. The Czar met them alone 'like old friends', questioned them about the Quaker faith, knelt and prayed with them, and volunteered his unity and sympathy with much that they said. He is depicted on the left of our panel, against a Petersburg background.

We shall shortly see (pp. 179–80) how Daniel Wheeler and his family had just started, at the request of the Emperor, to drain the marshes south of Petersburg, and Grellet and Allen met with the little Quaker group at Ochta. They visited prisons, hospitals and other institutions and reported on them to the Czar. They also had many contacts with the dissenting groups in Russia – Dukhobors, Molokhani, Old Believers – and with the German immigrants. They then went south through Turkey to Greece, but at Zante, while William Allen was 'very busy upon a plan for the education of the poor children', he was taken seriously ill and had to return to England.

Stephen Grellet now spent some time in Italy, being anxious to arrange a visit to the Pope. On the morning of his very last day in Rome, 9 December 1819, he had an audience of Pius VII – 'an old man; very thin, of a mild, serious countenance' (he was, indeed, 79 years old, and had been Pope for 19 years). Grellet, naturally for a Quaker of those days, had his hat on but 'as I was entering the door, some one behind me gently, but quickly, took off my hat, and before I could look for it, the door was quietly closed upon us three'.

With the aid of the priest who was interpreter, they covered much ground – prisons and reformatories, the inquisition, the nature of the church and the grounds of gospel ministry. At the end of the interview (much longer than he was accustomed to give in private audiences) the Pope rose and expressed a desire that 'the Lord would bless and protect me wherever I go'. This interview is commemorated on the right hand side of our panel, which also depicts Grellet with a group representing some of those for whom he felt a special concern – a ragged woman, a Jewish rabbi, and a prisoner in chains.

The visit to Rome over, Grellet returned by central Europe, Switzerland and France to England and thus by August 1820 to home at New York.

'Preaching to nobody' (B5)

While the children's section of our panel depicts Stephen Grellet preaching in a crowd, the centre shows him alone in front of a hut. Quaker legend treasures the story of how, one day, Grellet went to a now-deserted lumberman's camp, sat in an empty hut and against all reason felt impelled to rise and preach the gospel, which he did with much power though perhaps, humanly speaking, feeling a trifle foolish. But he had been faithful to the inward promptings; and faithfulness is all. He journeyed home and forgot the incident. But many years later he was in London and crossing London Bridge when he was accosted by a stranger. He had been, he explained, a lumberman of evil life; he had gone back to the camp to pick up some forgotten tools and, hearing the voice from within the hut he had remained riveted by what he had heard, so that his life had been transformed. And now he was thankful to meet again the man who had been the agency in that transformation.

As explained in the Prologue (pp. 19–20) the story has no firm grounding in history, and may be a misremembering of another, and rather less dramatic, story which Stephen Grellet himself once recounted. But it is worth the brief telling here, and the illustration in our tapestry, for it symbolizes Grellet's spiritual discernment and his obedient faithfulness to divine leadings, a faithfulness which often enabled him to discern the hidden anxieties and intentions of others and to 'speak to states' at times with uncomfortable directness but always with hope and with healing.

Grellet's later years

After the third European journey Stephen Grellet made an extensive visit in 1822 to Friends in the United States and Canada and two years later felt the duty laid upon him to visit the slave-holding states of the south. In his fourth European journey (1831–1834) he visited Great Britain, Holland, Germany, Austria, Hungary, Switzer-

E11. Friends' Provident Institution

land, France and Spain, travelling over 28,000 miles by land. His last 20 years were
spent at Burlington, New Jersey, where he died in the autumn of 1855. An English
Friend recalled him:

> Of very noble presence and singularly delightful intonation in speech, gentle, dignified,
> venerable, his words appealed to all our hearts . . . his manner, aspect and bearing were that
> of a man endued with power from on high, and I regarded him as an Apostle of the Lord,
> and his words as of Apostolic authority.

The Gurneys of Earlham (E5)

We all think we know much more about Elizabeth Fry (1780–1845) than we do about
most people; but all we know, and the more we know, does not answer the question
how this unstable, sensuous, flirtatious young woman, who when she married was no
great success in running her household or managing her children, won the trust of the
women prisoners in Newgate whom the turnkeys feared, and whom the politicians and
reformers had abandoned. If you don't want to call it Divine Grace, as she did, you
have to invent another label; to everyone then, and to anyone who thinks about it
now, it was quite simply miraculous. If you have ever faced a schoolroom, or a youth
club, full of rowdy teenagers, or a street crowd in a bad mood, you have only just
the faintest inkling of what it was like.

The Gurney family to whom she belonged were not 'plain Friends' but (in the
eighteenth century sense of the phrase) 'gay Friends' or as her early Memoir says
'hereditary members'; they belonged because they always had done. The plain Friends
sat secure within the walls of their traditions; the gay Friends adopted many of the
attitudes of 'the world's people' among whom they moved.

The Gurneys were wool-merchants, mill-owners, bankers who did move among 'the
world's people'. On one side Elizabeth was descended from John Gournay, merchant
of Norwich converted in the time of Fox; on the other from Robert Barclay the great
'Apologist', theorist and defender of Quakerism. The family went regularly to Goat's
Lane Meeting in Norwich; and at home their mother read to them from the Bible;
but they did *not* wear Quaker dress, and the twelve children had a very social life with
innumerable cousins and friends and wide contacts in East Anglian society and in
London, including the officers of the Norwich garrison. 'Is dancing wrong?' wrote
Betsy in her journal. 'I have just been dancing; I think there are many dangers
attending it, it may lead to vanity and intemperance. But I think in a family, and in
an innocent way, it may be of use by the bodily exercise; it animates the spirits and
produces good effects,' but as she goes on you can see that she has one foot in the
'plain' camp after all: 'The more the pleasures of life are given up, the less we love

the world, and our hearts will be set upon better things; not but that we are allowed, I believe, to enjoy the blessings Heaven has sent us.'

For the moment, high spirits prevailed; and the episode depicted at the foot of our panel E5, when the Gurney children made a chain across the road to stop the Norwich mail coach, is only one example of high spirits turning into dangerous mischief. The officers of the garrison up to and including George III's nephew Prince William clustered round this bevy of girls, 'all the eleven of us got round the Prince and sang and were very merry'. Flirtation turned to serious love; at 16 Elizabeth fell deeply for James Lloyd (from the family which founded Lloyd's Bank) and it came to an engagement which he broke off abruptly. A year later she wrote: 'This time last year how miserable I was,' and two years later, 'James Lloyd is ill. Do I owe him aught? I think he did me an injury in his time.' Still, there was the Prince and other distractions. 'Why do I wish so much for the Prince to come?' and then the other voice again: 'I am like one setting out on a journey: if I set out on the wrong road I shall lose my way for ever.'

The private emotions of adolescence were echoed by a terrifying public scene. We have seen endless revolutions; what was it like to see the first one? Elizabeth was in her tenth year when the French mob stormed the Bastille and set out to make all things new: government, the coinage, the calendar, the army and the state. The guillotine was set up and claimed its victims; Marat died and Robespierre; Napoleon became First Consul and then the Pope was summoned from Rome to crown him Emperor. These things were the background of Betsy Gurney's growing up, the collapse of the old order and the old faith; and every first-day she and the rest went to Goat's to face the disapproval of their red cloaks and purple boots and fidgets; the boredom of the long silence and the sing-song ministry of outworn phrases, which they parodied at home for their peer-group. The Prince came; the girls all ran up to Betsy's room with him, where Rachel gave them a sing-song sermon from Goats ('I never saw anything so droll'). 'I had a most dis Goats,' wrote Louisa in her diary; and, whatever their frequent use of 'dis' may have meant, it is damning enough.

So what turned Betsy into the plainest Quaker of them all? Surely it was a combination of things. First, her own sense of her unstable nature. Her fear of death, fuelled by her mother's death when she was 12; her terror of water, with recurrent dreams of drowning; her intense sensuality showing itself in the love of food, drink, flirtation and above all, dancing and music: 'It makes me almost beside myself.'

However 'dis' Goat's might be, it did provide an anchor, a degree of security in its solidity; faithfulness may be boring, but how much we owe to it! That sense of fidelity, of a faithful remnant in Israel, the Quakers gathered and borrowed from the Hebrew prophets and from Paul's letter to the Romans; it is in Isaiah, Jeremiah, Ezekiel, Joel, Micah and Zephaniah, persisting through every apostasy. Now Betsy Gurney was to meet it in the flesh in William Savery, Stephen Grellet, Rebecca Young, Deborah Darby and 'dear' Richard Reynolds, who one by one built and sealed her confidence and conviction.

William Savery visits England

William Savery (1750–1804) was a tanner from Philadelphia who like John Woolman, Daniel Wheeler and some others dreaded the fascination of making money. In youth, it was his brother Thomas who felt the call to speak, and it embarrassed William so much that he pulled Thomas down by the coat-tail. 'If thou dost that,' whispered Thomas fiercely, 'it will fall to thee', and so it proved; Thomas became a silent elder, and William the minister able to command large crowds by his eloquence.

He reached England as 'a celebrated preacher from America' – but, in fact, he rarely spoke in meeting on this visit. He was deeply discouraged by the state of British Friends, and never more so than in Norwich: 'I thought it the gayest Friends' Meeting I ever sat in and was grieved to see it. I expected to have passed it through in silent suffering, but at length believed it most for my peace to stand up with "Your fathers, where are they, and the prophets, do they live for ever?" ' (Zechariah 1:5).

Betsy, though recording that 'I had a very bad pain in my stomach' had been anxious to go to Goats that morning in the hopes that he would speak. After meeting she went to dine at Uncle Joseph's at the Grove, where Savery was staying – Joseph Gurney was a 'plain' Friend though his wife was described by Savery as 'a dressy woman'. Uncle Joseph put Betsy to ride alone with William Savery to the evening meeting at the Gildencroft, where Norwich Friends had their burial ground. She wrote in her journal: 'I was very low almost all meeting, I don't know why. I could not help considering how near my mother was in the burying-ground, which led me to think of death'. She drove back to the Grove alone in the carriage with William Savery: 'We had a sort of meeting all the way . . . as soon as we got to the Grove he had a regular one with me'. It was characteristic of travelling ministering Friends of the time that they often, as now, saw into the spiritual states of those they met with. Back at Earlham, she slept badly that night: 'I dreamt nor thought of anything but this man and what had passed'.

Her sisters watched with a mixture of dread and amusement Betsy's preoccupation with the American: 'Betsy, who spent all day yesterday with him, not only admires, but quite loves him', wrote Richenda (aged 15). Her father decided that Betsy needed a change of scene and sent her to London for a month. Savery was there and she saw

F1. Derby gaol

him again. She also went to Covent Garden and Drury Lane, to the opera and concerts, saw the Prince of Wales, talked scandal ('I own I love scandal, though I highly disapprove of it'), called on Mrs Siddons, went about with Amelia Opie, Quaker wife of a fashionable painter: 'I was painted a little and I had my hair dressed, and did look pretty, for me.' In several meetings she met Savery; 'It was like the casting die in my life.'

After a month she went home not feeling well; a farewell letter from Savery regretted that he had no chance 'to take thee affectionately by the hand'. With none of the narrowness she dreaded he encouraged her to 'an enjoyment, under the perfect law of liberty, of that serene state of mind wherein there is no condemnation'. He warned against 'formal professors of religion who think to obtain peace with God by a critical exactness and ever rigid austerity in outward observances' and many others who 'are always exhibiting the dark and gloomy side of religion, not having, in my humble opinion, their minds sufficiently expanded by just conceptions of the adorable love and mercy of God.'

Now came the sign of blessing. Ever since she was 14 years old Betsy had a recurring dream. 'I never missed a week or a few nights without dreaming, I was nearly being washed away by the sea, sometimes in one way, sometimes in another; and I felt all the terror of being drowned, or hope of being saved; at last I dreamt it so often, that I told many of the family what a strange dream I had, and how near I was to being lost.' After Savery's visit she went on dreaming, until on 21 April she could write in her journal:

> The day when I felt I had really and truly got true and real faith, that night I dreamed the sea was coming as usual to wash me away, but I was beyond its reach; beyond its powers to wash me away; since that night I do not remember having dreamed that dream. Odd! It did not strike me at the time so odd; but now it does.

She did not disguise from herself the nature of her feelings; if she had, her sisters would have prompted her:

> Rachel has just said she thinks *I am in love* with W. Savery, I answered I did not think I was, but I own I have not felt clear in my own mind respecting him. I think I may love a person without being in love, but I doubt it. I first loved him for his religion, but the feelings of human nature are very apt to join in with the superior feelings of the heart. I don't think I am in love with him. I should be grieved to think I was.

Betsy Gurney's call to the ministry

In the summer of 1798 John Gurney took his seven daughters on a 'romp' through the west country. Her dream might have gone, but Betsy still feared water, and sailing and bathing at Weymouth were a trial to her. Against this background of summer and sea, the turmoil in Betsy's heart went on. She tried Quaker caps, she tried saying 'thee' instead of 'you' and got mixed up and wondered whether it really mattered: 'Is it not better to be remarkable for excellence of conduct, than for such little peculiarities?' Would she have to turn 'plain Quaker'? 'I find it almost impossible to keep up the principles of Friends without altering my dress and speech . . . plainness appears to be a sort of protection to the principles of Christianity in the present state of the world.'

They visited Coalbrookdale in Shropshire to see the famous ironworks and the iron bridge and to meet all the Quakers who ran the place; the Darbys and Rebecca Young and Richard Reynolds whom everyone loved.

On 31 August 1798 Elizabeth wrote in her diary: 'This evening I am at Colebrooke Dale, the place I have so much wished to be at . . . It brings me into a sweet state, being with plain Friends like these, a sort of humility.' As the first days of September went by, she showed signs of the great emotional excitement which her father watched anxiously with no mother to turn to; he took her aside to warn her 'to beware of passion and enthusiasm, which I hope I do most earnestly pray I may be; for truly they are snares of the enemy.' Could the Coalbrookdale Friends help since they had heard about her from William Savery? Rebecca Young was out, but on 3 September when Betsy came down to breakfast, Deborah Darby was there, and she 'felt her heart beat much.' After breakfast silence fell, and Deborah Darby 'preached in a deep, clear and striking manner', first to the whole company, and then to Elizabeth herself. 'I do not remember her words, but she expressed first, I was, as I am, sick of the world; and looked higher (and I believe I do) and that I was to be dedicated to my God and should have peace in this world, and glory everlasting in the world to come.'

Next day, with 'dear' Richard Reynolds and her cousin Priscilla Hannah Gurney they went to the Darbys', and found Rebecca Young had returned. 'She touched my heart,' but it was Deborah Darby who challenged her once more. 'I only fear she says too much of what I am to be. A light to the blind; speech to the dumb; and feet to the lame; can it be? She seems as if she thought I was to be a minister of Christ. Can I ever be one? If I am obedient I believe I shall.' Next morning as they left she began to count the cost: 'There is a mountain for me to climb over; there is a sacrifice for me to make before I am favoured with faith, virtue, and assurance of immortality.'

Elizabeth Fry's married life

Elizabeth did not envisage marriage when she thought of the mountain; and when a new suitor appeared she had no immediate liking for him. For the family he had recommendations – Joseph Fry was the son of a wealthy, well-connected London merchant and banker, William Storrs Fry; his family were plain, which would suit Betsy, and his manner was exceedingly sober, even dry, which might calm her down. Although 'plain' he did not share Betsy's scruples; he loved music, sang beautifully, and joined in the family pleasures. Betsy would not encourage him: 'I have had many doubts, many risings and fallings about the affair' but they were doubts about marriage and her vocation: 'If I have any active duties to perform in the church . . . are they not rather incompatible with the duties of a wife and a mother?' Joseph refused to go away, and gradually his persistence impressed her; he seemed to be part of that rock of security she needed. Finally, one night in May 1800, he gave her a beautiful gold watch saying that if she gave it back by nine o'clock next morning 'he never more would renew the affair' but that if she kept it after that hour 'he never would receive it back'. 'I did not', she wrote in her journal, 'feel at liberty to return the watch'. In August they were married; Joseph was the youngest son and they had to live in the old Fry residence in the City of London, over the shop in Mildred's Court. 1800, a new century and a new life were beginning.

Settling to married life was not easy, especially with her husband's relatives all round her. Their ways were very different from Earlham life. On the whole she adjusted remarkably well. Her life was filled with acts of kindness – to her relatives on both sides in numerous illnesses and bereavements of the day; to the poor of London who clustered round her; to those in the Quaker school in Islington Road (part of John Bellers' scheme) where she was appointed a visitor and managed, in her first public utterance, to read a few verses and say a few words. There were frequent opportunities, in the war with France, to face unpopularity with courage: the Quaker dress and manner bore witness in opposition to war, and when there were victories to celebrate it was an act of defiance not to illuminate your windows, and risk having them broken; easy-going Joseph was willing to acquiesce (and there was the business to think of) but Elizabeth was not. From one childbirth to the next (there were 11 children), from one sick-bed to the next, from one slum to the next, Elizabeth Fry made her way. Her father-in-law died in the house with his hand in hers; and then they were all summoned to Earlham where, after an operation without anaesthetic, their father John Gurney lay dying, too weak to kiss Betsy when she arrived. 'Never mind, we have kissed in our hearts,' he said.

It was at her father's funeral that Elizabeth first 'appeared in the ministry', an anniversary that she remembered; and it was not long before she was 'recorded' as a minister and began to travel, attending Meetings round the country. For a time she was cheered because they moved out to Plashet in Essex, the estate which Joseph had

WILLIAM PENN + WILLIAM MEADE
were tried for preaching to an unlawful assembly
The jury refused to give a verdict against them
although fined + locked up without food. Their stand
established the right of Juries to give their verdict
according to their convictions. 1670

F2. The Penn and Meade trial

inherited; but when the war with Napoleon came to a crisis in 1812 and the blockade was biting, they were threatened with bankruptcy and had to return to Mildred's Court and what was, for them, penury. 'I fear my life is slipping away to little purpose . . . I do long not to be a drone,' she wrote, but the destiny which Elizabeth craved was near at hand, through one of those 'travelling ministers' whose visits she dreaded.

Elizabeth Fry in Newgate (E5)

We have seen (p. 162) how Stephen Grellet, after visiting the women's side in Newgate with William Forster and Peter Bedford in January 1813, went to see Elizabeth Fry to say that 'something must be done immediately for those poor suffering children'. Elizabeth Fry 'immediately sent for several pieces of flannel, and had speedily collected a number of our young women Friends, who went to work with such diligence, that on the very next day, she repaired to the prison with a bundle of made-up garments for the naked children'.

She was already interested in prisons: as a young girl she had persuaded her father to take her to the 'House of Correction' in Norwich. But she can hardly have been prepared, even after hearing Grellet and Forster, for the total anarchy and squalor which met her. In 1841, in old age and when she was perhaps the most famous woman in Europe, she told an audience of fashionable ladies in Berlin of the questions she had asked herself:

> Would it be possible to touch their hearts by religious truths? Shall I venture to read the Holy Scriptures to them? What effect will it produce?

On her first visit, she told that Berlin audience, she had chosen the fifteenth chapter of Luke, beginning with the Pharisees criticising Jesus for mixing with sinners and ending with the parable of the Prodigal Son; and she recalled the wonderful effect it had, so that afterwards, kneeling down and offering a prayer for them, she could hardly 'hear her own voice'. She assumed immediate and total control; it had to be then or never. Many who heard her tried to explain, or get her to explain, her secret, her peculiar voice and manner, her skill in arresting the attention of her auditors, and her power to touch their hearts.

Through her readings the Bible became the living Word and produced the changes at which the world marvelled, bringing the 'stillness and propriety' described by a male visitor:

> I was conducted by a decently dressed person, the newly-appointed yard-woman, to the door of a ward, where at head of a long table sat a lady belonging to the Society of Friends. She was reading aloud to about sixteen women prisoners, who were engaged in needlework. They

all rose on my entrance, curtsied respectfully, and then at a signal given, resumed their seats. Instead of a scowl, lear, or ill-suppressed laugh, I observed upon their countenances an air of self-respect and gravity, *a sort of consciousness of their improved characters, and the altered position in which they were placed.*

One of her helpers (for in 1817 she had formed a Ladies' Committee) describes how she and her companion went to the felons' door and were admitted to an ante-room,

the walls of which were covered with the different chains and fetters, suspended in readiness for the culprits: a block and hammer were placed in the centre of it, on which the chains were rivetted. I trembled and was sick, and my heart sunk within me, when a prisoner was brought forward to have his chain lightened, because he had an inflammation of the ankle.

The crowd waiting to see the prisoners were searched, and 'a young and pretty little Irish woman with an infant in her arms' was found to have a rope round her middle – she was committed to prison with the babe. Eventually the two young women reached the women's wards, and found 'women from every part of Great Britain, of every age and condition,' assembled in mute silence with their babies, 'innocent partakers in their parents' punishment'. The same helper wrote:

The matron read; I could not refrain from tears, the woman wept also, several were under the sentence of death. Swain, for forging, who had just received her respite, sat next to me; and on my left hand sat Lawrence, alias Woodman, surrounded by her four children, and only waiting for the birth of another, which she hourly expects, to pay the forfeit of her life as her husband has done for the same crime.

Such various, such acute, and such new feelings passed through my mind, that I could hardly support the reflection that what I saw was only to be compared to an atom in the vast abyss of vice, and consequently misery, of this vast metropolis. The hope of doing the least good seemed to vanish, and to leave me in fearful apathy.

The same member of the Ladies' Committee describes the visit of an official committee of inspection headed by the Lord Mayor and Sheriffs of London, to find Elizabeth Fry in the middle of reading a psalm. She stopped and looked at them; they stopped; there was silence – these great and important gentlemen who with jailers, fetters, guns, ropes and gibbets could do nothing with the prisoners, confronting the Quaker lady with her Bible, who could do anything with them. Mrs Fry explained that everything must wait until the reading was finished; she left them standing there, read on; there was silence. The women were dismissed and crowded round the visitors to beg little favours. Then there was a long conference. They cordially accepted the service of the ladies, and acknowledged the extent and importance of the improvements effected. They had themselves experienced insurmountable difficulties in the attempt to control, or introduce order amongst, the women in Newgate. 'Economy not parsimony was the theme of the Lord Mayor' but it was the weight of the influence and authority of these city dignitaries that ensured the establishment on a firm footing of Elizabeth Fry's efforts.

So now everyone came; and it is the wholehearted transatlantic exuberance of the American ambassador's tribute that is remembered:

> Two days ago I saw the greatest curiosity in London, and in England too, compared to which Westminster Abbey, the Tower, Somerset House, the British Museum, nay Parliament itself, sink into utter insignificance. I have seen Elizabeth Fry in Newgate, and I have witnessed there the miraculous effect of true Christianity upon the most depraved of human beings.

Well, the readings were miraculous, but equally incredible was the power of this woman to organize. It was an age when 'public' women were almost unknown, and she had no real previous experience. She gathered helpers, formed an Association, appointed a matron, coped with the filth and anarchy, organised rotas, set up schools in the prison. The prisoners were divided into squads under her helpers, and set to clean up the place. Materials were provided to make clothes for the children in the prison, and those who could sew helped those who could not. The children were taught to read by the helpers and by prisoners who were literate; adults also. The work was paid for by small privileges, and supplies of tea and sugar. Then came the inspired idea of the patchwork quilts.

Transportation Day: Elizabeth Fry's later years (E6)

One day Elizabeth Fry came into the prison to find a poisonous atmosphere, chaos, all her work undone. Anything that could be smashed was smashed; there were yells, screams and curses; and in the middle of it all turnkeys were handcuffing and chaining women together. It was 'Transportation Day'; 128 women and children were to be paraded through the streets in open wagons, crushed into a convict ship and sent to Botany Bay, to be sold into service on their arrival in Australia.

She coped with the situation bit by bit. She got the fetters struck off; she got the open carts changed to closed carriages; then she promised to organize work for the women during the long voyage, and later, help when they arrived. She promised to go personally with the women to the ship. As you can see at the foot of panel E6 (embroidered by children in Australia and Taunton, England), each woman was given a bag of useful things: a Bible, two aprons, a black cotton cap, a large hessian bag for her clothes, a small bag with a piece of tape; pins, one hundred needles, nine balls of different coloured sewing cotton, 24 hanks of coloured thread, 8 darning needles, one

DANIEL WHEELER was engaged in 1818 by Czar Alexander I to clear + drain 105,700 acres of the St Petersburg marshes.

God's love enableth me to call every country my country and every man my brother.

In later life he requested a ship that he might sail the South Seas to present the Quaker message.

F4. Daniel Wheeler

small bodkin, 2 stay laces, a thimble, a pair of scissors, a pair of spectacles if needed, 2 pounds of patchwork pieces, 2 combs, a knife and fork and a ball of string. There was everything required to make a patchwork quilt, and these could be sold for a guinea at Rio de Janeiro, or on arrival at Botany Bay; or used as proof of skill for those seeking work. From 1818 until 1843 Elizabeth Fry organized and visited, with one exception, every convict ship that left for the colonies with women on board, and talked to the officers and crew: 106 ships in all, carrying 12,000 convicts; sometimes four or five ships in convoy.

Elizabeth Fry was now a person of international fame. The King of Prussia knelt with her and her convicts on the clean floor of Newgate. She walked through the streets of Copenhagen with the Queen of Denmark on her arm. The Czar of Russia took note of her suggestions. Wherever she went she visited prisons, orphanages, asylums, took notes and reported on their state to those supposed to govern them; and she organized societies of ladies to continue her work, some of which persisted into the twentieth century. She gave written evidence to Royal Commissions, and advised on the construction of new prisons, though she disapproved of the new 'solitary system' and of cells where the prisoners could not see the sky. At home she was constantly under criticism – from her children who hated her absences, from the local Meeting for hobnobbing with royalty in fine clothes, from those who disapproved of molly-coddling the prisoners instead of punishing them as an example to others. She was also under constant criticism from herself, and often with justice; she was a snob, she loved kings and lords and being famous; she loved food, and, under the stress of continual toothache, there was a period when she loved wine too well; she loved praise and dreaded its effect on her; no wonder that she said that she never asked the women what they had done: 'we have all sinned and come short of the glory of God'.

What we would like to know is what Joseph made of it all. No doubt he knew from the start, as a Quaker, some of the penalties and privations of having a wife a minister – and such a minister; but who really understands such things until they experience them? We do not read that he visited the prison though doubtless he did so, or that he involved himself in the work: it was women's work. Wilberforce went to Newgate with Mrs Fry; her much-loved brother Joseph John Gurney was frequently in her company at home and abroad, sharing her ministry; other members of the family accompanied her; when she was away long letters flowed to her 'Beloved Husband' and the children; Joseph stayed at home and minded the shop.

As time went on Elizabeth became involved with other 'causes', large and small – let us instance libraries for coastguards, and a concern for trained nurses which anticipated Florence Nightingale – but we read between the lines growing divergence within the family. Joseph went off to concerts with the girls while Elizabeth, who in youth had loved music so passionately, refused to go. One by one nearly all the children left the Society. Financial troubles which had at various times beset the family business came to a head with the failure of Fry's Bank. Joseph was disowned by the monthly meeting but later was reinstated. In these days he abandoned his Quaker coat and strict Quaker ways.

Elizabeth herself never wavered, a Quaker and a minister to the end. Her last appearances in the ministry were at 'Draper's', the meeting-house near Margate (shown in our panel C4). She had gone to the coast in a last effort to regain her health, but she was dying. She had always been afraid of death; now she set him at defiance in 'a most powerful and remarkable sermon' in which she called on herself and all there, to repent and be ready 'at the eleventh hour of the day'. On Sunday morning, 12 October 1845, the day before her death, she said to her maid 'Oh, Mary, dear Mary, I am very ill!' 'I know it, dearest ma'am, I know it.' 'Pray for me – It is a strift, but I am safe,' *Strift*, that special Gurney word for a test, an ordeal; it was past, and she was safe.

Daniel Wheeler becomes a Quaker

Daniel Wheeler (1771–1840) was orphaned at the age of 12, and after two years as a cabin boy in a trading ship he joined first the navy and, six years later, the army. He endured many dangers and privations; he had several religious experiences; and in 1796 he turned against a military life for ever. He went to stay with his favourite sister, Barbara, who had gone to live in Yorkshire when she was orphaned, and who had by now married a Quaker. She had joined the Society of Friends herself and it was through her that Daniel first came in touch with Quakers and became a member. He set up in business as a seed merchant, married a farmer's daughter, and became a farmer himself.

Draining the Russian marshes (F4)

As a result of the consultations of William Allen and Stephen Grellet the Emperor Alexander I of Russia attended Westminster Meeting in 1814. A week later, travelling in Sussex, he stopped at a Quaker's farm, was hospitably but simply entertained, and was impressed by the careful management of the land. After his return to Russia he wrote requesting Quaker help in finding farmers, miners, engineers and doctors for him; and in especial for a Friend who would undertake the draining of the marshes south of Petersburg (Leningrad).

Daniel Wheeler was told of this, and as he had long had a sense that he would have work to do overseas, he offered himself for the work. He made an exploratory visit in

1817 to talk things over, and next year, with his wife and family, he set out. From then until 1832 he laboured at the draining of over 100,000 acres of marsh and waste land, extracting old tree stumps and roots, supervising the digging of ditches, the surveying and the levelling, as the land was reclaimed. He amazed the serfs provided for the labour by his humane attitude and his efforts to ameliorate their conditions.

For seven years he was helped by George Edmondson (1798–1863), younger brother of Thomas whom we recently met (p.134) as the inventor of the railway ticket. George came out in 1819 and, at the age of 21, was put in charge of the initial work at Volkova, 10 miles from the Wheelers' house at Shushari: living in a peasant's hut, he would rise at four, fending for himself, responsible for the welfare as well as directing the work of 200 men in the fields.

Meetings for worship were held on Sundays and midweek and George Edmondson would often walk the ten miles to join in worship with the Wheeler family and the occasional visitor. A meeting for worship held 'in the life', as Quakers would say, and with a united sense of being under the canopy of God's blessing, they would describe as a 'covered' meeting, and Daniel Wheeler could write:

> Last First-day, in our little meeting, the Master was pleased to preside, and it was indeed 'a feast of fat things' and the language which was in my heart was, 'Take, eat, this is my body'. I never remember such a covering, and my desire is that I may never forget it; and oh! that the fear of the Lord may so prevail amongst us, as to entitle us to his Love, which can alone enable us to 'run through a troop, or leap over a wall', and which at this time enableth me to call every country my country, and every man my brother.

These words are recalled in our panel, which also depicts on the left the fertile land which was the result of these years in Russia.

It was in July 1832 that Daniel Wheeler returned to England, the intention being that his family would follow him later or that he would return. But by the end of that year his wife had died: the Emperor provided a plot of land in which she could be buried, and in 1837 their daughter Jane had also died, her body being interred in the same plot, which yet remains, restored by the Soviet authorities, a memorial to the family who made those waste acres fertile.

Daniel Wheeler's voyage to the South Seas (F4)

On 13 September 1832 Daniel Wheeler was at his area monthly meeting at Doncaster and was 'strengthened to spread before Friends, the prospect which had been presented to the view of my mind, of visiting in the love of the gospel the inhabitants of some of the islands of the Pacific Ocean, New South Wales, and Van Diemen's Land',

F5. Friends visit the Czar

warning them 'not to let affectionate sympathy bias their minds' and recommending 'that all should endeavour to sink down to the precious gift in every heart, that a right judgment might be come to'.

It was indeed a weighty matter. But the monthly and quarterly meetings had united with it and before the end of the year it had been approved on behalf of the Yearly Meeting. Daniel Wheeler now returned to Russia briefly and then prepared for the long voyage. A post-office packet of 101 tons became available and a number of Friends contributed towards its purchase and fitting. Accompanied by his son Charles, Daniel Wheeler set sail on 13 November 1833.

The ship, the *Henry Freeling*, encountered fierce storms, especially off the Cape of Good Hope. Wheeler recorded in his journal one incident, portrayed on the right of our panel, when mountainous seas broke over the ship and she seemed in grave danger. But the watch on deck called them up to look at a school of some 200 whales ('black fish' each about 12 feet long) which had surrounded the ship:

> so near that some of them might have been struck by a harpoon; they remained constantly swimming in gentle and steady order . . . and I suggested that nothing be done to frighten them away. Not one sea had broken on board while they occupied their useful post . . . these friends in need and friends indeed filled up a sufficiently wide space upon two of the large swells of the ocean, completely to obstruct the approach of each succeeding wave opposed to the vessel.

Half a century later, in the streets of Sydney, Australia, some Quaker visitors met an old man in Quaker garb, 'the very picture of an ancient Friend'. He was Daniel Wheeler's former cabin-boy, John Mohringk, and he confirmed, to the letter, Wheeler's story of the whales that saved the ship.

At Hobart Daniel and Charles Wheeler met James Backhouse and George Washington Walker (whom we shall meet again towards the close of this book) and they travelled together in Tasmania and New South Wales, visiting isolated Friends, encouraging missionaries, and giving hope to the transported convicts. Daniel and Charles then returned through the Pacific, visiting Tahiti, Hawaii and other islands on their way home to England. It was on 1 May 1838 that they returned to London.

Two more years remained to him, during which he twice responded to a concern he felt to travel in the ministry in America, and it was on the second of these visits that, on 13 June 1840, he died in the city of New York.

10. A witness for peace

George Fox in Derby gaol (F1)

In our description of George Fox's early travels in the midlands we referred (p.43) to his imprisonment at Derby. It came about like this. In October 1650 he was in the town and heard a steeplehouse bell – 'and it struck at my life at the very hearing of it'. He found it was a lecture day 'and abundance of the officers of the army, and priests, and preachers were to be there, and a colonel that was a preacher'. Fox went along and, when the preacher had done, spoke of 'the day of the Lord, and the light within them, and the spirit to teach and lead them to God'. Though 'they were pretty quiet' an officer came and took him by the hand and said he must go before the magistrates.

He was committed to the House of Correction for six months and it was towards the end of this time that he was offered a captaincy in the commonwealth army: 'But I told them I lived in the virtue of that life and power that took away the occasion of all wars'. Not realizing that Fox had early learned 'to keep to "yea" and "nay" in all things', they 'courted me to accept of their offer and thought that I did but compliment with them', but he told them he 'was come into the covenant of peace which was before wars and strifes were'.

The result was dramatic. Crying 'Take him away gaoler' they cast him into a dungeon 'amongst thirty felons in a lousy, stinking low place in the ground without any bed' and here he was kept, save for occasional walks in the garden, another six months. Justice Bennet, who had committed him, sent constables to press him for a soldier seeing that he would not take a command, offering press-money which he refused. They continued their efforts but Fox stood firm, well knowing the dungeon conditions he had to face again for doing so. The episode is a reminder of the cost, both to oneself and to others (for his relations were distressed) of obedience and faithfulness.

The experience of Thomas Lurting

It must not be thought that all Quakers saw at once what they were called to witness. A number of members of the Parliamentary army became Friends and if they left it, it was on account of the testimony against oaths rather than any testimony against war. There were also Quakers in the Royalist army. The rejection of war was not a matter of theoretical debate. It was reached as a result of immediate experience, as we may see in the life of Thomas Lurting, the 'fighting sailor turn'd peaceable Christian'.

Born in 1632, he was at the age of 14 pressed into the wars in Ireland and then fought by sea against the Dutch and Spaniards, becoming in 1657 boatswain's mate upon the *Bristol* frigate, where he had oversight of the crew of 200 men. One of his duties was to see that the crew were at the ship's worship, and those who met in Quaker fashion for silent worship he beat and maltreated for their obstinacy. But he became dissatisfied with the official worship and began to wonder whether the truth did not rest with the Quakers after all. But 'the Reasoning Part got up. What to such a People, that both Priest and Professors are against! What to such a People, that I have been so long Beating and Abusing, and that without just Cause! Death would be more welcome to me'.

He confided in one of the Friends, who received him lovingly, but Lurting's first attendance at their little meeting caused a great stir on board, calling forth remonstrance from both chaplain and captain. But the Quakers, not yet seeing the unlawfulness of war, proved the hardiest men on the ship and, moreover, refused to take any plunder. And now, being come to Leghorn, they were ordered to Barcelona to take or burn a Spanish man-of-war – 'And we called Quakers fought with as much Courage as any, feeling then no farther'.

Lurting went into the forecastle and levelled the guns, then going out to check whether to level higher or lower, but 'as I was coming out of the Fore-Castle Door, to see where the Shot fell, the Word of the Lord run through me, how if I had kill'd a Man'. He took aside two of the Quakers that night and 'queried much with them about Fighting; to which they gave me little answer, but said, if the Lord sent them well home, they would never go to it again'. And as for Lurting, he 'plainly saw, that inasmuch as we had been so great Actors in it, now we must bear our Testimony against Fighting'.

It is out of individual experiences such as this that the Quaker testimony against all war became a corporate witness.

The experience of Richard Sellar (A4)

We turn now to another episode, this time in the changed atmosphere of the

F6. Relief work: British Isles

F9. Reconciliation

Restoration. Quakers were now seen as a growing menace which the Navy could no longer tolerate in a life and death struggle with the Dutch.

Richard Sellar was a long-shore fisherman from Kilnsea, far out toward Spurn Head in east Yorkshire. He was pressganged during the campaign of 1665 and assigned to the Admiral's flagship *Royal Prince*. He refused orders, saying that he durst not fight with carnal weapons, for his war was within, and spiritual, and that 'As I was not free to do the King's Work, I could not live at his Charge for Victuals'.

He was beaten by most of those in authority and at last put in irons for 12 days, but his patient endurance won him some friends, for the boatswain's mate declared that he would never beat a Quaker again or anyone else for conscience' sake ('and lost his place for it') while the carpenter's mate brought him food secretly 'for, said he, I have Meat of my own, which is not at the King's charge'.

But the captain had to deal with this stubborn passive resister and Sellar was brought before a court-martial: the account of this trial leaves the impression that it was intended to frighten him into submission, the judge having pleasantly said 'I should be put into a Barrel or Cask full of Nails, with their Points inwards, and so roll'd to Death'. But the Council of War, thinking this 'too much unchristian-like', decided to hang him. 'I am', Sellar replied, 'at Peace with God and all Men, and you my Adversaries'. Next morning he was brought on deck, prepared for execution, and central character in a curious scene.

The interchange between the Judge and Sir Edward Spragg, the Admiral ('Sir Edward is a merciful Man, that puts that Heretick to no worse death than hanging'; 'he is more a Christian than thyself; for I do believe thou wouldst hang me, if it were in thy Power') was a prelude to the Admiral's thrice-uttered words, that 'If any Man or Men on board of the Ship, would come and give Evidence, that I had done any Thing that I deserved Death for, I should have it, provided they were credible Persons'. 'But', Sellar continued, 'no Body came, neither opened a Mouth against me then'. The Admiral then proclaimed him a free man, 'So the Men heaved up their Hats, and with a loud Voice cried, God bless Sir Edward, he is a merciful Man: The Shrouds, and Tops, and Decks being full of Men, several of their Hats flew over board, and were lost'.

Whether Sellar's life had been in serious jeopardy may be doubted, but his own calm courage can never be in doubt. He had great kindness shown by all men on board and continued in the ship, undertaking such non-combatant duties as carrying down the wounded in battle and acting as look-out. We shall see, throughout Quaker history, the tradition of uncompromising absolutism in refusal to have anything to do with the conduct of war and the tradition of alternative service, of undertaking those tasks that conscience permits. Perhaps, at this early juncture, Lurting stands for the one and Sellar for the other.

The prophet and the reconciler

We have seen (pp. 71–2) how Margaret Fell, in June 1660, presented a paper to the King rebutting any suggestion that Quakers were involved in plots and stating that Friends 'do deny and bear our testimony against all strife and wars and contentions'. After the Fifth Monarchy Rising of January 1661 an even stronger (and longer) declaration was issued 'from the harmless and innocent people of God, called Quakers, against all plotters and fighters in the world': 'we do certainly know, and so testify to the world, that the spirit of Christ, which leads us into all Truth, will never move us to fight and war against any man with outward weapons, neither for the kingdom of Christ, nor for the kingdoms of this world'.

This was a statement of personal conviction, and to remove grounds of jealousy and suspicion. Within 20 years its implications in political action had been seen, for in 1678 a work of Robert Barclay's was presented to the ambassadors negotiating the Peace of Nijmegen 'wherein the true cause of the present war is discovered, and the right remedy and means for a firm and settled peace is proposed'.

It is not enough, then, to maintain a personal testimony against participation in war and Friends early found their energies focussed on building the institutions of peace. We have already mentioned, for example (pp. 98–100) William Penn's *Essay towards the present and future peace of Europe* (1693) and John Bellers' *Some reasons for an European state* (1710). But there is also personal service in those places where reconciliation may be possible. When in 1748 the plenipotentiaries met to conclude the peace of Aix-la-Chapelle, they found amongst them a Dutch Quaker, Jan van der Werf, acting as emissary of the Meeting for Sufferings in London. He was quietly delivering a statement on the nature of a durable peace and presenting copies of Robert Barclay's *Apology for the true Christian divinity* in Latin and Spanish, in French and Low Dutch. The French ambassador 'gave the Letter to his Secretary, who read it, and said to the Ambassador, it is about Religious Affairs: On which St Severin said to me, he had no Occasion for it, and thanked me, giving them back again'. The conversations, if at times amusingly negative, were at others rewarding.

There have, then, been these different, yet complementary, strands in the Quaker witness for peace. They have not always been seen as complementary: the prophets have at times accused the reconcilers of compromising, and the reconcilers have at times accused the prophets of being unrealistic. And in every generation there have been those who have found faithfulness too demanding, as when Yearly Meeting 1693 learned of 'some shipmasters (who profess the truth, and are esteemed Quakers) carrying guns in their ships, supposing thereby to defend and secure themselves and their ships, contrary to their former principle and practice'. That said, let us turn to the problems that beset the Quaker whalers of Nantucket during the American War of Independence.

The Nantucket whalers (F12)

There had been Quakers on Nantucket island since 1659, but it was from the beginning of the eighteenth century that Quakerism flourished so that by the middle of the century visiting ministering Friends could report that the meeting house, seating 1500, was filled. It was a whaling community and at one time two-thirds of the islanders were Friends. It is no wonder that the 1770s saw substantial emigration to North Carolina and other southern states.

William Rotch (1734–1828) was a leading Friend. 'When the war began we declared against taking any part of it' he wrote. But he could not avoid the implications of his stand. He had taken a large stock of muskets and bayonets in payment of a debt. The muskets he converted into fowling-pieces and sold but the bayonets he refused to sell. At the outbreak of war both the British and the Americans wished to get hold of his stock and the Americans sent over to requisition them, but Rotch refused: 'The time was now come to endeavour to support our Testimony against War, or abandon it'. There were repeated requests and repeated refusals, so that it 'made a great noise in the Country, and my life was threatened'. Not being able to beat them into pruning hooks, Rotch took 'an early opportunity of throwing them into the sea'.

For his refusal he was summoned before a committee of investigation, where he explained his position. The chairman, after hearing him, declared that 'every man has a right to act consistently with his religious principles', and the major asked more of Quaker convictions, but 'One of the Committee in a pert manner observed "then your principles are passive Obedience and non-resistance". I replied, "No, my friend, our principles are active Obedience or passive suffering"'.

A variety of reasons led the Nantucket whalers to seek a base in Europe and about 1786 William Rotch, his son Benjamin and others of the family settled at Dunkirk. But the French Revolution, three years later, brought fresh trials. The group joined with the newly-discovered group in and around Congénies (see p. 235) in presenting in 1791 a petition to the National Assembly: it is hardly surprising that Mirabeau, in reply, commended the Quaker view of religion as a lofty one but did not take at all kindly to their opposition to war. A little later the group had an interview with Robespierre, who 'made no reply, but let us pass silently away'.

[188]

F7. Relief of suffering

In 1795 William Rotch returned to America, making New Bedford, Massachusetts, the centre of extensive whaling operations. His son and some 15 other families had three years earlier settled in the newly developed port of Milford Haven, and the town took shape under a Nova Scotian architect, a market place and three main roads parallel to the shore, lanes crossing at right angles. The meeting house, shown in our panel, was built in 1811. The whale-oil trade did not succeed, however, and most of the community left or turned to other employments. By 1851 the attendance at Milford Haven Meeting was down to five.

Our panel also commemorates Waldo Williams (1904-1971), a Welsh poet of high merit. In 1939 he had declared himself a conscientious objector and, after the war he transferred to extra-mural lecturing so that his income-tax would not be deducted from his salary at source and he could withhold a proportion of his tax: his goods were distrained and he twice suffered imprisonment. When peacetime conscription was abolished he returned to primary school teaching.

For several years he walked the seven miles from his home to Milford Haven Meeting, though he did not join Friends until 1953. There was a mystical streak in him but he was deeply concerned for practicalities, like the improvement of living conditions in rural Wales and the restoration to legal status of the Welsh language. After his death a local paper headed its obituary of him, 'A man without malice'.

Deputation to Czar Nicholas 1854 (F5)

Our panel commemorates the Quaker deputation to Russia in January and February 1854: the journey was undertaken by three Friends – Henry Pease (1807–1881) of Darlington, son of Edward Pease 'the father of railways' whom we have already met (pp. 131–2); Robert Charleton (1809–1872), a pin manufacturer in Bristol; and Joseph Sturge (1793–1859) a corn-factor in Birmingham. It was with Sturge, the senior member of the party, that the concern originated.

He came of a farming family from Olveston in Gloucestershire and he early had to recognize that if his peace principles were to be worth anything, they must be costing. In 1813, when he was 20, he was balloted for the militia and, refusing to serve or to hire a substitute, his property was distrained and he returned home one day to see sheep being driven off his farm. He had moved to Birmingham where he became in due time the wealthy head of a thriving grain firm, living unostentatiously and less committed to getting and spending than to philanthropic and social concerns.

He had been active in the anti-slavery movement, in the Anti-Corn Law League, and in campaign for franchise reform. He had also thrown his energies into the Peace Society, founded in 1816. In 1850, when Denmark was at war with Prussia over

Schleswig-Holstein, he had with two others visited the heads of both factions in an attempt to prevent bloodshed, and had earned the commendation of the Anglican MP Cobden: 'You have done good service by breaking through the flimsy veil with which the diplomatists of the world try to conceal their shallow craft . . . You have done good work . . . never mind the sneerers'.

By December 1853, when the general war fever in Britain was being fanned by a Russophobe press, and agitation to join the conflict on the side of Turkey was at its height, Joseph Sturge in conversation began to wonder whether, even as a last ditch effort, any good might be effected by a Quaker deputation to the Czar. This time, Cobden was far from encouraging: 'I rather think you overrate the effect of deputating to crowned heads. "Friends" have been charged with being too fond of the "great", and the memoirs of Allen and other biographies give some colourable sanction to the suspicion that you have *tuft-hunters* among your body'.

Sturge was not deterred: he brought his concern before Meeting for Sufferings on 6 January 1854 when it was agreed to appoint 17 Friends to draft an address to the Czar; at an adjournment on 11 January it was approved and at a further meeting on 17 January Charleton and Sturge were appointed to present it, Pease being added within the next day or two. And on Friday 20 January the deputation left London. Quakers are sometimes accused of being unduly slow and cautious: it is not always so.

It was a taxing journey, perhaps particularly for Sturge, who was now 60. As our panel shows, they went by train through Berlin to Königsburg (Kaliningrad), then in a hired carriage to Riga. Now it was a sledge journey of three days to Petersburg (Leningrad), with a team of six horses, constantly changed. But they encountered no serious mishaps, despite deep snowdrifts on the banks of Lake Peipus, and they reached Petersburg at seven in the evening of Thursday 2 February.

We must pause to look at the diplomatic situation. On 22 December England and France had issued a joint demand that the Russian fleet take no action against Turkey and on 3 January sent their own fleets to the Black Sea to ensure this. This the Quakers knew. What they could not have known was that on 16 January the Russian Chancellor ordered the ambassador in London to ask whether the allies meant to keep Turkey from attacking Russia, whether, in his words, there would be *'juste réciprocité'*. On 31 January the British Foreign Secretary gave what would prove an unsatisfactory answer: but this news, of course, had not yet reached Petersburg.

The deputation was kindly received in the capital in general, by the Chancellor on Monday 6 and the Czar on Friday 10 February, Sturge then reading the address of Meeting for Sufferings: 'It is not our business, nor do we presume to offer any opinion upon the question now at issue between the Imperial Government of Russia and that of any other country'. The address went on to state the Christian duty for the promotion of a peaceable spirit, for magnanimity, and for forbearance: 'May the Lord make thee the honoured instrument of exemplifying this true nobility . . . Thus, O mighty Prince, may the miseries and devastation of war be averted'.

They now purposed to return home. They were, however, asked to remain a few more days as the Czar wished to present a written reply to the address and the Duchess of Leuchtenberg, his daughter, wanted them to call on her the following Tuesday. But, in the event, their reception there was very different, being 'with merely formal politeness': 'Her sorrowful air and the depressed look of the gentleman in waiting, made it evident that a great change had come over the whole aspect of affairs'.

They left for London immediately, the return journey lasting only nine days, so that they arrived on Thursday evening, 23 February. They believed that the change in atmosphere had been caused by the arrival of the English papers with news of the warlike speeches in the House of Commons. They were mistaken, for that news had probably reached Petersburg before the Quakers met the Czar. What changed the atmosphere, but what they could not know, was that the previous afternoon the reply of the British Foreign Office had been received saying there was to be no '*juste réciprocité*', so that diplomatic relations were suspended.

The British press had meanwhile had a field day. Among the mildest of the comments were the lines:

> Joseph Sturge
> Went over to urge
> Peace on the Emperor Nicholas.
> Henry Pease
> Went over the seas
> On the same errand ridiculous.

The Times and *John Bull* were far more scathing. And other papers, such as the *Herald of peace*, which might have offered moral support at the time, did not do so until all was over. The Quakers had not gone in any mood of false optimism. They had gone because they believed it was their religious duty in a deteriorating situation. And they learned, through continuing unpopularity and ridicule, that they had to pay the cost of their convictions.

Now it is time to turn to another sort of experience, and to see a nineteenth century Quaker in Parliament.

F8. Friends Ambulance Unit

John Bright's Quaker background

John Bright (1811–1889) drew great strength from his Quaker faith. He was proud of his descent from a prominent seventeenth century Derbyshire Friend and he remained keenly aware of his Quaker heritage. He regularly attended meeting when at home in Rochdale, and when in London, at Westminster; and took part in the business of the Society up to Yearly Meeting. When he died, a politician of national stature, he was buried in Rochdale with a Quaker lack of fuss. Every morning before breakfast, when at home, he read the Bible to his household, 'and so greatly did we delight in his reading that we were always down in time to hear him,' wrote his son Philip, though he added: 'I never heard my father mention religious questions in our home.'

Although deeply affected by the ministry of other Friends, Bright never spoke in meeting for worship. However, he traced his Liberalism to his Quakerism, with its 'belief in the equality of all men in the sight of heaven, and in the equal rights of all men before earthly governments'. But he was not a democrat nor did he support votes for women. Outwardly so often aggressive in political conflict he was inwardly possessed of a deep spiritual humility. Worried by the compliments paid him after his 'Angel of Death' speech in February 1855 he reminded himself 'to avoid vanity' and 'to be grateful' for the opportunity to address Parliament 'on behalf of peace and of political morality.' Writing to J. Bevan Braithwaite in 1859 Bright declared: 'I believe I am not moved by ambition or the desire for personal advantage. I feel a strong love of what is just and a strong sympathy with those who suffer. I endeavour to base our government and policy on morality and truth.' In 1875 he told the American Quaker Allen Jay 'that he believed that he was called to his work as a statesman . . . he thought that the Lord had led him in the course that he had pursued.'

Bright could be critical of the 'little Church' he loved and remained faithful to. He had no patience with the narrower rules of the 'Discipline' in his time. He was saddened and angry when his sister Priscilla was expelled in 1849 for marriage before the superintendent registrar: 'The Society may well not extend . . . It keeps out multitudes by the imposition of tests and observances which can never be of real importance'. He lived to see the rules changed and his sister re-admitted to membership in 1887.

After education at several Quaker schools, Bright entered his father's cotton mill at the age of 15. From 1839 to his death in 1889 the firm bore the name of John Bright & Brothers, although after 1840 his brother Thomas managed the mill. Bright was thus left free to make a career in national politics. But this was not without difficulty, for Quaker attitudes were only slowly changing towards an active Quaker participation in public affairs. Bright entered Parliament in 1843 and in time became the greatest Quaker parliamentarian amongst nineteenth century Friends.

The Corn Laws and the Factory Acts (B3)

Bright had taken a leading part in the campaign against church rates in Rochdale before becoming involved in the Anti-Corn Law League. By 1841 Cobden had recognized Bright as an indispensable speaking partner in the campaign against agricultural protection. The tragic death of his first wife, Elizabeth Priestman, in that year, led Bright temporarily to withdraw from the League's activities. By 1843 he was again active and the second Quaker member of the House of Commons. London Yearly Meeting's epistle urged Friends to be 'quiet in the land', but Bright's spirited protest in Yearly Meeting in support of action against 'unjust laws' won him polite approval from the Friends present. The working class was denied cheap bread by the high price of corn whilst protection restrained freedom of trade with other countries. 'I be protected and I be starving' said a Dorset labourer, and he was made into a slogan straight away. 'Give us this day our daily bread' was borrowed from Holy Writ to be printed around plates and platters. The penny post, the new railways made national campaigns practicable and ensured the maximum publicity for Cobden and Bright's vigorous advocacy of the League's objectives. They effectively led the first modern political pressure group but victory was only secured when the Prime Minister, Peel, decided for himself that the Corn Laws must go. Nonetheless Cobden and Bright became national figures and their busts in Staffordshire ware adorned cottage chimney pieces.

Bright strongly opposed Lord Ashley's (later Lord Shaftesbury) efforts to gain limitation of working hours for factory workers. Bright's father had taken an active interest in the material well-being and education of his work force and Bright continued the tradition. His work force rallied to his defence when political opponents made unjust allegations about Bright's treatment of them. He never opposed restriction of children's hours but he otherwise felt that working hours was a matter best left to employer and employee to decide. There should be no parliamentary interference with the worker's right to determine how long he or she should work. In his sincere but pugnacious defence of laissez-faire Bright ignored the economic power of the employer and seriously misunderstood Ashley's position and motives.

John Bright and peace (B3)

In an age of independent members of Parliament Bright made his mark but he was never able, between 1846 and 1868, to find an alternative power base outside the main political parties of the day. His political career was brought to a temporary end by his courageous opposition to the Crimean War of 1854–6. Bright was not alone in opposing a war forced upon a weak British government by a public opinion deeply hostile to Russia. That opinion already supported Quakers after Joseph Sturge's peace mission to St Petersburg in February 1854 (see p. 191). Bright believed that the war could have been diplomatically averted. In a parliamentary speech opposing the declaration of war on 31 March 1854 he said he would not argue the case 'on the abstract principle of peace at any price' but on grounds of general policy: 'Alliances are dangerous things . . . I would not advise alliances with any nation, but I would cultivate friendship with all nations . . . I am told that the war is popular and that it is foolish and eccentric to oppose it' but 'I do not trouble myself whether my conduct in Parliament is popular or not.'

Bright persisted in this view despite the opposition of his constituents at Manchester, the clear support for the war in the country and the openly expressed contempt of Palmerston, who became Prime Minister in 1855. His greatest impact was in the House of Commons, whose respect he won, despite the unpopularity of his views. His most notable effort came on 23 February 1855 when he made an appeal to Palmerston for a negotiated peace, in a conciliatory speech containing a celebrated Scriptural allusion (Exodus 12, Psalm 78: 49):

> . . .I am certain that many homes in England in which there now exists a fond hope that the distant one may return – many such homes may be rendered desolate when the next mail shall arrive. The Angel of Death has been abroad throughout the land; you may almost hear the beating of his wings. There is no one, as when the first-born were slain of old, to sprinkle with blood the lintel and the two sideposts of our doors, that he may spare and pass on; he takes his victims from the castle of the noble, the mansion of the wealthy, and the cottage of the poor and the lowly, and it is on behalf of all these classes that I make this solemn appeal.

The Commons were deeply moved but the speech had no effect on Palmerston. Peace was not concluded until March 1856. Bright had exercised no effective role either in the conduct of the war or in the making of peace. He collapsed in total breakdown, mental and physical. For two years he wandered in Britain and abroad in search of health. In March 1857 he lost his seat at Manchester but was elected as MP for Birmingham in August 1857.

Bright was not an absolute pacifist. In September 1857 he told Joseph Sturge: 'I have never advocated the extreme peace principle, the non-resistance principle, in public or in private. I don't know whether I could logically maintain it.' In March 1884 he told an Irish visitor: . . . 'do not suppose that I object to violence. I do not,

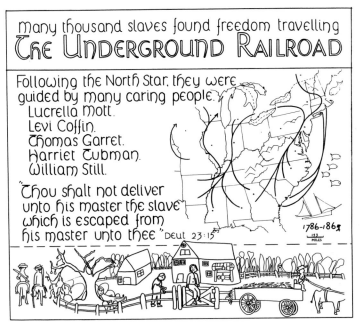

F10. The Underground Railroad

F13. Quakers in Dolgellau

if it rests on a moral basis'. When the American Civil War began in April 1861 the British upper class was sympathetic to the southern slave states. Bright consistently supported the northern states. Through correspondence with the influential Senator Charles Sumner both Cobden and Bright played an important part in preventing the 'Trent' crisis of December 1861 provoking war between Britain and the United States. Bright believed that the American democratic experiment gave freedom a wide expression, a freedom made complete when President Lincoln identified the Union cause with the abolition of slavery in September 1862. Bright had no doubt that the removal of slavery was a proper cause to fight for. Northern victory saw considerable expressions of gratitude to Bright for his persistent advocacy of their cause. Yet he refused all invitations to visit the United States because he did not desire the publicity and adulation which would clearly have been given him if he had accepted.

Bright as a politician (B3)

Bright's great political strength was his oratory, a command of spoken English which could both move and impress all who heard him. The tapestry panel shows a characteristic speaking pose. He used his oratory very effectively between 1865 and 1867 in mobilizing public opinion for an increase in the electorate, secured in the Reform Act of 1867. The new electorate returned the Liberals to power in 1868. Bright found himself the first Quaker cabinet minister, at the Board of Trade, in Gladstone's first government. It was on this occasion, in expressing his reluctance to leave a position of simple citizenship for high office, that Bright used the words from II Kings 4: 13 – 'I dwell among mine own people'.

Gladstone and Bright had a deep respect for each other, which survived the serious political differences of the 1880s. Bright was unhappy in government and a second breakdown occurred in 1870. Thereafter he became a respected Liberal elder statesman. He accepted a minor post, the Chancellor of the Duchy of Lancaster, in Gladstone's government of 1880 but resigned, in July 1882, in protest against the British naval bombardment of Alexandria. He declared the action to be 'a manifest violation of international law, and of the moral law', which he had long publicly upheld as the basis of conduct for states as well as individuals. Gladstone noted: 'splendid old fellow . . . such a grand moral tone'.

From the tragedy of the Famine (see p. 211) Bright had taken a serious interest in Irish issues, looking to religious equality and land reform as a means of securing a more effective Act of Union. 'Force', he declared, 'is no remedy'. He could not, however, trust Parnell and the Irish Nationalist Party and was unable to support Gladstone's Home Rule Bill of 1886. His decision to vote against its second reading encouraged sufficient Liberal dissentients to join with the Conservatives in defeating the Bill. Bright saw no alternative but felt deep pain at the separation from his colleagues and his party.

Bright could not escape the many tensions involved in a political career, especially on occasion conflict between the principles of his Quaker faith and practical politics. He did, however, try to make exercise of political power a serious individual and corporate commitment. 'In working out our political problem, we should take for our foundation that which recommends itself to our conscience as just and moral'. Friends keenly missed him during the Anglo-Boer War of 1899–1903, to which we shall now turn.

Friends and the Anglo-Boer War (F19)

With the outbreak of the Anglo-Boer War in October 1899, Friends found themselves expressing their peace witness in a variety of ways. First, there were public statements like *A plea for a peaceable spirit*. Then, there were public meetings, even if these sometimes proved stormy. Later, as the British military command, faced with the success of Boer commando tactics, turned to a 'scorched earth' policy, burning and destroying Boer homesteads and farmlands and gathering the homeless into camps, there was relief work to be done in those camps. Finally, there was the exercise of trying to understand, so that W. H. F. Alexander, then of Brighton, and Lawrence Richardson of Newcastle upon Tyne could write of their ten-week visit: 'Throughout we made it our custom to talk to all sorts of persons, listening to their views rather than expressing our own. We thus got a very great variety of opinions, often distorted by racial feeling or partial information, and in consequence contradictory, but from which we were gradually able to sift the facts material to our purpose'.

On their return they told the Friends South African Relief Fund Committee on 1 January 1903 of work which Friends might do — land reclamation, help for widows and orphans, support of other general aid. Two small schemes shall be mentioned here, because they were seen not just as relief but as small gestures of reconciliation.

They appealed for money and books to try to replace the destroyed libraries of ministers of the Dutch Reformed Church, helping what others were also doing. The letters received in response expressed not only gratitude for the books but for the restoration of spiritual values and 'a belief once more in the decency of men'. One minister, who had lost all his valuable library, had recovered from the wreckage only one smoke-stained page including the words 'You shall have peace amid the severest trials', a page he had framed in testimony.

The family Bibles of many Boer households had been looted and, learning of the deep bitterness this had caused, two Friends undertook to get reliable information and to try to recover and restore the treasured Bibles. They advertised, using a tactful euphemism, for the return of those Bibles 'which have found their way to England as curiosities', and in July Lord Roberts himself added his word of encouragement to the appeal. The Quakers appealed not only in Britain but in Australia, New Zealand, and Canada.

By the end of March the first Bible had been offered, followed by a steady stream during the next two years. One pocket Bible had been carried by an English soldier killed at Nicholson's Nek, and W. H. F. Alexander was able to return it to the dead man's sister in Natal – she it was who had given it to him. As late as 1927 it had been possible to return a Bible, but in 1933 the appeal was officially ended. About 175 Bibles had passed through the committee's hands, some 20 or 25 being returned to the donors when it proved impossible to find claimants in South Africa; some 130 returned to the families from whom they had been taken; and about a score remaining.

It was a small, undramatic piece of work, involving considerable correspondence, pertinacity, patience, and scrutiny of all manner of records, and conversation with those who might know of neighbours or friends who might help in tracing the owners. But the reward was not only in the gratitude of the Boers who were reunited with their treasured heritage which they had despaired of seeing again; it was with those returning the Bibles who often expressed pleasure at being able to restore them to the rightful owner or family.

And the score which remained? They were handed over to the High Commissioner for South Africa, for dispatch to Pretoria, and they now rest among the Transvaal archives in the Union Building there. A Friend who sought them out in 1977 has written: 'The way in which Afrikaner faces light up when the visitor in search of Boer Bibles is identified as a Quaker from London is today's witness of how much that service meant to the Boers'.

Conscientious objection 1916–1919 (A7)

We saw at the very outset of this chapter the way in which, in the midst of fighting, Thomas Lurting was suddenly convinced of the moral unlawfulness of war. This experience has been re-echoed down the years. In 1914 a young Territorial Army officer, John Hunter, son of a lieutenant-colonel, was automatically called up for service and went out to France in January 1915. He had three years in the trenches, he had been twice mentioned in dispatches, and he had the rank of captain when in 1918, after much heart-searching, he found he could do no other than witness against

F11. Penn and Pennsylvania

all wars and fighting. He was court-martialled and sentenced to death but, following questions in Parliament, had this commuted to imprisonment.

Released after nine months' imprisonment in May 1919, he went almost at once to Poland with the Friends War Victims Relief Committee, concerned to do something practical to repair the ravages of war by providing farmers and peasants with horses, agricultural machinery and seed. In his spare time he learned to knit beautifully patterned pullovers so that even his leisure should be of service to the destitute children around him. He was able to see these devastated lands again yielding a harvest. It was a few years later that John Hunter and his wife joined the Society of Friends.

There have been far more who, like Richard Sellar, were already clear in their conviction that they could not fight when they were pressganged or caught up in Militia or Conscription Acts. Conscription in France, Germany and Norway in the nineteenth century made more severe demands on Quakers in those lands than Friends in Britain suffered from the Militia Acts, though here, too, there were prison sentences. In the Civil War many American Quakers suffered dire punishment for their refusal to take part. But our panel concentrates on the First World War. Let us turn to it.

At first, service was voluntary – and we recall Lord Kitchener's famous recruiting poster, as also those women who offered white feathers, symbolizing cowardice, to young men who were not in uniform. But at the outset of the war British Quakers set up a War Victims Relief Committee to help the civilian sufferers, initially in France; at the same time an unofficial Friends Ambulance Unit was established so that young men who were prepared (as Richard Sellar had been) to undertake non-combatant duties had a ready way to fulfil this willingness. We shall return to this work in our next chapter.

Conscription was introduced in 1916, the Act including a conscience clause and also providing for tribunals (including, as our panel shows, a military representative) who considered applications for exemption alike on grounds of hardship and on those of conscience. London Yearly Meeting, meeting especially to consider the situation, recorded that 'we cannot admit that a human tribunal is an adequate judge of any man's conscience [for the] final appeal can only be to the source from which the conscientious convictions themselves spring'.

Some Quakers, now and in the Second World War, therefore refused to go before a tribunal and were arrested. Those who faced tribunals might receive absolute exemption; or exemption conditional on (for example) joining the Friends Ambulance Unit or undertaking work in hospitals or on the land; or they might have their application dismissed.

Those who refused to go before a tribunal or were unable to accept its verdict were, technically, soldiers. They would be taken to barracks, told to don uniform and refuse. They then found themselves in army detention or prison cells, like the one (from an original sketch) on the right of the panel. By the 'cat and mouse' policy they served short sentences but, on release, were again submitted to the same process and recommitted. There were those who had served in France with the Friends Ambulance Unit who, in 1916, returned to England and to prison, believing that this was their best service in fighting conscription.

Our panel is concerned to stress the different, and equally valid, forms of witness – the absolutist in the prison cell; those who worked in this country in hospitals or on the land; those who undertook civilian relief overseas or ambulance work close to the army. All had different difficulties to face in their witness: many found that their experiences led to a different pattern in their later lives.

Work camps (F15)

Our panel carries quotations from two Friends, the British Jack Hoyland and the Swiss Pierre Ceresole. How did they come to see work camps as a form of witnessing for peace?

Both in thought and action Pierre Ceresole (1879–1945) is an outstanding figure among twentieth-century Quakers, an iconoclast, a radical, as courageous as George Fox himself; and like George Fox a man who kept a journal (from which selections in French and English have been published). He was the son of a former President of the Swiss Confederation, trained as an engineer, and a brilliant mathematician.

When he was 17 he had a mystical experience in the Forest of Gantenaz, a place to which he returned from time to time and at the end of his life. He called the experience *la vision-verité*, a solemn consecration to Truth; and being suspicious of accepted standard names, he preferred to call God *'l'Éternel'*. At 30 he abandoned his promising academic career to travel round the world, working with his hands on a chicken farm, an oil-rig, a three-masted schooner. He returned to Switzerland in 1914 and went to work in the famous firm of Brown-Boveri at Baden, but became more and more troubled by the course of the war, and in 1917, inspired by the faithfulness of a pacifist school teacher, he made a public declaration of unity with him. He now refused to pay the tax on those exempt (as he was) from military service and served his first imprisonment.

The war over, he joined a new international community at Bilthoven, in Holland, the community's objects being to attack and resist conscription and to apply the Gospel consistently to their lives. It was soon after this, in the early 1920s, that he founded what he called 'an army of men without hatred' who would replace conscription by voluntary constructive service. He called it *Le Service Civil International* – International Voluntary Service. It has operated in many countries from Wales (during the mass unemployment of the 1930s) to India (in Gandhi's time) and Kenya (during the painful transfer to self-government) as well as in direct relief during and after the Second World War.

Ceresole himself, after hesitation and a period of dialogue, joined the Society of Friends in 1936. During the Second World War he was again and again imprisoned. He was a troubled and sometimes troubling presence among the small group of Swiss Quakers to which he now belonged. Faithful to his conscience he suffered many hardships and, returning home late in 1944, he did so to face a terminal illness. He survived to know that peace had come and that IVS teams were in the field, coping with the debris of war. 'God', he had written, 'God is the search, the struggle, the life . . . we must not limit God to anything else'.

The other Friend whose words form part of our panel is John S. Hoyland (1887–1957). He worked for 12 years as a missionary in India and had an abiding love for that country and its peoples. From the time of his own undergraduate days Jack Hoyland had a lifelong concern for the service of youth and organized Quaker tramps and also visits between young Friends in Britain and America. For 24 years he was a lecturer at Woodbrooke College in Birmingham (see p. 239) and it was during this time that he published *Digging with the unemployed* (1934) and *Digging for a new England* (1936).

He wrote out of experience. He dug with the unemployed in South Wales because he knew that work done *with* people is of much greater value – and to both parties – than work done *for* them. Tremendous worker though he was, he was prepared to sacrifice some measure of efficiency to achieve this ideal. He gave to the work camp movement a new and more personal meaning, which helped to inspire numerous off-shoots, all of them concerned with the sacramental quality of the work, the camp life, and the relations between the volunteers and the local inhabitants where the work was done.

In 1935, at Marienthal, near Vienna, Austrian and British Friends co-operated with the local unemployed in preparing land for allotments so as to improve the living conditions in that very distressed area. Jack Hoyland reflected on the experience, which had attracted nearly 70 British volunteers:

[It] opens up visions of a new form of Quaker international service. Hitherto our work in Europe has been chiefly among the 'intellectuals'. Perhaps the allotment work is going to open up much wider spheres of service among the 'dispossessed'. It will be service of a John

F12. America and Milford Haven meeting

Woolman type; we shall be working with our hands at the task of international and inter-class reconciliation, as the unpaid servants of the poorest classes of other nations.

There was a second Marienthal camp in 1937 but Jack's efforts to obtain permission for a third in 1938 were, understandably, unsuccessful. He was always concerned to ensure that the free labour of the camps should never conflict with the interest of paid labour and the jobs undertaken were always ones that would either be done by voluntary labour or not at all. By the time he was 65 he was medically unfit for hard manual work and those who heard that he had spent a week at a work camp were alarmed, knowing he would never care to be a 'non-working visitor'. Characteristically he had quietly relieved other members of the camp and spent the time scrubbing vegetables and washing up dirty plates and dishes. It was after such a camp, in August 1953, that he received a letter: 'Dear Jack, We are so very glad you came to camp with us. We cannot say how much your presence and guiding love helped us . . .'

Every weed uprooted and every nail driven home in such an atmosphere was, Jack believed, a contribution to a better world. His towering figure, sounding laughter and large warm handgrip convinced many British Quakers that understanding those of other nationalities is often best achieved through working together.

Vigils for peace (F17)

Early Quakers might well have declared that it was not in accord with Truth to describe as a vigil a gathering for silent witness arranged for a summer afternoon. And the gathering arranged in 1968 was indeed more accurately styled 'Witness for peace'.

It was far from the first time that Quakers had met in public places in silent witness, so what was unusual about it? First, it was seen as an integral part of our Yearly Meeting so that it received the loyal support of many who might not have attended had they seen it as an optional extra. And second, it followed hard upon the Yearly Meeting's consideration of the right sharing of the world's resources, thus giving an added depth of meaning to the witness, which was conceived 'not simply as witness against war but as witness to the need for justice in the world and against disparities of wealth between nations and peoples'.

Some 600 to 700 Friends gathered outside Westminster Abbey at 4.30 on the Sunday afternoon, greyheads standing side by side with members of Junior Yearly Meeting, while a few older Friends, including one of 93, sat in the Abbey. The dean and sub-dean stood with Friends throughout. The St John's Ambulance men in waiting surveyed the ranks of older Friends and, 45 minutes later, murmured surprise to one another as, without a single hint of anyone fainting, the gathering broke and the long procession of Friends moved into the Abbey and slowly and quietly down the nave, standing for a few further moments of quiet prayer until, led by the dean, the company joined in the Lord's Prayer.

Our panel recalls another witness of the whole Yearly Meeting, this time in Trafalgar Square in 1980 and attended by about 1000 Friends, most of whom walked, two by two, in an exceedingly long crocodile, in groups of 40 badged and bannered fore and aft. As 6 o'clock struck from St Martin-in-the-Fields the last group of 40 reached the crossing into the Square and the little supporting group of saffron-robed Buddhists, old friends by now, courteously ceased their drumming, as essential to their witness in the streets of London as silence is to the Quakers. And, as one commentator wrote, 'The "rude boys" lounging high on Landseer's lions gradually ran out of squeaky comments as they contemplated the silent assemblies of God's people'.

It is not for us to estimate what the result was, whether, indeed, there was a result, of these silent witnesses for peace, nor of any other in any other place at any other time. These things are not judged by results as the world accounts results. They are valid only if they are entered into, neither counting the cost nor expecting return, because we are impelled by the holy spirit which will not be denied.

Q-PAC (B8)

It was in May 1980 that the Quaker Peace Action Caravan began its travels, travels which ended in December 1985. Our panel therefore celebrates a short-lived piece of work but one which touched the imaginations – and the lives – of many British Quakers.

The description (a 'mobile resource centre for peace education') may sound stuffy. Q-PAC decidedly was not. It was alive. And the message on the van – 'working for a less violent world' – brought peace into everyday life, for the team defined violence as anything which damages, degrades or destroys human beings. We were taught to explore the connections between the violence we do to each other in our everyday lives, violence in the community in which we live, and the global violence which threatens the existence of the human race and of our planet.

'Working for a less violent world' – not a world without violence, an aim which too many people would think of as unattainable. But Q-PAC's foundation stone was nonviolence – the search for creative, constructive and peaceful means of resolving conflict. The team did not reject conflict, for through conflict we can change and grow; but it urged that violence is just one option for trying to solve problems, and that there are others.

Our panel reminds us that whether it is street theatre, or work in schools, or putting new heart into tired and dispirited peace workers, it is always the individual encounter that is important. There is a place for the large-scale campaign, for media coverage, for the mass meeting; but Q-PAC sought always the small gatherings and the personal contact. In a world that seems to be in the grip of far-off decision-makers and impersonal forces, it is above all necessary to stress the worth of the individual and the conviction that, in the long run, individuals can change things. Let us close with the words which our panel quotes from Q-PAC's van: 'World peace will only come through action by ordinary people like yourself'.

Building the institutions of peace (F16)

Our panel on vigils for peace reminded us that peace begins in the hearts of the people. But practical steps towards successful peace-keeping are often worked out round the conference table, and our last panel in this chapter serves to remind us of this.

We have already seen how William Penn and John Bellers each had plans for institutions to ensure the stable peace of Europe, how Meeting for Sufferings in 1748 asked the Dutch Quaker Jan van der Werf to talk on its behalf with the ambassadors negotiating the Peace of Aix-la-Chapelle, and how at the time of the likely outbreak of the Crimean War, three Friends travelled to Russia in an effort to avert it. Now let us turn to our own century.

It was in 1917 that Carl Heath, secretary of the National Peace Council, a man who had recently joined the Society of Friends, urged Quakers to establish 'an embassy of the city of God in every great city of men'. And thus the seed of Quaker centres was sown — some (Berlin, Paris, Geneva) lasting for many years, others meeting a passing need only.

Geneva enabled Quakers to be close to those places where decisions are made affecting many peoples so that, for instance, Quaker relief workers were able to report their experiences so that their knowledge and judgment could be transmitted to international refugee organizations. And, with the coming of the United Nations and, later, the European Community, New York and Brussels became obvious places for a Quaker presence.

And if there are military academies, why should there not be schools of peace studies? We have seen that goodwill is not enough: we need a disciplined mind to face the problems that confront us. We might have commemorated Lewis Fry Richardson (1881–1953), the meteorologist who resigned his post when the Meteoro-logical Office became part of the Air Ministry, the brilliant mathematician and physicist who in 1940 refused a professorship because he felt a concern to devote

F14. Quakerism in New Zealand

himself more fully to a study of the causes and results of war, publishing (usually on microfilm) works with such alluring titles as *Statistics of deadly quarrels*.

But we have chosen to recall the fact that the University of Bradford was the first university in this country to establish a full chair in peace studies. There had been, for example, departments of conflict resolution elsewhere, but here in 1972 is recognition that the study of peace issues is a serious academic discipline. We have travelled a long way since the commonwealth commissioners confronted George Fox in Derby gaol in 1651: and there is a long way yet to travel. But we shall not despair.

11. Quaker relief

The Society of Friends is sometimes (to its embarrassment) thought to be a relief agency. Quakers would stress that any work they have undertaken for the relief of suffering springs directly from the personal concern and insights of individuals, tested by the corporate guidance and judgment of the group. Perhaps it is significant that one of the first pieces of Quaker relief work – in Massachusetts in 1775–6 – was a direct response to a recognition of the needs of the civilian population in an area ravaged by the War of Independence. The very fact that Quakers have maintained a testimony against all war has often led them to attempt, in however small a way, to help in binding up the wounds which war creates.

But wounds are caused not only by war, but by natural disasters and by such social evils as unemployment and poverty. Yearly Meeting 1812 decided to present an address to the Prince Regent on the war then raging. William Allen, whom we met earlier as an eminent pharmacist, was one of those appointed to present the address. He was also at that time correlating information on the extent of poverty throughout this country. And he had other preoccupations. On 8 June 1812 he wrote in his journal:

> Most of my time is taken up with societies for the relief of the distressed poor, engaged also about an arbitration, the African Institution committee, &c, &c. The times are very awful, the wheels of government can hardly go on, great fears of a war with America. On occasions of public calamity, Friends' post must be the care of the poor and the relief of distress.

With that in mind, let us turn to look at some of the panels.

Ireland: the Great Hunger (E8)

The 1841 census of Ireland showed that of a population of eight million, nearly three and a half million occupied 'the lowest class of house accommodation', the potato being almost their only food as well as being their chief means of obtaining the other necessities of life. If the labourer kept a pig it was, as like as not, destined not for home consumption but for the market to help clear his debt to the farmer to help clear *his* debt to the landlord.

When, therefore, in the summer of 1846, though the potatoes looked remarkably well, the whole crop throughout the land was destroyed by blight within one week, it was a blow of first magnitude.

It was not, of course, the first time that the crop had failed – there had been 1822, 1831–2 and 1845. But none had been on the scale of 1846 when, as well as the potato failure, wheat was barely an average crop and barley and oats deficient. Moreover, the announcement did not immediately produce alarm, for many believed the accounts exaggerated and others that the consequences would, after all, not be so very serious.

And, as in all crises, there were those who did not believe that any existed, the folk who had met someone who had met someone who had seen an Irishman who looked well-fed. The Quaker committee which had been set up in Britain noted that 'many persons, when they reflect upon the stores of all kinds yet to be found in the ports and warehouses and markets of that fruitful island, deny the existence of famine altogether'. 'But', the committee went on, 'as famine may exist in one town or province, though plenty may be found elsewhere in the same kingdom; so famine may exist for one class of the community, whilst the rest may have the command, in adequate quantity, though at an increased price, of all the necessaries of life. This is exactly the state of the case in Ireland'.

Various relief organizations had been set up, and funds raised, in the late summer and autumn of 1846. It was in November that Irish Quakers formed a Central Relief Committee in Dublin, with corresponding members from Belfast in the north to Waterford in the south and Limerick in the west, and four auxiliary committees. At almost the same time a committee of 20 British Friends was appointed and William Forster (1784–1854), then of Norwich, set out to make a personal visit, under the guidance of the Dublin committee, of some of the worst-hit districts.

He saw children 'worn to skeletons, their features sharpened with hunger, and their limbs wasted almost to the bone'; he saw a widow with two children who had for a week subsisted on one meal of cabbage each day; he saw another woman, again with two children, who had lived the whole of the week on two quarts of meal and two heads of cabbage; he saw how pigs and poultry had disappeared because the poor no longer could feed them. No wonder that, a few months later, other British Quakers saw 'multitudes of emigrants, mostly on foot, with their bundles on their backs, proceeding to Dublin' – they saw several hundred in the course of one morning and were assured that it was the same, day after day.

F15. Work camps

One of the Dublin Quaker committee's first efforts was the establishment of a soup kitchen in the city, which was soon dispensing 1000 quarts a day and was a model for others to be set up elsewhere (a penny a quart or three halfpence with bread, and special arrangements for those who could not afford it). Relief arrangements were bedevilled, for the Quakers and others, by practical difficulties – vessels to bring food to Ireland were hard to come by; Indian meal which was sent in was unsuitable because there was not sufficient grinding power to cope with the quantity and for want of that, and of adequate instruction on cooking it, a prejudice grew up against it. There was a steady increase in dysentery which weakened the hardest-hit still further.

The pattern of relief operations throughout the island grew – clothing distributions; over 36,000 lbs of seeds distributed to 40,000 destitute people, so that nearly 10,000 acres were sown; assistance to industrial schools; promotion of fisheries; an attempt to encourage the manufacture of flannel in Galway and the establishment there of a model farm. Not all efforts were equally successful, and the farm, for example, was short-lived. But by the time the committee had finished its work in 1852 it had, in the course of nearly eight years, handled just under £200,000, a very considerable sum for those days – this included the value of much food received from America and, nearer home, the value of 56 boilers given by the Coalbrookdale Iron Company (see pp. 124–7).

The committee's final report ran to some 130 pages, with a further 350 closely-printed pages of evidence and detail. The committee went further than relief, feeling a duty 'to advert to some circumstances in the condition of Ireland prior to 1846, which appear to us to have aggravated the difficulties arising from the loss of the potato' and to express its views 'as to the injurious effects which these defective social arrangements must continue to produce, so long as they exist'.

The committee attempted to forestall criticism which they anticipated – and which successive relief organizations down the next century and a half have received:

> In venturing thus to place before the public our opinions on social and economical questions of great moment, respecting some of which the public mind is deeply interested, we feel that we are going beyond what some may consider the duty of the Committee of a charitable association; and that in so doing we may expose ourselves to censure, as outstepping our province, and interfering in matters in which we have no proper concern.

Successive relief organizations – Quaker and other – have been told to keep their hands out of political matters. Yet they cannot. Immediate relief involves long-term responsibility and that responsibility may be a practical step (like the effort to set up a model farm) or it may be, as here, an outright criticism of the Irish land laws, injurious, in the committee's judgment, alike to landlord and tenant. A careful analysis of the position occupied much of the final chapter of the report and, as the committee contemplated the vast emigration in the wake of the disaster, diminishing a population 'which, in the midst of peace, has experienced a decrease such as the ravages of war have rarely or never produced', it could but say, 'There is no time to lose in effecting these reforms'.

The need on our doorstep (F6)

We now turn from this vast piece of work on the part of Irish Quakers to some of the needs which British Friends have found on their own doorsteps. Our panel depicts the response of Manchester Friends in 1819 to a need for immediate relief, for their 1795-vintage meeting house in South Street was close to St Peter's Fields where, on 16 August, a large demonstration for parliamentary reform was put down by the Manchester Yeomanry, at a cost of 11 killed and 400 injured, and the meeting house was the refuge for those swept before the advancing cavalry.

Eleven years later, in 1830, a new meeting house was built, facing Mount Street, and the lower part of our panel reminds us that the basement (whose roofline is recalled to us) was the centre of varied continuing relief work. On the left we are reminded of the Manchester & District Refugee Committee, set up by local Quakers in 1938, which continued in being until 1949. On its books were some 2250 refugees from Germany and Austria, most of them non-Aryan Christians, and it ran or cooperated in running five or six hostels. It was, moreover, extremely active in raising money for its work, a special feature of its fundraising being an annual exhibition and sale of refugee handicrafts, as depicted in our panel: in 1944 this brought in some £700, well above many people's annual salary.

The centre may serve to remind us of an outstanding educational experiment. The overseers of the Manchester and Liverpool areas decided at the outset of the Second World War to run an evacuation school at Yealand Manor in north Lancashire – 'with none of the recognised essentials in school equipment excepting children!' The adult members of the community (who worked on a bare pocket-money allowance) used whatever was to hand; small children pooled their toys to form the nucleus of nursery and kindergarten equipment; older children sat cross-legged on the floor for lessons, and did their written work lying prone on their tummies, heels waving in the air, each with an old copy of the *Hibbert journal* in lieu of a desk.

From these beginnings a reasonably-equipped school was evolved able to satisfy the Board of Education inspector both as regards equipment and attainment; its record for scholarships was high in proportion to its numbers and age range; and if at times it was uncertain where fees, or replacement staff, were coming from, and if this hand-to-mouth existence did not always make life easy, at least it saved Yealand from any temptation to sink into the rut of the commonplace.

On the right we are transported from Manchester to London, but again to the Second World War. It was mainly – but certainly not entirely – members of the Friends Ambulance Unit who were involved in Quaker service in shelters in east London. And we shall return to this work shortly. But shelter work is all very well for those who need to be in target areas and it was early clear that there were many who wanted to get away or ought to get away, but who could not do so because they did not fit into government evacuation schemes. Chief among these were old people and mothers accompanied by their children.

Old people were picked up almost at random by Quakers who were working in target areas and transported to the midlands where a 'reception committee' allocated them to rapidly-converted meeting houses, hop-pickers' barracks and whatever other accommodation could be found. Gradually things sorted themselves out and a more regular system was adopted, alike for the elderly and for mothers and children, so that by the end of the war Friends Relief Service had run some 80 hostels of one sort or another for evacuees. But the start had been with the immediate need seen by Friends, as depicted in our panel, who were working on the spot.

Patterns of overseas relief (F7)

In July 1870 the Franco-Prussian War broke out. In October Meeting for Sufferings set up a committee of 58 Friends to meet every week (with an executive of seven meeting every day) to administer a Friends War Victims Fund. Though, as we have seen, far from the first Quaker effort at relief work, it was, apart from the Irish famine, the first on so large a scale. For the first time the red and black eight-pointed star, as shown in our panel, was used as a symbol.

Some 40 commissioners, many of them Friends advanced in life, undertook work in the field – in the neighbourhood of Metz, in Paris, in the Loire valley. Notices in French and German made clear (a fundamental principle) that relief was given without discrimination: 'Société Britannique de secours aux paysans non-combattants (français ou allemands) qui ont souffert de la guerre'. It was a principle not always easy to apply and always liable to be misunderstood.

Similar relief committees were appointed by British Quakers during the Balkan wars, and during and after the two World Wars. Of the work done during and after the First World War (it included France, Holland, Russia, Germany, Austria, Poland) we have selected the Maternité Anglaise at Chalons-sur-Marne. It was in November

F16. Peace embassies

1914 that the first party of 33 workers left this country for France and, while the main body set to the creation of wooden housing for the homeless ('Monsieur', said eight-year-old Antoinette to the 'War Vics' architect, 'je demande pour Maman le prix d'un abri de deux pièces, une cuisine et une chambre à coucher'), it was a woman doctor who wrestled with the authorities to set up a maternity hospital, securing at last a wing of the gaunt, stone-floored Asile des Vieillards, the home of the aged, the imbecile and the epileptic. By December it was scrubbed, disinfected, painted and ready for the first baby to be born there; in just over five years there were to be 980 more births, with the death of only one mother. And in 1919 the hospital was handed over to a French committee, new buildings being opened in 1922 as the Maison Maternelle de la Marne.

Chalons remained as a monument to Dr Hilda Clark ('1881–1955), who 'lit up sparks in others and released in them powers they did not know they possessed', and to Edith Pye (1875–1965), sometime president of the College of Midwives who once, questioned about why she spent so much time on relief work, replied in simple words, 'We do it because we must'. It was she who, in her seventieth year, was one of the first three Quakers to enter Paris in 1944, personifying to her host of French acquaintances the interest of the outside world, so that 'in the light of her encouragement, they took up again with renewed conviction their tremendous struggle to make relief bricks without straw'.

During and after the Second World War Friends Relief Service had worked in France, Greece, Germany, Austria, Poland. One of the German teams was among the first to enter the concentration camp at Belsen, but besides the victims of concentration camps Germany was full of foreigners brought in compulsorily to work in German factories – Poles, Balts, Ukranians, Yugoslavs, as well as western Europeans. The air was full of questions from these 'displaced persons' – 'When can I go home?' or 'Must I go home?' or 'Have I a home to go to?'

The Belsen team moved to Brunswick where for three years they helped in the care of some 17,500 displaced persons – and just outside the city was a large aerodrome barracks which was adapted and filled with 3000 Poles. And at Goslar and elsewhere Quaker teams worked among DPs until, in February 1948, the number in the British Zone had fallen to 212,000: increasingly the task would be not of preparation for repatriation, but of integration into the German community.

The foot of our panel reminds us again that goodwill is not enough; effective training, whether for work in this country or overseas, is essential – it may be cooking, or languages, or hygiene, or the complexities of international organizations. Beyond all this, whether at Spiceland in Devon, or at Mount Waltham in Hampstead, there was the discipline of learning to live with one another, quirks and all — a discipline clearly so well learned that relief workers tended to look back on either with tremendous affection.

Finally, our panel reminds us that the Friends Service Council (which was then the continuing body for the overseas work of British Quakers) and the American Friends Service Committee in 1947 were awarded the Nobel Peace Prize. 'If', said Henry J. Cadbury on behalf of both bodies, 'If any should question the appropriateness of bestowing the peace prize upon groups rather than upon outstanding individuals, we may say this. The common people of all nations want peace. In the presence of great impersonal forces they feel individually helpless to promote it. You are saying to them today that common folk — not statesmen nor generals, nor great men of affairs, but just simple plain men and women like the few thousand Quakers and their friends, if they devote themselves to resolute insistence on goodwill in place of force, can do something to build a better, peaceful world'.

Friends Ambulance Unit (F8)

In August 1914 there was set up, unofficially rather than as part of regular Quaker administration, a Friends Ambulance Unit, and by the next month the first training camp was in full swing. By the end of October the first party of 43 members set out from London: it included three doctors and six dressers, and they took with them eight ambulance cars and several tons of stores. When the party reached Dunkirk they found, in the half-darkness of bare sheds, hundreds upon hundreds of wounded men stretched on the straw-covered floor — Frenchmen, Belgians, and here and there a few British and Germans.

For five years the Unit worked in civilian hospitals in France, mainly in and around Ypres, in military hospitals in France, with French convoys, and on ambulance trains; while its work in England centred on four hospitals. There were some 1700 members of the Unit, far from all of them Quakers, and their work is commemorated in the left-hand part of our panel.

The rest of our panel touches on the work of the Friends Ambulance Unit when it was revived with the Second World War. The older Friends who had brought it into being left it to the members to run — again, far from all of them Quakers — so that it was a body of young workers with young leaders, among whom anyone over 35, and at first even over 30, was rare.

Unit teams found themselves in the freezing Arctic forests of the north of Finland, in the desert sands of Tobruk and Alamein, in the malaria-ridden villages of Syria, in hospitals in the mountainous capital of Ethiopia. They experienced the perilous convoys of the Burma Road; they served in famine-stricken India; and they followed in the wake of the advancing armies into Italy, the Balkans, the Dodecanese, north-west Europe, and Austria.

But all this is ahead of the air raid shelter in a London Underground station which our panel depicts. In 1940 the Unit had teams working in a number of East End hospitals. On Saturday 7 September, 65 Unit members went to their work as usual. That night, as terrible as unexpected, came the London blitz. East Enders took refuge by tens and hundreds of thousands in basements, under railway arches, in church crypts, in large warehouses that looked more adequate, or at least less inadequate, than their own flimsy dwellings. And every dawn, families emerged to find their homes no longer there: they poured into rest centres, bewildered and full of unanswerable questions.

The Unit had not envisaged that it would devote itself so largely to civilian relief work. But the need was there. All over the following weekend, with Quakers who lived in the area, they toured settlements, shelters, rest centres – trying to get a grip on the facts. All the same, it was unnerving when the Ministry of Health rang up and said that they understood the Unit could supply 65 men to work in rest centres immediately. But, by the end of the year, 200 men were engaged in air-raid relief.

Very soon many shelters became community centres. And at Christmas 1940 there was to be a party in one of the wharves. The day before the event, the manager of the wharf phoned the Unit in consternation. He had heard that decorations were being hung; he was terrified lest they be set on fire and burn the whole warehouse, packed with valuable foods. A Unit officer went to the wharf to talk with him, returning an hour later not only with official sanction for the decorations but with a ten shilling note towards the party expenses.

The bottom of our panel celebrates, in concentrated form, the varied overseas work of the Unit, which continued until 1946, and in which 1300 people served. We are reminded of the China Convoy – in 1942, with 11 trucks lost in Burma, the Unit faced the fact that the age of petrol and plentiful spare parts was over, and that the age of the charcoal-burner, skin and hair ingrained with charcoal dust, had arrived, for lying under a lorry attempting repairs was 'more the rule than the exception in west China'. We are reminded, in our panel, of so much more.

One man, who eventually found his way into the Unit, was brought up in Bethnal Green on stories of 'derring do' by his relatives – how they killed a policeman in Essex Street by dropping a chimney pot from the roof onto his head, how Uncle Dan cracked safes and stole bullion from the airport, how Aunt Kit lived by shoplifting. But he

F17. Quaker vigils for peace

was a 'joiner' – the library, cubs, scouts, evening classes, and the Friends Hall social club at Barnet Grove. It was 'The Hall' and he never thought who or what Friends were until he began to think about the sanctity of human life. When war broke out he realized he was a pacifist. His father said, 'If you are not prepared to shed a drop of blood in the defence of your mother and sisters, there is no reason why you should be allowed to share their roof'.

Forty years later he was to reflect on this crisis moment. 'I slunk off', he wrote, 'and joined the FAU'. Air-raids, ward duties in hospital, organizing a boy's camp, assisting in the operating theatre, quartermaster at a 'homeless' shelter, driving ambulances – and then – coveted but unbelievable – the China Convoy. It was in the Unit that 'I was to learn I could do a great deal more than I believed possible of myself', that he saw demonstrated 'the success of living without threatening or being threatened', so that, looking back over 40 years, he could write: 'I salute dear comrades and extend my gratitude to them and the people like them who supplied the jewels in London's East End'.

Northern Ireland: relief and reconciliation (F9)

We began this series of panels with Ireland in the 1840s. We return to Ireland of the 1970s and 1980s. Our panel recalls two small, imaginative projects which the Ulster Quaker Service Committee has established. Visitors to those detained at the Maze Prison were found often to be bewildered, not knowing how to control children equally bewildered, overwhelmed by a sense of impersonality. By providing a canteen and a playroom for the children, Friends have been able to build relationships, to listen, to explain sometimes that prison regulations have been misunderstood, to enhearten the despairing.

At the foot of our panel we have pictured Quaker Cottage, which gives children from both sides of the torn community the opportunity for holiday activities together. For, as we recalled early on in our chapter, Quakers have sought to administer relief 'without discrimination'. As people from different backgrounds learn to work or play together they can learn that they do in fact belong together. We are not, therefore, much impressed by vast numbers, for we are concerned with relationships, and relationship is possible only between individuals.

In the last years of his long life, Joseph Rowntree of York, he who founded the cocoa business and who served so long in his adult school, looked from a house in Downshire Hill to half of London spread before him – 'It's too big', he said aloud, 'No one person can do anything for it'. And, just over a decade later, an experienced and much-loved American Quaker re-echoed the same sentiment: 'I pin my hopes to quiet processes and small circles in which vital and transforming events take place'.

And it is to these quiet processes in Northern Ireland that we commend our readers' prayers.

12. 'The Gospel must be social'

We have already seen (p. 136) how at the end of the nineteenth century John Wilhelm Rowntree was urging that 'the gospel must be social'. These words did but restate in different language what had always been a Quaker conviction, that religion must permeate the whole of life. Not that there is anything uniquely Quaker about this insight, for it was one proclaimed by the Hebrew prophets of the eighth century BC.

Thus Amos declared that the Lord rejected the formal worship of a corrupt and luxury-loving society: 'Though ye offer me burnt offerings and your meat offerings, I will not accept them: neither will I regard the peace offerings of your fat beasts. Take thou away from me the noise of thy songs; for I will not hear the melody of thy viols. But let judgment run down as waters, and righteousness as a mighty stream' (Amos 5: 22–4). Or Micah: 'Will the Lord be pleased with thousands of rams, or with ten thousands of rivers of oil? Shall I give my firstborn for my transgressions, the fruit of my body for the sin of my soul? He hath shewed thee, O man, what is good; and what doth the Lord require of thee, but to do justly, and to love mercy, and to walk humbly with thy God?' (Micah 6: 7–8).

A witness for peace involves a witness against those things in our own personal lives and in our community life that make for discord. John Woolman pertinently asked, 'May we look upon our treasures and the furniture of our houses and the garments in which we array ourselves and try whether the seeds of war have any nourishment in these our possessions or not'. And our Yearly Meeting of 1940 reflected that the 'dissensions of the world reflect the divisions of our own minds; belief is separated from service, religion from politics, and Christian faith from social practice. Before we are able to heal the world's divisions, we must ourselves find the undivided mind of Christ'.

Testimony concerning simplicity (D2)
Pride is the great enemy to the vision of the Inward Light of Christ in every one and,

[224]

TASMANIA
The first Meeting for Worship in Hobart was held in 1832
Two Quakers James Backhouse and George Washington Walker came to Van Diemen's Land in 1832 to investigate the condition of Convicts and Aborigines

F20. Tasmania

as we have seen (p. 123), the early Quakers sought to overcome that pride which expresses itself in ostentation, flaunting elaborate clothes and jewelry. Truth required that they dress simply, avoid flattering titles and language, and keep to plainness in all things. Not only did the testimony concerning simplicity aim to help conquer personal pride, but it was also an economic witness in an unjust society: 'The trimmings of the vain world', wrote William Penn, 'would clothe the naked one'.

But human nature always finds it easier to judge by outward yardsticks than to discern what are the fruits of the spirit and, alike in dress and address, Quaker simplicity gradually became ossified into Quaker uniformity, into a world of broad-brimmed hat and collarless coat, of coalscuttle bonnet, of thee and thou, of first-day and sixth-month. There was in fact 'more variety in dress than at first sight appeared, but beyond that small variety there were those in each generation who were rebels. Margaret Fell in her late eighties became worried about the way in which things were going and in 1700 wrote against Friends 'minding altogether outward things, neglecting the inward work of Almighty God in our hearts':

> we must look at no colours, nor make anything that is changeable colours as the hills are, nor sell them, nor wear them: but we must be all in one dress and one colour: this is a silly poor Gospel. It is more fit for us, to be covered with God's Eternal Spirit, and clothed with his Eternal Light.

It was as late as 1860 that our Yearly Meeting decided no longer to ask the various meetings for church affairs each year whether Friends were faithful in maintaining 'plainness of speech, behaviour and apparel' and whether the 'remiss herein' had been admonished, for year by year the exceptions and guarded answers had increased ('most Friends endeavour', 'with some exception, Friends endeavour', 'do in degree endeavour'; 'But little advice appears to have been given', 'very little recent admonition').

The abandonment was a gradual one, traditional Quaker speech continuing longer than the uniform dress – which, more than a century later, many folk still believe that Quakers wear. And if the plain dress and plain speech sometimes made a complexity of intended simplicity, if there was sometimes a judging spirit on the part of some Friends insisting that some detail in the dress of their fellow-members was 'inconsistent with Truth', then, when all is said and done, the plain dress did testify to a standard of simplicity when, as our panel shows, it was set against the dazzle of the world, and the plain language, though a sore burden to many and a potential social embarrassment, did witness to spiritual equality and to values other than worldly ones. But let us turn to our panel and learn the story.

David Barclay (1682–1769), son of Robert Barclay of the *Apology*, whom we have already met, had come from Scotland to London as a young man; he became an opulent export merchant and lived in Cheapside, opposite to the Church of St Mary-le-Bow. This house contained 'Warehouse, Counting-houses, parlour and Kitchen on the ground floor, with a large Drawing-room and Balcony above'. In the days of his predecessors in the house successive monarchs had used it as a vantage point to watch the Lord Mayor's procession, and in 1761 George III asked Barclay to be his host.

Barclay's brother-in-law wrote that 'Brother Barclay spared no expense in repairing his house both inside and out, as well as decorating it in a suitable manner' and that 'Lord Bruce came several times to teach them their duty and to give directions about the apartments and furniture'. David Barclay, even if he did install panelling attributed to Grinling Gibbons, was firm on one point, the family should be dressed as 'plain Friends'. His brother-in-law wryly remarked that 'on the whole they made a very genteel appearance, and acted their part in the masquerade very well'. One of Barclay's granddaughters is reputed to have amused the Court who were there by apologizing for not making a curtsey, as her grandfather would not permit it; we are assured, however, that George III had let it be known that he understood Quaker scruples and did not expect any of the family to kneel when they were presented.

Our panel, then, depicts the Queen (whose dress drove one of Barclay's daughters into raptures, plain Quaker that she was) and some of the Court in their splendour with, either side, the Barclay family in their plainness. If it seems to us now to be an opulent plainness, then it is all the more remarkable that David Barclay, despite his wealth, despite his position in the City, was willing to risk misunderstanding and criticism in order to stand firm to his principles. But for few does the working out of what Truth and simplicity require come in so dramatic a manner.

For most, the challenge to live simply will come most persuasively when experience brings understanding of deprivations which others suffer. 'Do you', one of our queries used to read, 'as disciples of the Lord Jesus take a living interest in the social conditions of those around you? What place do you give to personal service, and do you undertake this in the spirit of friendship?' Perhaps nowhere in Quaker history was this answered so affirmatively as in the lives of those who were drawn into the adult school movement.

Personal service: adult schools (E7)

Adult education had a long uneventful period of growth, carried on by individuals and groups of various religious denominations or none, before the deep concern of a few Quakers set a nationwide movement into dedicated activity. Robert Raikes had established his Sunday schools in 1782, adult classes for Bible study (or, more accurately, learning to read by means of the Bible) following shortly after: the most famous of these was begun in Nottingham in 1798 and the work spread, many schools being in operation before Friends had any large part in the work.

Joseph Sturge, William White and Joseph Rowntree are the names on our panel: two of them we have briefly met (see pp. 136, 191). All three contributed their ideas, time, hard work, enthusiasm and character to plant and nurture a seedling which grew into a healthy and health-giving tree with widespread branches.

Joseph Sturge (1793–1859) made the first step when he founded in 1845 the Severn Street Adult School in Birmingham. It was started for boys but men soon came, anxious to learn, and the adult school soon became a distinct movement. After a conference of Quaker teachers in these schools, called by Joseph Sturge in 1847, the Friends First Day School Association was set up.

If Sturge planted, it was William White (1820–1900), the Birmingham printer, whose green fingers caused the plant to flourish. He had had experience of a tough Sunday school of boys in Reading: he brought that experience and his innate helpfulness, tact and kindness to the new work. His was not a dominating character – he led, he encouraged, he persuaded, but he did not drive. Men came to the schools because they were illiterate, driven by the hunger to learn and to know, or because their neighbours were attending, or because they met William White in the street and he talked to them.

It was the success of the Severn Street School and the enthusiasm of William White that took the adult school movement into Quaker meetings up and down the country and involved countless men – and women – Friends in teaching and in other activities that grew around the schools. When William White began his work in Birmingham there were perhaps 500 men and women in adult classes; when he died 50 years later there were 50,000 members in England.

Joseph Rowntree (1836–1925) was 21 when he first took charge of an adult school class at York, where Friends had begun a first-day school in 1848. He started with a class of nine men, most of them older than himself; he was nearly 60 when he gave up. He once wrote to a friend: 'To prepare a bright and practical address once a week may be of immense educational value to oneself, but it is an onerous task'.

The first adult classes were evening ones, but the pattern soon changed to Sunday mornings, and early at that – 7.30, with a breakfast for the teachers at 7.00 in some schools. The arrangements for the schools varied, as also did the classes themselves, depending on the abilities of the teachers and the needs of the class. Joseph Rowntree's brother John, for instance, who started at the same time, began by handing

F21. Friends in Canada

round a plum cake to the men, and announcing that they would read the Bible straight through, whereas Joseph, as we have seen, produced carefully-thought-out addresses.

But the basic work was much the same everywhere, however the presentations varied – the teaching of reading and writing to those who had had little if any instruction; and some arithmetic. But no good movement stands still and from about 1860 there was a steady growth in the range of activities – savings clubs, holiday outings, discussion groups on a variety of subjects. The movement became, in some measure, an unsectarian working-men's church, developing gifts and skills and interests in many men and women who would otherwise have never found them, fostering responsibility and a strong sense of fellowship, exerting an influence on the scholars, their families and friends which we cannot possibly estimate.

But the influence was not on them alone. The teachers, and through them the Society of Friends as a whole, were profoundly affected by involvement in the adult schools. When you teach grown men the unaccustomed arts of reading and writing you have to be patient with them. When you give them plum cake and start them ploughing through Genesis, you see them, as John Bellers always saw others, not as a group but as individual people, as real as yourself. When a scholar failed to attend, the teacher would visit the home, meet the family, and learn at first hand the conditions in which they had to live, the temptations and deprivations they endured, the destitution wrought by unemployment, the terror of 'coming on the parish', of the workhouse. No teacher could be successful who showed any priggishness or condescension. They were appalled by what they came to know and they brought their experience to their Quaker Meetings, so that the adult school movement became a deeply-felt commitment of the whole Society and brought about a changed attitude to the social structure, a change based not on 'notions' but on experience.

The hard work and devotion of the teachers is something to make us wonder. Joseph Rowntree's 40 years' service was while he was building up and running a successful business, employing several thousands by the end of his time as a teacher. George Cadbury likewise gave much of his spare time to the Severn Street School in Birmingham, riding five miles on horseback – in later years, on a bicycle – to join the 7.00 o'clock breakfast for the 7.30 class. To these two, and to hundreds like them, it was not a tight-lipped duty which took them walking, riding or cycling through all weathers to the early Sunday class, but a knowledge that the words of the early Quaker Francis Howgill were indeed true in their experience: 'The Kingdom of Heaven did gather us and catch us all, as in a net, and his heavenly power at one time drew many hundreds to land'.

[230]

The witness of Mary Hughes (E9)

'Comrade is dead'. So passed the word from one to another in East London one April day in 1941. There was only one person east of Aldgate pump who was simply 'Comrade' without any further appellation, and that was Mary Hughes of Whitechapel, where she had lived since 1895.

But why 'Comrade'? Her West End Friends remonstrated with her (for she had indeed, as our panel reminds us, been born in Mayfair) – 'Why do you live in the East End?', they asked, 'You should live away from the people you want to help and you would come back to them so much fresher. And why do you call yourself Comrade? Such affectation!'

Mary Hughes began to wonder if she was wrong. Then it began to rain. And there were two children outside, wondering if they could come in. Suppose, she reflected to herself, they had knocked on the door and said, 'Can we come in Miss Hughes?', then she would have answered, 'No, darlings, Miss Hughes is busy. Miss Hughes will see you another day, but now Miss Hughes is busy – so take these sweeties and run away and don't bother her'. But it wasn't like that: 'They padded on the door with their soft little hands and they shouted, "Tan we tome in, Tomrade?" – and then I knew it was all right'.

Her father, Thomas Hughes, was a judge, one of the group of Christian socialists, alongside F. D. Maurice and Charles Kingsley, and author of *Tom Brown's schooldays*. In her early twenties Mary went to be housekeeper for her uncle, vicar of a parish in the Vale of White Horse: here she met poverty for the first time, and here she became a Poor Law guardian, visiting the workhouse and getting to know the people and their needs.

When she came to London it was to her sister, whose husband was curate at St Jude's, Whitechapel. They were drowned in the loss of the *Titanic*, and Mary moved a few times before settling in 1926 in a converted public house in Vallance Road which, since the message she wanted to give her neighbours was 'Do drop in' she christened in an excruciating pun, the "Dew Drop Inn" – and it is commemorated with a blue plaque.

She had become a member of the Stepney Board of Guardians, then a Labour councillor, and then a magistrate. On the council she was respected by all, but feared by some – but her real work was done outside. She tirelessly visited and encouraged people, spending little time or energy on herself: tea, margarine, onions, bread, cabbage and milkless cocoa were her staple diet. This small, wiry, energetic woman often seemed eccentric. Her letters in a mixture of red and black ink on tiny scraps of paper were characterized by her own weird spelling and punctuation, and the envelopes could be equally eccentric, as when she wrote to a fellow-Quaker at 'The Great Big Joy House, Shadwell'.

Disgusted at the attitude of the churches towards the First World War, she had joined the Society of Friends in 1918. To the end of her life she would be regular in her attendance at the Yearly Meeting, sitting in her red cloak in the front row. Our panel reminds us of her saying that 'Once we have said "Our Father" in the morning we can treat no one as a stranger for the rest of the day'. Nor did she. On the kitchen wall at the Dew Drop Inn there was painted:

> Thinking of things gets mouldier and mouldier
> But thinking of blokes gets more and more absorbing.

And Father Groser, an Anglican priest in a nearby parish, recalled: 'She was always there. That is why she came to the East End and that is why she stayed. It did not matter to her what she did and I don't think she was aware that she did much. But she was always there and there are countless people in the East End who are eternally grateful for that and who have reason to know how much it meant'.

But we must look at the bottom of our panel. It is a story that belongs to Mary Hughes in her mid seventies. There was to be a march of the unemployed ('the Devil's unemployment' she used to call it) to the Houses of Parliament and she said she would go with them. But they said 'You are too old'. 'Nonsense', she replied and they met at the Seamen's Mission. The police said there must be someone to lead them and she said that if there was nobody else, she would: 'And what do you think they said then? They said "You're too slow!" '.

Westminster is a long slog and by the time the procession reached Whitehall there was a great crowd pushing and jostling and she was urged to go on the pavement, but she shouted, 'No! Cowards go on the pavement. I am going to walk on the road'. And near Parliament Square the police tried to split the procession up, sending some one way and some another, so that none knew where the rest were:

> And then quite suddenly I was knocked down by a tram car. The ambulance came as I was lying in the road and I called loudly as they were going to put me in the ambulance, 'Stop! I must see the tramdriver'. So they fetched him and I said to him, 'Look here young man. I'm a JP. I know I don't look like one, but I am, and I want you to write down what I say'. I told him to write, 'I am entirely responsible for this accident, The tramdriver is in no way to blame'. Then I signed it 'Mary Hughes JP' and then I said, 'Now you can do what you like with me'.

And perhaps that, too, is where we should leave her.

Final Panel. World family of Friends

13. Quakers as a world family

We said at the outset that neither this book nor the tapestry pretends to do more than touch on a few episodes from the history of the small company of Quakers in Great Britain and to reflect on some of the insights which these Friends have come to share corporately as a result of their experience and their search. But we cannot conclude without renewed recognition that British Friends are but one group among a far larger number of Quakers worldwide, and that other groups within that world family will have different backgrounds, different experiences, different emphases, so that the unity of the family is found through great diversity.

Our tapestry, therefore, has a few panels which point to this larger family, and in this chapter we shall mention some of them, recognizing that in small space we cannot do them full justice and that, in any event, these Friends must speak for themselves.

It was two years after that memorable Whitsun fortnight of 1652, that fortnight in and around Sedbergh and Ulverston in the north-west of England, that the first of the Valiant Sixty began their work in the south of England. In July 1654 Anthony Pearson, he who had been convinced of Truth as he sat on the bench at Appleby with James Nayler a prisoner before him, was telling Oliver Cromwell 'what great things the Lord had done in the north, which was going over England, and should pass over the whole earth'.

Within a year another of the Valiant Sixty was writing back to Swarthmoor Hall that 'many are raised up and moved for several parts; here are four from hereaway moved to go for New England, two men and two women; some are gone for France and some for Holland'. We have already recounted some of these journeys — to Barbados and New England and to the Great Turk, for example. By the end of the seventeenth century there were Quaker communities the length of the eastern seaboard of America, in Antigua and Jamaica, Bermuda and Nevis, and small groups in the Netherlands, in Friedrichstadt and in Danzig.

We have followed the travels of some of those Friends who crossed the Atlantic to publish Truth; we have seen how William Penn in 1681 founded Pennsylvania as a 'Holy Experiment'. Now is the time to remember all those Friends who went to America as emigrants. Our panel F13 recalls the Friends of Dolgellau – and, indeed, elsewhere in Wales – who, partly on account of persecution and partly because of land hunger, went in successive waves to America, and particularly to the Welsh Tract in Pennsylvania, where such place names as Merion, Bryn Mawr, Gwynedd, Haverford, Radnor, are a lasting monument to the places whence the emigrants came.

Our panel recalls Rowland Ellis (1650–1731) of Brynmawr. In 1686 he and many others from Dolgellau emigrated to Pennsylvania, his family following him later. The centre of our panel shows Tyddynygarreg, the home of the Owen family, where Friends met for worship until a meeting house was built. It is estimated that some 4000– 5000 Friends emigrated from Wales to America and perhaps it is not surprising that the Yearly Meeting for Wales lamented the 'runnings off to Pennsylvania'.

We have also touched on the part played by Friends 'travelling in the ministry' across the Atlantic, recalling American Friends like John Woolman visiting England and British Quakers like Daniel Wheeler journeying to America. These are but two of a continuing and varied company who kept the links alive between otherwise distant communities: they not only gave the ministry of the word in meetings for worship (in which, in point of fact, they often sat silent), but the pastoral ministry of the family visit and the social ministry of the sharing of news. They bound the Atlantic community of Quakerdom into an entity.

For it was as yet almost entirely Anglo-Saxon. The Quaker meetings on the continent of Europe did not long flourish, those in the Netherlands perhaps lasting longest – and we have seen the Dutch Friend Jan van der Werf acting as emissary for British Friends in 1748. But two continental groups were to be 'discovered' in the later eighteenth century.

One was a company of *inspirés* in and around Congénies and Nîmes. They had been in existence from the early eighteenth century and one of their number had in 1769 attended a Quaker meeting in London. In the 1780s, by some curious chances, they had learned afresh of these folk in Britain who thought along the same lines as themselves. One member of the group travelled to London to learn more. Thus it came about that on 23 May 1788 there arrived at Congénies a small party of English and American Quakers, overjoyed to discover this 'hidden precious seed of God'. Our panel C5 depicts the meeting house (1822) at Congénies.

The same Anglo-American party, as they had travelled through Germany, heard of some mystical groups, often called Quakers by their neighbours, and in 1790 British Friends discovered in and around Pyrmont and Minden companies of Pietists 'weary of the ceremonial part of religion', who were already 'true worshippers in spirit'. And we have already seen how Benjamin Seebohm, who grew up in the Pyrmont group, became as a boy the interpreter when Stephen Grellet visited Friends there.

Representing Norway in our panel C5 is the meeting house at Röldal. During the Napoleonic wars some Danish prisoners of war in ships in the Medway came upon a copy of Robert Barclay's *Apology* and made contact with English Friends as a result. On their release they formed the first groups of Norwegian Quakers and were visited by William Allen and Stephen Grellet in 1818. Among later visits paid to the groups was one in 1853 by Lindley Murray Hoag (1808–1880) of New England and James Backhouse (1794–1869), a nurseryman of York. But first we must go back a few years.

Back in America, some time before this visit, Lindley Murray Hoag dreamed that he was in Norway, with a view of a beautiful lake, houses and fields, and snow mountains beyond – a definite landscape – and that he ate fish from the lake. Now, in 1853, he and Backhouse, with a Norwegian Friend as interpreter, visited all the Quaker groups. Back at Stavanger, Lindley Murray Hoag did not feel his service was complete, so a map was produced and he pointed to some mountains to the east. The party set off and appointed a meeting at Sövde.

Now, unknown to Norwegian Quakers or the visitors, some four years earlier a young man in Röldal called Knud Botnen had, entirely as a result of inward illumination, come to deny clerical authority and Lutheran orthodoxy, and to resist war and tithes. A company had gathered round him, abandoning the church, and meeting for silent worship and Bible reading. The priest called them Quakers, but they attached no meaning to the word. Now, two of them wanted to get married, but would not be married by the priest. The group was troubled what to do, but Knud had a vision of light in the darkness and told them that if they waited all would be well. Then some of the group heard of the meeting appointed to be held at Sövde and journeyed thither – only to hear from the visiting Quakers their own faith restated.

Next day Backhouse and Hoag went over to Röldal. On the top of the hill above it the American Quaker stood like a statue, for before him was his dream landscape. They descended the hill and met a man with fish, newly caught, and this constituted their first meal. The group explained their predicament about the marriage; the visitors told them of Quaker procedures; and the couple were married after the manner of Friends in Knud Botnen's house.

But, not only in Norway but in Germany and France, the issue of conscription made life difficult for these small Quaker groups. Nearly all the Röldal Quakers emigrated and their descendants are to be found among the conservative Quakers of Iowa. Others, too, emigrated, so that by the beginning of the twentieth century there were very few

Friends in any of the groups on the continent. But now we must go to the other side of the world.

If we turn to our panel F20 we shall find James Backhouse again, this time in company with George Washington Walker (1800–1859). With the full backing of British Quakers they remained in Van Dieman's Land (Tasmania) from 1832 until 1837, broken only by two visits to New South Wales. As a result of their labours Quaker Meetings were established in Hobart and in Sydney, but the importance of their visit in relation alike to penal reform and to aboriginal policy is perhaps greater. Neither was robust, yet, of 4260 miles travelled in Australia and Mauritius, 3000 were on foot, 1000 on horseback, and the small remainder by coach or row-boat. They saw the transported convicts in the ships which Elizabeth Fry had witnessed at the London end. And Backhouse, as a considerable botanist, inbetweenwhiles recorded all the new plants that he saw. We cannot begin to recount their adventures or their achievements, but we must always remember their effective devotion.

The Australian meeting house shown in our panel C5 is Adelaide, a prefabricated building sent out from London in 1839 in 69 packages and received in South Australia early the following year. And New Zealand is represented by the first Auckland meeting house of 1890. As our panel F14 reminds us, it was in 1840 that the first Quakers settled in New Zealand, and Thomas Mason and his wife are depicted with a Maori chief. The continuing concern of Friends in those islands for a bi-cultural society is expressed in their Yearly Meeting's epistle of 1988 as they began on this panel:

> As we begin working on the New Zealand panel of Quaker Tapestry, initiated by English Friends, we remember the stories of our heritage and the continuing messages they hold for the meeting. Hidden in the fabric of our Quaker life are threads of beauty which we have neglected and which we have seen afresh in our struggle towards a vision of a truly bi-cultural society. Our contact with Maori people has revealed these threads to us, for we see and appreciate in their culture a spirituality and a sense of belonging to an extended family, which we also value.

Thus it is that our panel, like the Yearly Meeting, speaks of Aotearoa/New Zealand. And perhaps, in a wider sense, the extended family is represented in the summer gathering, depicted here, for these gatherings, held in various places each December-January for a 10-day period and attended by 60–200 Friends, are increasingly seen as an integral part of the life of the New Zealand Quaker community.

A summer camp is also part of our panel F21, which celebrates the life of Canadian Quakers. And, just as our Australian panel reminded us of concern for aborigines and that for New Zealand the Maoris, so here, too, we are reminded of Canadian Friends' concern to support the efforts of native people to regain their rights. Earlier on, Canadian Quakers had been involved in the communities of Doukhobors who in the 1880s and 1890s had been driven out of Russia for their radical views.

Quakerism in Canada owes its origin to those Loyalists who migrated there after the American War of Independence, augmented by later migrations from upper New York state in search of land. Our panel commemorates the 1810 meeting house at Yonge Street, Ontario. It had been in 1797 that Timothy Rogers, then living near Vergennes, Vermont, had expressed a concern to go westward 'to open a door for a meeting of Friends in a new settlement'. In 1800, with his son-in-law, he travelled into Upper Canada and from York (Toronto) he struck 30 or 40 miles into the back country, impressed that this was the place in which he was to settle. He came home to settle his affairs and again set out, in the late winter of 1801, with his wife, family and effects 'loaded on seven sleighs', the journey starting on 17 January and ending not until 1 May. And thus was Yonge Street settled. The many scattered Quakers in Canada were enabled to feel part of the family by pastoral visits and our panel recalls the devoted travels, at the end of the nineteenth century and into our own, of Alma Dale, drawn long distances by her cream horses to support and encourage the isolated.

The nineteenth century saw the beginnings of missionary endeavour. British Quakers undertook work in mid-India, Madagascar, west China, the Lebanon, and, at the end of the century, Pemba. To the left of our panel B7 we see the buildings of the West China Union University, Chengtu (Chengdu), opened in 1910, while below the long journey to west China is recalled. From Shanghai nearly 1000 miles up the Yangtze (Yangzi) to Ichang (Yichang); then a further 500 miles through the magnificent but then dangerous gorges with their treacherous rapids – the boats pulled by trackers whose bamboo ropes cut into the rock. As an 86-year-old Quaker traveller wrote: 'There is some excitement in passing the rapids, for if the rope breaks the vessel drifts away, and may easily go on the rocks'. And then, at the end, Chung-king (Chongqing), the entrance to the province of Szechwan (Sichuan) where work was concentrated.

To the right of the same panel B7 we are reminded of clove plantations in Pemba. It was in 1890 that Britain gave Germany Heligoland in exchange for Zanzibar and Pemba; seven years later the legal status of slavery was abolished and more than half the 400,000 population of the two islands was set at liberty. Two Quakers at that time set sail for Pemba, concerned to show how plantations could be run with free labour, and to help the manumitted slaves to rise to the position of free and useful citizens. At Banani a clove and coconut plantation was established and in Chake Chake a day school for boys and a boarding school for girls were started, the latter being moved to Mtambile and leaving in Chake Chake (whose meeting house is pictured in our panel C5) an industrial school.

Other meeting houses in our panel C5 represent other movements and traditions – for Germany, Bad Pyrmont (1933), rebuilt on the site of an earlier building, reminds us of the regrowth of continental Quakerism after the First World War; Bolivia of the missionary work of American Quakers, in this case by Friends of Oregon (now Northwest) Yearly Meeting; Brumanna, Lebanon, of long years of Friends' service in the Middle East; while South Africa is represented by Cape Town and Ghana by Hill House, the one traditional, the other open to the outside world, recalling diversities of conditions of worship.

As Quakerism spread geographically it was but natural that different emphases should develop, alike in theology and practice – there were evangelical Friends, those of the mystical tradition, and those who stressed the place of reason in religion. In Britain the 1895 Manchester Conference (A8) gave impetus to a movement that sought to draw out the best in each tradition, relating each to the current discoveries of science and biblical scholarship and to the rediscovery of the historical setting of Quakerism and the relevance of its seventeenth-century message to twentieth-century needs.

One of the results of this movement has been the establishment in 1903 of Wood-brooke College (B6) in Birmingham, where students – Quaker and non-Quaker – of all ages, nations, traditions and convictions have stretched their minds and spirits as they have learned from one another's insights. And our panel C9 reminds us that Quakers the world over have a common heritage and that there is a place in life for the pilgrimage, to walk and talk in 'the Galilee of Quakerism' so that there may be fresh realization that the roots of the present lie deep in the past.

But the time has come to look at our final panel, the world family of Quakers. It was in 1928 that the recently-formed Germany Yearly Meeting, not yet in its restored meeting house at Bad Pyrmont, asked: 'Does Quakerism consist only of individual Yearly Meetings, which independent of one another manage their own affairs in their own districts, or is it a great Society of Friends reaching away over all boundaries and nations?' There have been world conferences; there is, as our panel shows, a Friends World Committee for Consultation, working through triennial meetings and through sections for The Americas; for Europe & the Near East; and for Asia & the West Pacific. But organization exists only as a means, and our children's section at the bottom of the panel represents the end beyond the means – that as individuals of all nations and backgrounds and temperaments we may listen one to another, learn one from another, and enjoy one another, and all to the glory of God.

Sources and references

It is quite impracticable to give here detailed references to every quotation in this book. A complete list of sources and references is available at the Library of the Religious Society of Friends, London. The principal books used are listed below. It should be noted that in many cases quotations have been taken from secondary rather than primary sources: in particular, many are taken from London Yearly Meeting's *Christian faith and practice in the experience of the Society of Friends*, 1960, and readers are reminded that this work gives full bibliographical details of all works cited. The listing below is 'in order of appearance' rather than alphabetical.

George Fox, *Journal*, ed. John L Nickalls, 1952

Mabel R. Brailsford, *A Quaker from Cromwell's army: James Nayler*, 1927

Norman Penney (ed.), *The first publishers of Truth*, 1907

Joseph Besse, *A collection of the sufferings of the people called Quakers*, 2 vol., 1753

James Bowden, *The history of the Society of Friends in America*, 2 vol., 1850–4

George Fox, *A collection of many select and Christian epistles*, 1698

William Charles Braithwaite, *The beginnings of Quakerism*, 1912

William Charles Braithwaite, *The second period of Quakerism*, 1919

Norman Penney (ed.), *Extracts from state papers relating to Friends*, 1913

Edgar B. Castle, *Approach to Quakerism*, 1961

George Whitehead, *The Christian progress of that ancient servant and minister of Jesus Christ*, 1725

Thomas Ellwood, *The history of the life*, 1714

George Clarke (ed.), *John Bellers: his life, times and writings*, 1987

Thomas E. Drake, *Quakers and slavery in America*, 1950

John Woolman, *The journal and major essays*, ed. Phillips P. Moulton, 1971

Henry J. Cadbury, *John Woolman in England: a documentary supplement*, 1971

Judith G. Jennings, *The campaign for the abolition of the British slave trade: the Quaker contribution, 1757–1807*, unpublished thesis, 1975

Arthur Raistrick, *Quakers in science and industry*, 1950

Arthur Raistrick, *Dynasty of iron founders: the Darbys and Coalbrookdale*, 1953

William K. and E. Margaret Sessions, *The Tukes of York*, 1971

Arthur Raistrick, *Two centuries of industrial welfare*, 1938

Anne Vernon, *A Quaker business man: the life of Joseph Rowntree, 1836–1925*, 1958

SOURCES AND REFERENCES

David Tregoning and Hugh Cockerell, *Friends for life: the Friends' Provident Life Office 1832–1982*, 1982

E. Jean Whittaker, *Thomas Lawson, 1630–1691: north country botanist, Quaker and schoolmaster*, 1986

R. Hingston Fox, *Dr John Fothergill and his friends*, 1919

William Allen, *Life, with selections from his correspondence*, 3 vol., 1846–7

Amalie M. and Edward H. Kass, *Perfecting the world: the life and times of Thomas Hodgkin, 1798–1866*, 1988

Richard B. Fisher, *Joseph Lister, 1827–1912*, 1977

Fenner Brockway, *Bermondsey story: the life of Alfred Salter*, 1949

Stephen Grellet, *Memoirs of the life and gospel labours*, ed. Benjamin Seebohm, 2 vol., 1860

June Rose, *Elizabeth Fry*, 1980

Daniel Wheeler, *Memoirs of the life and gospel labours*, 1842

Margaret E. Hirst, *The Quakers in peace and war*, 1923

Hope Hay Hewison, *Hedge of wild almonds: South Africa, the pro-Boers and the Quaker conscience*, 1989

Reginald Reynolds, *John Somervell Hoyland*, 1958

Dublin Yearly Meeting, *Transactions of the Central Relief Committee of the Society of Friends during the famine in Ireland in 1846 and 1847*, 1852

Edward H. Milligan, *The past is prologue: 100 years of Quaker overseas work, 1868–1968*, 1968

A. Tegla Davies, *Friends Ambulance Unit*, 1947

Christopher B. Barber (ed.), *FAU postscript: some reflections of some former Friends Ambulance Unit members*, 1984

Charles W. Barclay *et al.*, *A history of the Barclay family*, 3 vol., 1924–34

Oliver Morland, *William White, a brother of men*, 1903

Rosa Hobhouse, *Mary Hughes: her life for the dispossessed*, 1949

Hugh S. Pyper, *Mary Hughes: a friend to all in need*, 1985

John William Graham, *Psychical experiences of Quaker ministers*, 1933

Index

This index does not pretend to be comprehensive. It does not, for instance, include persons or places where there is only passing mention in the text, and it does not attempt full subject coverage. The needs, interests, and approach of readers will vary and users of this book are invited to supplement this index with their own personal one on the back endpapers.

In place of biographical notes the persons in the index are briefly identified. To help readers find half-recalled quotations key words to some of the best-known have been included in the index.